LACI PETERSON
The Whole Story

LACI PETERSON
The Whole Story

◆

Laci, Scott, and Amber's Deadly Love Triangle

Brad Knight

iUniverse, Inc.
New York Lincoln Shanghai

LACI PETERSON The Whole Story
Laci, Scott, and Amber's Deadly Love Triangle

Copyright © 2005 by Brad Knight

All rights reserved. No part of this book may be used or reproduced by any means, graphic, electronic, or mechanical, including photocopying, recording, taping or by any information storage retrieval system without the written permission of the publisher except in the case of brief quotations embodied in critical articles and reviews.

iUniverse books may be ordered through booksellers or by contacting:

iUniverse
2021 Pine Lake Road, Suite 100
Lincoln, NE 68512
www.iuniverse.com
1-800-Authors (1-800-288-4677)

ISBN-13: 978-0-595-34750-6
ISBN-10: 0-595-34750-9

Printed in the United States of America

To Laci

Contents

Editor's Note ix
Acknowledgments xiii
Prologue 1

PART I

Chapter 1	Missing in Modesto 11
Chapter 2	The Search 44
Chapter 3	The Affair 73
Chapter 4	Murder in the Air 111

PART II

Chapter 5	Bodies Are Found 141
Chapter 6	Riding On Laci's Coattails 196
Chapter 7	DNA—The Forensic Evidence 240
Chapter 8	Scott Peterson vs. O.J. 268

PART III

Chapter 9	The Preliminary Hearing 277
Chapter 10	Into the Realm of Nightmare 312
Chapter 11	Potential Closing Arguments 339
Chapter 12	End for Now 379

APPENDIX 399
   Article A - Arrest Warrant *400*
   Article B - Probable Cause Declaration . *401*
   Article C - Booking Register *402*
   Article D - Criminal Complaint *403*

Index *405*

Editor's Note

It was the publishing process that the author of this book began which brought me into contact with him for the beginning of a very fascinating and rewarding professional relationship.

I began a telephone conversation with freelance writer Brad Knight. Mr. Knight described his book as a true-crime, non-fiction work. As it so happens, I am an avid reader of non-fiction, and my own home library contains 20 or more books of this genré. I happened to mention to him that I had read several non-fiction works by various well-known prosecutors. With these revelations from me, Brad began to discuss more information. He particularly admired some of these same attorneys, and had a broad and deep historical knowledge of many notorious murder cases. We each offered opinions on the various past murder cases that had caught our attention, and I could tell that Brad was clearly in his element.

It was at this point that he revealed that his book was on the Laci Peterson murder case.

When I first met Mr. Knight, he was, naturally, somewhat cautious about providing the details of his book right away. Over the course of the next hour, he gradually revealed the details of his work, and I described my editing methodology to him.

Well, I considered myself to be very well acquainted with the Peterson case, and most of the other cases that Brad and I discussed. I had videotaped portions of the O.J. Simpson trial, followed closely the more recent Chandra Levy—Gary Condit investigation, and was avidly reading all I could lay my hands on about the Laci Peterson case. Brad and I saw eye to eye.

Privately though, I was a bit skeptical of his or anyone else's ability to bring a sense of freshness to the material available, since the Laci case was in the news virtually daily. However, this did not dampen my eagerness to assist this author in editing his book; we agreed that I would edit just Chapter One as a test in order to finalize our working relationship. He then emailed his first chapter to me.

As I mentioned, I was doubtful that I would find anything new or enlightening in his account of this gruesome and heartbreaking case. To my astonishment and pleasure, by page two of his original manuscript, I was forced to change this opinion—Brad presented facts about the Laci Peterson case that I had never before heard or seen in print. I was so impressed that I immediately called him to let him know that he definitely had my attention.

I don't always have the opportunity to spend time with my writers; luckily, Brad was working not too far from where I live, and he was nice enough to come visit me at my home to discuss Chapter One modifications and to get organized. I found him to be as animated and energized in person as he had been on the telephone. He was quite serious about his writing, having invested many months on this book, but he was always courteous and respectful of my knowledge of advanced editing.

Over the course of the next few weeks, we worked together to polish Laci's story. Mr. Knight continued to attend Scott Peterson's trial a couple of days a week in preparation for his sequel. At night, he worked late preparing his current manuscript and sometimes until the next morning in order to get me the material for final editing by our deadlines. Again, he had already invested numerous months in this book, but he never failed in his determination and follow through.

Brad brings personal insights and perspective to this tale that are not available elsewhere—he joined the searches for Laci, he interviewed many participants, and he examined all sides of the story. In addition, he adds layers of depth through his examination of the societal issues that lay below the surface of this case; these issues are not pretty to examine and are generally ignored in the traditional media. But Brad does not shy away from uncomfortable subject matter here and, for that, I applaud him.

There are no other first-hand, personalized accounts of the Laci case available at this time; what you are about to read is unique in that respect. Enjoy...

Chris Jones
Editor

ACKNOWLEDGMENTS

The author would like to thank the following:

Chris Jones—Editor, you brought me up to date and always on track. Thanks for that extra edge and tolerance needed for these higher stress pressures that are consistent with a project of this magnitude.

Edward Holmes—Senior Editor, thank you for bringing us to this level. Your career expertise in this field is clearly demonstrated.

Marc Klaas—For his generous efforts to the Rocha family in their time of grief and his persistence for justice. It's been a pleasure working with him. His friendship and insightfulness was a tremendous inspiration that kept me going throughout this project.

Ted Rowlands—His reporting skills, from the get-go, in this case have been outstanding. He's been straightforward, fair, and accurate throughout the ordeal and has been devoted since the start to delivering all the breaking developments as they unfolded.

Sharon and Ron Grantski—As well as Dennis, Brent, and Amy Rocha. It is people like you that the local community, as well as the nation, feel deserve the best justice has to offer. This book cannot bring Laci back, but perhaps, in some way, it may help.

Dr. Henry Lee—His forensic expertise was invaluable in showing step-by-step how investigators use tools and trace evidence at hand to lead a case of this nature to its current status.

Kim Petersen—Along with the staff at the Sund/Carrington Foundation—The expertise of this organization helped stimulate and maintain a great deal of the mass media attention the case received, which resulted in constant pressure on investigative agencies furthering the chance of a resolution. I'd especially like to thank Kim to whom much of this establishment's success can be attributed.

The Modesto Police Department—I'd like to thank Roy Wasden and staff. A highly trained, experienced, and skilled organization. Your homicide division is among the best in the nation.

Stanislaus County District Attorney's Office—It's reassuring to see good old-fashioned traditional values still in practice. All right-minded people are here behind you.

The Modesto Bee—For their insightful, fair, and thorough coverage of the case from day one. The staff has been very accommodating to me, and I appreciate all you've done. I'd especially like to thank Molly Dugan, Judy Sly, Richard Estrada, Ty Phillips, Patrick Giblin, Lisa Millegan, John Cote, Michael Mooney, Jeff Jardine, and Garth Stapley.

Renee Tomlinson—Your presence as a volunteer organizer from day one in the disappearance of your best friend has contributed markedly toward the case getting that extra needed exposure that was imperative in getting it solved.

Larry King, Greta Van Susteren, Nancy Grace and Geraldo Rivera—Your week-to-week coverage of the case and expert panels gave me a unique interest in pursuing this project even that much more. As always, a job well done.

The San Francisco Examiner—Good coverage. Consistently new and different perspectives to ponder.

People Magazine—Great people, great case coverage, and new information all the time.

Time Magazine—As usual, excellent material and very credible case coverage.

Gregg Chavaria—My longtime friend from college who in 1996 made the connection between Marc Klaas and I that resulted in our involvement together in charitable activities. Gregg also had been a journalist for the *Contra Costa Times* during those years.

Stanislaus County Sheriff's Department—As well as the countless hundreds of volunteers that came out to participate in the searches for Laci. Without you, we as a nation could not have remained focused on the daughter of Modesto, California—the one and only Laci.

PROLOGUE

Within the first six months of the investigation, just before one of the press conferences, a few reporters and I received a handshake and a thank you from several members of the Rocha family for our contribution to the incredible media effort that ultimately led to their daughter's case being solved. Some people have voiced concerns about how the family may be taking all the case exposure with coverage from nightly cable programs, regular network news, almost all newspapers locally and nationally, many national magazines as well as radio, especially since some have criticized the role the media have taken in this case. Fortunately, however, the family of the victims (Laci and Conner) have applauded our hard work and role in finding justice for their tragedy, because if it were *not* for the intensive media exposure, this case may have simply gone *unsolved*, as was the Evelyn Hernandez case. Evelyn Hernandez, who was 8 months pregnant, was found floating dead in the San Francisco Bay several months after she disappeared with no real suspects to speak of. Why did that investigation go cold? The reason: Lack of media exposure. It seemed no one really cared. There was only one small article about that case in the back of a local paper.

Detectives have praised us in the media as a very important and effective tool for law enforcement during this investigation, and others. It is clear that in the Laci Peterson case, if it were not for such intense media scrutiny, her body too may have only washed up when it did, without any solid suspects or evidence of any kind. The perpetrator may have successfully...gotten away with murder. Even though the *police* investigation may be over, it is commentary of this nature that keeps pressure on prosecutors during criminal trials, in a further search for the truth. This particular literary work may not bring Laci back, but I hope, at least in some way, it may help the Rocha family in their overall quest for justice.

Forensic crime analysis based on real cases, I've always found riveting. Sometimes even when I have to be up early the next morning for work, I find it hard to put a case down until I get to the conclusion. Although I had a tremendous amount of interest in the Peterson case itself, I originally had no interest in writing a book on the subject. Then, during discussions I had with several people associated with the families, it was apparent that they were impressed with my style of commentary regarding the circumstances of the investigation and asked if I would consider writing a book on this case. At the time, I said, "no," mainly because to take on a project of this magnitude would be an enormous undertaking to try to fit into an already overloaded time schedule. But as the weeks went by, I spoke to more and more people who had independently made similar comments in a subtle effort to persuade me into doing it. I finally conceded and agreed to write the book.

With the tremendous volume of information and details surrounding the Laci Peterson case, I knew the facts could not be contained in only one book; hence it was decided to produce a two-volume set, which worked out very well in this instance, given that a large number of people were hungering for an all-encompassing literary work on the case, even though it hadn't gone to trial yet. Thus, the second volume naturally would contain an even more explosive wealth of complicated facts, information, and circumstances since it would encompass the trial itself.

I had coordinated with Marc Klaas on several different events throughout the years, promoting safe Halloweens and raising funds for child recovery programs. I spoke at several universities on crime study analysis, and have been a writer most of my life. In addition, business associates and family were pressuring me to publish more of my works on this same subject. With all of this, and the fact that I lived less than one mile from the Peterson home, I concluded that I would commit to the project. I'd channel my efforts to this one endeavor and begin the large undertaking that would, no doubt, consume numerous months of intensive research.

Unlike the O.J. Simpson or other high-profile cases, Scott and Laci Peterson were not famous before Laci disappeared. This particular case took the country by storm largely based on one factor…the "good looks" of the key participants involved. In addition, they were a young, suburban California couple of some prosperity, which is actually a main premise certain programs have used to retain their popularity, such as *Melrose Place, Bay Watch* or *90210*. Also, the recent Chandra Levy—Gary Condit scandal paved the way for the national media to find Modesto very inviting.

I've always been consciously aware of this general fascination people have with "looks," which remains fairly consistent anywhere you go, for as long as people have existed. Why? Common sense would indicate: People prefer images that are more pleasing to view.

In fact, I've been somewhat disappointed with Hollywood over the last fifteen years or so, because there has been a general trend in films that have moved away from the "classic" elements and replaced them with political correctness. A lot of this movement was created as a result of subtle criticisms made in recent years, in which it had been implied that films haven't changed that much in the last hundred years because directors continue to use "good-looking" good guys and "bad-looking" bad guys. Even at the end of the *Pee Wee's Big Adventure* movie, he tries to make a mockery of Hollywood over-glamorizing characters that might otherwise be seemingly average people.

As a result, some film producers in recent years have steered away from the use of above-average looking actors and actresses for main characters and subsequently lost Academy Award nomination opportunities. Or in other words, simple typecasting mistakes made by some producers just to be different, thinking the characters would look more historically correct (although quite the opposite was actually true in history) by using actors and actresses that were homelier than what had been traditionally used in years past, gambling that the modern high-tech special effects of the film would make up for it in the end. Wrong. I remember seeing one movie recently that was based on the life of a great female leader in medieval history. It had all the markings of a great film—a dungeon queen rising to power in the Dark Ages and ultimately being burned alive at the stake as a witch. What a plot. How much more dramatic could you get? And based on actual events, no less. On top of that, you could tell this producer must've had an enormous budget to work with, equal to any major motion picture because of the orchestrated music soundtrack, the tremendous castle settings, majestic backdrops, extravagant costumes, and computerized graphics, etc. So here, you would think they would have used no less than an "A" quality actress, whose appearance would've been so stunning, that one could realistically picture her influence over the men being intense enough that they would become willing to die for her in battle. But, no; instead, the actress they did use, in my opinion, was about a C+ in both looks and acting skills. If the director had in mind (which I'm sure he did not) using an actress who portrayed what the actual look of this historical figure might have been, who for God's sake, watching this movie, is going to remember what this particular character from their high school history textbook actually looked like. And because this was supposed to be taking place about 1300 years ago in Medieval Europe, how accurate an image from possible ancient art, or whatever, could have realistically replicated what she may have actually looked like? So the directors were not bound by knowledge of her appearance, like they would have been with a more modern leader's image, and therefore, they could have picked a lead actress however they pleased, keeping in mind what has proven to be most in the public's interest, of course—her looks first and foremost.

Furthermore, they used extras in the battle scenes who could not of been more than amateur actors themselves. There's nothing wrong with using amateurs, but in these particular types of scenes, it's not really *acting* that's required, it is more just simply glorified "posing." So why not use amateur models instead? And those models who don't have long hair? No problem, simply give them wigs to wear. I don't think any amateur model getting a call from a major producer to be in a major motion picture would refuse. Thus, the most important part of the silver screen movie, the visual impact, would be improved ten-fold. And how hard would it be for a producer with a 200 million dollar budget for the film, to get a list of, say, a few hundred amateur models? Not hard, I'm sure. The point is, imagine this movie with a starring cast that included the likes of Scott, Laci, and Amber. When Scott had the highlighted goatee right before he was arrested, all he needed was a long wig that matched and to be on horseback with a sword at his side. Laci and Amber could be dressed as Renaissance maids.

Obviously, Polly Klaas was not the first young girl to be abducted in America; however, her story fit the classic fairytale of the beautiful young princess stolen by the grotesque boogie man (Richard Allen Davis), thus America was whole-heartedly captivated and the case instantly went national. Many producers are now reminded of the incredible power this seemingly superficial factor of classic sentiment actually has on the ratings of public popularity. So much so that someone brought to my attention that even some of the talk-show hosts were bringing on experts to discuss the Peterson case who undoubtedly were chosen more for their good looks than perhaps the level of accomplishment in their field.

Besides being a freelance writer and living less than a mile from Scott & Laci Peterson, I, too, bought my first home here in Modesto at about the same price range that Scott bought his, and also, within the exact same few months. I, too, am a reasonably successful All-American male in my 30's, as is he. Scott had a small warehouse for his business. I, too, happen to have a small warehouse for my business. Scott was driving (before he was arrested) a new white Dodge truck. I happen to drive a new white Dodge truck. Scott professed he was an avid fisherman. I, too, am an avid fisherman, outdoorsman, etc. Scott has his bachelor's degree from a California University. I have my bachelor's degree from a California University. And the list of commonalities between Scott and me seems to go on and on which, I believe, only made me that much more interested in the story. So, I've committed myself in this project to be as fair and balanced as possible in my analysis to both sides of the case. After carefully weighing and examining the evidence, I will give my formal opinion as to what I believe actually occurred Christmas Eve, 2002, in Modesto, California.

—The Author—

Part I

1

Missing in Modesto

I was in the drive-thru at a local fast-food place near my house in Modesto, California. The date was December 26, 2002, the day after Christmas. Like many thousands of San Francisco Bay Area residents, I had moved to Modesto just two years earlier because I was drawn by the affordable real estate prices; Bay Area real estate had shot up astronomically in the late 90's, but homes were still affordable here in the Modesto area.

Hanging from the menu speaker was a picture of Laci Peterson; it was a missing persons flyer. I don't know if it was that famous Laci smile we've all grown to know, or what other element drew my attention to a moment that would forever be embedded in my memory. I thought for a minute as I looked at the photo whether this young woman, like many others, would be cast to the wayside like numerous milk-carton images of missing kids, or post cards of the same thing that usually just get tossed out with the junk mail. I concluded at that time, "Probably so." With a taco salad steaming on the passenger seat, I proceeded to drive off.

Since I lived less than a mile from the Peterson home, my first impulse, as with many others here in the area, was to volunteer for the searches that were starting to build. But because the demands of my work at the time were consuming much more of me than usual, I wasn't able to get out and join the forces right away. Fortunately, however, by living in the community, I did know several people who participated, which in turn gave me a generous portion of hands-on insight into the beginnings of one incredible case.

I do have a personal understanding of why so many people poured out from the local community to help out in the searches. For many of the reasons I've tried to list here in my analysis, as well as other reasons I just haven't thought of, I personally felt more eager to contribute to this effort than I have in other situations like it. The people involved, family members, friends, and neighbors, etc., I'm sure, played a significant part in my interest. This was when the case was still local, and it was unknown at the time that the national mega-media were going to converge down on Modesto like a tornado. But soon enough, Modesto would be in the front-page headlines all over again, as we were in the Chandra Levy-Gary Condit scandal.

We here in Modesto were no strangers to the national media. Since this was Chandra's hometown and Condit's congressional district, the media began to surge with increasing momentum day by day, like a massive flock of eagles and vultures swirling down on us in a dark cloud of feeding frenzy.

Laci Denise Rocha (Peterson) was born May 4, 1975, at Doctors Medical Center in Modesto, California, and spent the first two years of her life in Escalon, a neighboring town. This is where her father had a dairy farm where she was raised as a young child. After her parents, Dennis and Sharon, divorced while Laci was still only two, she moved with her mother and older brother, Brent, to neighboring Modesto, where she spent most of her life, although she and her brother continued to spend many weekends back at the dairy farm. Laci's mother Sharon soon met Ron Grantski, who cared for Laci as his own, and together they raised the girl who would later become a nationwide icon. In the meantime, her father Dennis also met someone and eventually remarried, and together they had another daughter, Amy, when Laci was 6 years old.

Laci fit in quite well with her older brother and his friends, even though he was four years older than she. As they continued through their teenage years, Laci developed into quite an attractive young woman. Brent mentioned that his friends were among the first to notice.

Her father Dennis stores a keepsake box with many cherished photos of Laci as she grew up. These pictures include one of Laci frolicking in the snow, one of her riding a horse, and another with a coyote puppy she raised, named "Princess." The heartbroken Mr. Rocha has referred to Laci as "the perfect daughter to have in all ways."

Here in Modesto, she attended Sonoma Elementary School, La Loma Junior High, and eventually, Downey High School, where she became a cheerleader as well as establishing a close group of friends. Among those friends were Stacy Boyers, Rene Tomlinson, Renee Garza, and Lori Ellsworth, as well as several others, some of whom were cheerleaders with her, and others played sports. Those who knew her said she was very well liked and had become somewhat popular, which of course, is quite natural for a cheerleader. Most of the squad members I knew from high school, you could say, dominated the social hierarchy.

Bob Starling, her physical science teacher when she was a freshmen at Downey High, vividly remembered her. He said

Laci stood out from the cast of thousands with her vibrant personality, not to mention that she was also a good student academically. Mr. Starling elaborated, "She was always energetic, always bubbly and always in a good mood. Laci was one you'd never forget."

While in high school, Laci and her friends met at Rose Avenue Park on Friday nights. She and her other friends, who also were cheerleaders, were, of course, obligated to be at the football games, since they were running part of the show, and often planned the rest of their evenings from this location. Their plans usually included exclusive parties after the games, as well as other privileged functions.

When Laci was almost sixteen she started seeing her first long-term boyfriend, Kent Gaines. Kent was two years older than Laci and she began occasionally bringing the young man over to her father's dairy farm. Kent was from San Jose, California originally, but had been in Modesto at least several years. On the farm, Laci taught her boyfriend how to ride an all-terrain vehicle as well as other rural activities. In an interview about Laci, Gaines said, "She was brought up real well. She was real respectful to her parents and elders." He said that even in high school when many kids pull away from their families, Laci stayed close to her parents.

She graduated from Downey in 1993 and left for San Luis Obispo where she had been accepted into the horticulture program at California Polytechnic State University, also known as Cal Poly. She and Kent decided to move in together in nearby Morro Bay, where they found a small house that they rented. According to Virginia Walker, a horticulture professor at Cal Poly, Laci was a strong student and her studies paid off. During her first year there, she received the outstanding freshman award in the ornamental horticulture division. The professor said, "Laci was a classic student here, a high achiever." She was an industrious person, as well; during her education there she held several jobs. For a time, she managed the college-owned Poly Plant & Floral shop, which was a small on-campus retail outlet.

From a very young age Laci had shown a unique interest in horticulture, according to her mother, Sharon. When Laci was still quite small, Sharon remembered, she would often ask if she could go pull weeds. Naturally, her mother wasn't going to say no, and she'd watch her daughter through the window, working and playing in the dirt for hours on end. From then on, she could see that Laci had a green thumb and was surrounding herself with the greenery of plants, trees, and flowers. Later on, she was described by some of the neighbors as always having fresh flowers in her home and making crafts from flowers and berries she picked on her daily walks.

Laci's boyfriend Kent was with her on her 19th birthday, when she got a small tattoo of some daisies on her ankle, which she later covered with a larger tattoo. He said that with Laci, they were different from the average college students regarding their lifestyle—no beer bashes or much fast-food consumption. He said they mostly stayed at home to cook and tend to the garden.

However, friends of Laci more recently have said that Gaines didn't always treat her respectfully. Occasionally he'd talk to her in condescending tones. As things go, the two eventually broke up. One of Laci's closest friends while she was at Cal Poly was Katerina Pike. Regarding Kent and Laci's break-up, Katerina said, "She wasn't tearful about it. We were all happy they were going their separate ways."

Kent Gaines said that he and Laci were with each other for 3 years, 4 months, and 17 days. Regarding Scott Peterson, here is what Laci's long-term boyfriend had to say: "Scott screwed up bad. That guy's a moron...to have somebody like that and blow it. Even if he didn't do it and was cheating on her—what is he, stupid? It's like finding the rarest diamond in the world and hitting it to see what's inside."

Laci's boyfriend Kent Gaines, believe it or not, gave this interview from his prison cell in Washington State Prison, where he is now serving a 15-year sentence after being convicted of shooting his girlfriend. He is inmate No. 802862. Laci's family did not find this out until after the murder of *their* daughter. They were flabbergasted. Dennis Rocha said he was "blown away" when he heard about his daughter's ex-boyfriend's crime. He said, "He didn't seem that way. He looked like a nice guy."

Kent also pointed out during the interview that he didn't think Laci had ever found out about his current predicament.

The latest report on this finding indicated that Kent was convicted of "shooting" his girlfriend, which leads one to assume that he killed her, and, assuming that Scott will likely be convicted (with the propensity of evidence currently against him, it would be difficult to think that he wouldn't), then that prompts one to consider another point. For a case ripe with coincidences, it appears that Laci Peterson, who has had only *two* serious boyfriends, managed to acquire not *one*, but *two* spousal murderers within her short lifetime. If such random probability could actually fall on someone as wholesome as Laci, it makes one ponder momentarily about what kind of a world we actually live in.

At the time she disappeared on or about Tuesday, December 24, 2002, Laci was described as 5-feet 1 inch, about

140 pounds, 27 years old, with shoulder length brown hair and brown eyes. She had dimples on both cheeks and a tattoo of a sunflower on her ankle. (This just happened to remind me that I once dated a girl who had a tattoo of a mushroom also on her ankle. She, like Laci, was also very popular and successful in school.)

Scott Lee Peterson was born at Sharp Hospital in San Diego, California, on October 24, 1972. Growing up in San Diego, he was the youngest of seven half-siblings—five boys and two girls—of Lee and Jacqueline Peterson. His parents were similar to the Brady Bunch in that they both brought 3 kids from other marriages. Out of seven kids, Scott was the only child Lee and Jackie had *together*.

Scott has been described as a happy, healthy boy as a child. Despite having so many siblings, he enjoyed no shortage of attention at a young age, according to his mother. When he was 6 or 7 years old, Jacqueline remembered, they used to all go fishing together. Lee liked to spend time with his boys as they were growing up, taking them hunting and fishing on a regular basis, then eventually, golfing. As Scott got a little older, his father would often take him and his brothers on fishing trips to the mountains and, over time, Scott even talked his dad into getting a fishing boat. There were even a few times, they remembered, that Scott had brought his fishing pole along with him when they went golfing where the course ran alongside the San Diego River. Jacqueline remembered, "By the second hole, he'd stop golfing and start fishing." She continued, "He'd usually fish until they were done golfing." But as he got a little older, he began to show more interest in golfing, partly, Jacqueline said, because they enticed him by letting him drive the golf cart once in a while.

Scott was on the golf team when he attended the University of San Diego High School. There he played with Phil Mickelson, who now plays on the professional circuit. Scott graduated from high school in 1990. He earned a partial golf scholarship to Arizona State and attended there for a short period of time before moving back in with his parents, who had just recently purchased a new home in Morro Bay. That lasted for about 6 months until he said he was really too old to be living at home. So, he tried to put himself through college by juggling 2 to 3 jobs at a time, one of which was at the Pacific Café, where he worked as a waiter and ultimately met Laci. He attended Cuesta College and was eventually accepted at California Polytechnic State University, San Luis Obispo, as an agricultural major.

In July of 1994, when Scott was still a waiter at the Pacific Café (571 Embarcadero, Morro Bay), he was working with a friend of his, who was actually a neighbor of Laci's. Having come by to socialize with her neighbor at the cafe, Laci noticed Scott and became interested. To get to know him better, she would come in from time to time, order coffee and have small conversations over the counter with him. Her interest in Scott was perking, so one day she handed her phone number to her friend, so he could hand it to Scott. When Scott was told what it was for, he assumed his co-worker was pulling a joke and wasn't about to make a complete fool of himself by phoning some girl who wasn't even expecting his call and may not be at all interested, so he crumpled up Laci's phone number and threw it away. But once his friend convinced him that this truly was from Laci, he recovered it from the trash and figured he'd give her a call.

Laci was just 19 years old at the time, having just finished her first year in college at San Luis Obispo. Scott was 22. Laci was also working at another café at the time, which was in Morro Bay, as well.

Their first date, however, proved to be a bit of a fiasco. Scott decided to take Laci out on a commercial fishing boat—it was her first time and ended up being her last. She got seasick about halfway into the trip. Although she didn't go on any more fishing trips with Scott (except, perhaps, one more), their relationship together began to flourish, and the young couple continued to see more of each other. One time, in fact, Laci had called her mother to tell her that she thought she had met the man she was going to marry and invited her to come down and meet Scott. The introduction was to take place at Scott's workplace, the Pacific Café. To both Laci's and her mother's surprise, Scott had bought them each a bouquet of roses, which he had waiting at their table—Laci's were red and Sharon's were white. Scott eventually took Laci to San Diego to meet his brothers and sisters, who remembered him smiling quite a bit and that he appeared happier with Laci than what they remembered him being with previous girlfriends.

Those who knew Laci and Scott back then described them as the perfect couple and that they appeared to be sincerely falling in love. Laci's best friend in college was Heather Richardson. Heather said that, after having gone out with Scott for awhile, Laci brought him over to meet her and her boyfriend, Mike Richardson, whom Heather later married. Heather said, "She brought him over to meet us, and she was very proud. We didn't like him at first. He was very cocky." She then said that she and her boyfriend grew to like Scott as the two couples all became closer friends.

Only one month after their first date, Scott and Laci were living together. Richardson said the couple adored each other. She said Scott had a taste for fine things; he even drove a black Porsche while still in college. Laci, apparently having been influenced by Scott, began to refine her taste for more exquisite things, as well. Heather said, "He was very into portraying that image, and once you get a taste of that, you really like it. He set her in that direction and she ran with it, and it suited her. That was her."

Scott and Laci were together for a couple years and recently graduated before getting married on August 9, 1997, in a quaint ceremony filled with flowers and friends and held at a coastal area hot springs. It was here in the lush gardens at this Avila Beach resort in Central California where the Mr. and Mrs. Peterson-to-be exchanged vows on a sunny summer day. Heather Richardson was the matron of honor, and her husband Mike was Scott's best man. The wedding included, among other things, a live string quartet, a three-tiered white cake, an aisle made of rolled green carpet sprinkled with flower petals, and a large white gazebo in which the ceremony was officiated. Laci was wearing a flowing snow-white wedding dress, and Scott wore a black tuxedo with a white bow tie. Scott's brother-in-law, Ed Caudillo, said he remembered him carrying Laci up to the room at the end of the wedding. He said they were both loudly talking and laughing and even said they, for a second, were worried he might drop her in all the excitement, but that Scott had her safely in his arms. The couple spent their honeymoon in Tahiti.

Laci took a job at a wine distribution firm in Prunedale, Monterey County, which was a two-hour drive from where she and Scott were living at the time. To avoid the commute, Laci temporarily moved there. Scott, however, stayed in San Luis Obispo and shared a house with roommates. Laci visited on weekends. This was the time, according to Heather Richardson, when the first incident of Scott cheating on Laci occurred. It was Scott's graduation weekend in 1998. Naturally, Laci was there and was actually in the middle of making love to her husband, when suddenly another girl she didn't know barged in. This girl, evidently, was one Scott had begun a relationship with during the weekdays while Laci was gone. Unaware that Scott was married, the girl immediately accused him of cheating. I'm sure Scott had a rough time trying to explain this mess to the two young women. The couple did, however, manage to stay together and work through the sticky entanglement.

Shortly before his arrest, Scott had been staying with different family members and friends, as a possible way of eluding the authorities, who he knew had been monitoring his every move and whereabouts at all times. One of the places where he stayed was the home of Heather and Mike Richardson. He told Heather at this time all about the cheating incident that had occurred on his graduation weekend. In fact, Heather had actually been there at the time, because she had spent that weekend over at Scott's. However, Scott was surprised to find out that Heather didn't actually know about the affair. He thought for sure that Laci would have probably told her close friend on that day, if not later on. Heather said she remembered the weekend, but mentioned only that Laci had seemed irritated. She remembered Laci and Scott locking themselves in the bathroom, and yelling. When Laci came out, she had apparently only said, "Scott's not acting like he's married."

Regarding this little episode of infidelity, I had a bit of a concern prodding at me, something slightly ruffling my feathers the wrong way. What I'm talking about is the stereotype Scott represents being associated on a general basis with the kind of relationship behaviors he was exhibiting, which, I don't believe, has any substantial connection. I was concerned Scott might be giving the rest of us a bad name. Scott has been referred to by many as an "All-American Guy." This concerns me because I too have been attributed this same status by a few acquaintances for many of the same reasons that Scott's been associated with it. For instance, the way I look, the way I dress, and the activities I'm involved in. But my concern is that people who saw Scott as someone they wouldn't mind being like, i.e., good-looking, successful, owning his own home and driving newer vehicles, might also think carefree infidelity is common among, or a part of being an idealistic, achieving person. Or worse yet, females may become more leery of this particular kind of character, because of Peterson's nonchalant attitudes toward adultery, as we are seeing from his past. I personally was a little set back when I heard about this occurrence, not to mention feeling a little nauseated. What I mean is that, if Scott just goes ahead and marries a person with no intention whatsoever of being faithful, or, in other words—if he's just thinking, "Hey, whatever happens, happens. If someone wants to do me, and she doesn't know I'm really married, what she doesn't know won't hurt her, so I'll just partake. I mean, why not? Laci would never divorce me anyway. She loves me too much." In other words, Scott is taking advantage of the fortifications of marriage itself, and any way you slice it, this is extremely disrespectful to

Laci, or anyone with whom he chooses to carry out this kind of relationship. He obviously doesn't even care whether he has the other partner's approval or not. He doesn't care at all what the other person thinks, if she doesn't like it, oh well, he's just going to do it anyway. C'est la vie.

This is the complete opposite of my character. I've always believed that the whole reason you wait until you've found just the right person before saying our vows, is so that, naturally, you wouldn't want to cheat on this person. Isn't that the whole reason you married this person in the first place, that you've finally found someone worth being faithful to? Apparently with Scott, the complete opposite principle applies: find someone to marry who loves you more than you love her. That way you can feel free to cheat like hell knowing full well nothing tangible will ever come of it anyway.

It makes me wonder what family values have influenced Scott—what family role models he's had. His parents seem to be very upstanding people by most accounts. Could it possibly be from his mother's side of the family? The reason I'm curious is because not only am I appalled by this apparent way of thinking Scott embraces, but I also know from within both branches of my own family, such behavior is just simply unthinkable. Certainly we're not perfect, as nobody is, but this is an area that simply hasn't become an issue.

My long-time friends who are now married, and who have a similar image, seem to be as equally strong in their marital loyalty, as well. I myself tend to associate Scott's type of behavior, casual marital cheating, more with low-lifes, and certainly this trait disqualifies him from being an All-American Guy.

Both having graduated from Cal Poly, Scott and Laci managed to open their own business, a burger place they called "The Shack," which did reasonably well under the circumstances. The small restaurant was a renovated bakery in a strip mall which they decorated with barrels of peanuts, wood-chips all over the floor and several television sets playing the latest sporting events, definitely a college atmosphere the couple chose to market to. They eventually did sell "The Shack" two years later inorder to move to Modesto, Laci's hometown.

According to one source, Scott declared bankruptcy before they left, even though he only had $5,000.00 of credit card debt. Assuming this to be fairly accurate, or at least within that range, I thought this information was particularly interesting. I've known people who have considered bankruptcy as an option upon reaching about $20,000.00 or $25,000.00 in credit card debt, but I, quite frankly, would not even consider this an option, if I had $100,000.00 of debt; I simply value my credit rating more than that. But, as we know, Scott and Laci very shortly thereafter were able to buy their own home. This, I believe, was possible only because both sides of the family were naturally willing to co-sign the mortgage. No bank would possibly approve a new home loan with the black hole of a bankruptcy on their record, without the use of a prominent co-signer. Not only must it be a nice feeling to know you can run up a large debt without legally ever having to pay it back, but to have peace-of-mind that this action will not in any way hinder the future approval of a home-loan, car loan, or even boat loan, because all you need is an approving parent to co-sign.

A few days after Laci disappeared, the police were still examining Scott's truck in the lab, so he went ahead, without telling anyone, and traded in Laci's Land Rover, at the local

Dodge dealership, towards the purchase price of a new 4x4 Dodge Dakota. After a few days, the Rochas noticed Scott's new truck in the driveway and that Laci's vehicle was gone. When they asked Scott about this, he told them that he traded it in, like it was no big thing. The Rochas immediately went down to the dealership and, without question, the vehicle was returned. If the case hadn't been experiencing the national spotlight, it would be interesting to think how this dealership may have handled the situation.

In addition, the life insurance policy Scott took out on Laci, as well as possible alimony/child support avoidance, it's no wonder Sharon Rocha filed the wrongful death lawsuit as early as she did, now seeing the financial hustler her son-in-law turned out to be. (More about the lawsuit later, see Chapter 9). It makes sense that she wants to seize those assets, including Scott's home, before there's any chance of him getting out of jail. Who knows what'll be the next thing he's liable to sell before it's too late? To me, filing an entire Chapter Eleven bankruptcy, which destroys an individual's personal credit history for the next seven years, all over a measly $5,000.00 debt, is catastrophic. But then again, actually killing your wife and child to avoid alimony and child support payments for the next eighteen years because you found someone you like better is also, in my opinion, catastrophic, assuming, of course, that this is what happened.

There might, however, be another side of the coin regarding Scott's financial situation. With the searches, he couldn't very easily work to make a living while in the spotlight. Also, any income Laci had generated as a substitute teacher now would be gone (although she could not have continued working while pregnant for very long anyway). From this standpoint, it makes sense that the grieving husband needed to do some serious financial maneuvering in order to stay out of debt.

The young couple made the move to Laci's hometown of Modesto in May of 2000, to start a family and to be closer to Laci's parents. Laci's grandmother had recently died in 1999. The couple rented another place for a while before buying their home at 523 Covena Avenue in October 2000, which was in a slightly older neighborhood and was in need of some repair, which contributed to the couple getting a fairly reasonable deal on the purchase price. The cost of the house totaled $177,000; it is a 1,500-square foot, green, one-story, single family home with a shingle roof. It has a pool in the back yard, palm trees in the front, a large brick-laid chimney rising up the side, and sits in what is considered to be an upper-middle class neighborhood.

On my way to work, I took Yosemite Blvd. west toward the freeway and passed Covena Avenue on the right every morning. When the investigation first broke, I knew Modesto was fairly large and spread out, but I was curious about where the Peterson home was located. I was surprised to find out it was Covena Avenue, which I was already familiar with. This was one of the neighborhoods that lined La Loma Park, which we've heard so much about in the media (the place of the supposed dog-walk from which Laci never returned). I occasionally rode through La Loma Park when I went mountain-bike riding in the area. It's a rather large, wooded, open space, very green with many old but very large oak trees, a lot of thick foliage, and a creek running through it. Just the park alone, I can see, consumed a large amount of the search in the beginning in terms of time and manpower. Like a needle in a haystack, one could search for days or even weeks and still not be confident that every portion of this park was combed. Since then I've only visited the park for research-related purposes.

When the young couple first moved to Modesto, it wasn't long before Scott took a job with Tradecorp, where he became the California-Arizona territory sales representative, and Laci began working as a substitute teacher in the Modesto area schools. One year before Laci's disappearance, Scott joined the Modesto Rotary Club. The president of the chapter, Kenni Friedman, when asked later about Peterson's character, spoke very highly of him, which, I believe, is normal because anytime people newly join a fraternal organization, naturally they put their best foot forward.

Tradecorp, the company Scott worked for (and still does, according to their personnel), is based in Madrid, Spain. The company produces fertilizer and distributes it internationally. Those who spoke publicly on the subject of the fertilizer industry said Peterson did not have as easy a job as some have speculated. In the Central Valley, specifically San Joaquin and Stanislaus counties, where agriculture is the number one industry, the field is lucrative yet very competitive. One of Peterson's functions is to spread the Tradecorp name, reputation, and products through the agricultural community, getting these supplies into use by local farmers or planting the seeds of future growth for the company. Peterson worked within the wholesale distribution channels, establishing new accounts by getting various retailers to offer his company's products to their final consumers. According to a few of these retailers, they encounter sometimes what appear to be hundreds of these types of salespersons pushing a sizable variety of lines of chemicals.

The Central Valley's agriculture is a 15 billion dollar per year industry, which makes it no wonder that these companies are positioning themselves against each other for larger market shares. It helps to have a rock-solid ego to be successful as a salesman in this industry, given the frequent level of rejection they face. Tradecorp exports to 30 countries including France, Chile, South Africa, and Turkey, which are among their chief markets, but has very little presence currently in California. This is largely due to the fact that Tradecorp products cost 15 to 25 percent more than the average wholesale price for similar supplies, according to dealers, rendering Scott's job that much more difficult. He did have one fairly strong selling point with this line of products, however, and that was the fact that the company's solid fertilizers dissolve rapidly in water, allowing greater distribution to the crops through drip and micro-irrigation systems.

Peterson's employer's products specifically target the horticultural end of the valley's agriculture industry, including citrus fruit and other large orchard segments. Among the inventory Scott promoted are premium fertilizers and minerals, including acids, boron, iron, and other materials that are applied to crops on a wide scale to protect them from normal weather conditions, which leads to more bountiful harvests. Peterson has proven to be one of Tradecorp's better performing reps over the years, which is demonstrative of the company's faithful support of him throughout his tragic ordeal.

In the last few years before Laci's disappearance, the Petersons held frequent holiday dinner parties. According to the individuals who spoke about Laci's cooking and hospitality, she had developed quite a little reputation among this circle of people that included mostly neighbors and friends. Some called her the Martha Stewart of Covena Avenue. Her guests had come to know what to anticipate when spending an evening at one of

Laci's holiday fiestas. Be sure to dress nice, and you can expect to be impressed.

She was remembered as the lively spirited young woman who enjoyed gardening, cooking, and entertaining crowds of people in her humble abode. Some people commented that, if you were coming to Laci's house you could expect to be well fed, and you'd always learn something new. In fact, those who attended her previous year's Christmas party remembered her serving a recipe of her own creation, called "figs in a blanket," which was exactly that—figs wrapped in a slice of bacon, cooked and prepared, of course, with the Laci magic touch. She's also been described as a gracious, calm, and organized hostess, never stressed or breaking a sweat on those occasions that included visitors. Laci often had the cooking all completed in advance so rather than spending time in the kitchen, she could spend more time with the guests. They've even said they didn't feel like a burden on her during these functions because entertaining was clearly something Laci enjoyed.

Friends of the mother-to-be had not expected to spend Christmas searching for her and posting flyers all around. Ironically, they were planning to present Laci with an award honoring her spirit as the host of the year.

It was Laci who got her old high school girlfriends got the girls back together for a few slumber parties, just like old times. Except this time there was no checking in with parents or sneaking champagne, some of the girls cleared it with their husbands instead. Her sister Amy expressed that Laci liked to live life to the fullest. If she could, she'd do anything to help someone else and has been just the best role model Amy ever could've had.

After almost two years of trying, Laci Denise Peterson finally got the news she'd been hoping for—she discovered she was pregnant in June 2002. Part of the reason for her long wait before getting pregnant was due to the fact that she only had one ovary. She was so jubilant, she started calling friends and relatives to make her blissful announcement at 7 a.m. in the morning of the day she found out. This was after taking a home pregnancy test.

At the Village Yoga Center in Modesto, Laci started going to pre-natal yoga classes two times per week.

The extra bedroom in the house was converted into Conner's room. There was a crib, a rocking chair, and a changing table in the decorated, bright blue nursery. The couple had picked a maritime theme for the room that included scenes of the sea and a life preserver hanging above the crib (Ironically, this became somewhat symbolic of Connor's death considering where his body was found). In addition to working on the baby's room, Scott, with some help, had fixed up other parts of the house as well, doing a little bit of everything, but mostly painting and landscaping.

Here was something I could relate to. The house I had purchased in Modesto only a few months before the Petersons bought theirs, was also, a fixer-upper. Even though the house itself was only nine years old, it previously had been occupied by renters with pets and young children, so it was in definite need of much basic repair. I remember that the original cabinets were peeling and the floors were grungey with brown stains as were the walls, which had a lot of improper patchwork. I had devoted a lot of my weekends and time after work, but in about three months, I had single-handedly remodeled my entire house, a 3-bedroom 2-bath layout.

In preparation for the baby, Laci stopped working early in December. A few weeks before she disappeared, Laci spoke on the phone with her college friend Heather Richardson. Heather reported that she had learned from their phone conversations before Laci was pregnant, that because she had only the one ovary, Laci had to methodically track her cycle constantly, if she wanted to get pregnant. But Laci had indicated her disappointment to Richardson that Scott always seemed to be traveling right during her only fertile periods of the month. (This, perhaps, could be pointed out by a prosecutor to demonstrate that Scott was making a conscientious effort to avoid being a father.)

Laci seemed disappointed to have to tell Heather that she and Scott wouldn't be making it to the couple's annual Christmas party that year. She told her friend that Scott had been traveling a lot for his job recently, that his boss was in town, and Scott couldn't miss an important meeting. This phone call was the last time Heather would ever speak to her close friend. Prosecutors would later contend that Scott had spent this particular evening (of the Richardson's party) at another Christmas party in Fresno, at the home of one of Amber Frey's best friends. Heather later recalled that Laci had sounded disheartened, but if she had been aware of her husband's infidelity, Laci didn't elaborate.

On December 24, 2002, Christmas Eve day, Scott Peterson left his home in Modesto for the Berkeley Marina, 90 miles away, allegedly to go sturgeon fishing. He had to stop over at his business warehouse on North Emerald Avenue near Kansas Avenue, also in Modesto, so he could hook-up his 14-foot aluminum boat he had purchased only two weeks earlier. He claimed, later on that day, that his wife Laci was planning to walk their golden retriever, McKenzie, that morning in nearby East La Loma Park, as well as go grocery shopping.

Scott returned from the Berkeley Marina, after supposedly fishing in the San Francisco Bay for only 90 minutes, to find Laci's Land Rover parked in the driveway and her purse still in the house. He then, having reported this information to detectives later, took off his clothes, including a t-shirt, jeans, and a pull-over sweatshirt, and placed them in the washing machine, added soap and started the cycle. He then said he had a couple slices of pizza and got into the shower.

I found this interesting, and I'm certain the detectives thought so too, that Peterson felt the necessity to wash the clothes he was wearing immediately upon returning from his un-collaborated alibi. It would be one thing if he had simply put his clothes he'd been wearing into a hamper with other clothes to be washed, or even if he had washed his "alibi" clothing with other items, but that wasn't the situation here. Having researched many missing persons, abductions, and homicide cases, when the prime suspect returns from a rather distant and rugged area alibi and right away decides to wash only the clothes he was wearing from that particular trip and sometimes even including his *shoes*, naturally this raises an element of suspicion.

Neighbor Karen Servas, earlier that day, after Scott had already left for his solo-outing, said she saw the Peterson's dog with his leash still attached and muddy at about 10:30 a.m. Not thinking anything of it, she returned the golden retriever to the yard. Since the side gate was still open, she figured that that was probably how he got out. It wasn't until a reporting officer, later that day, asked her if she remembered seeing anything unusual, before this circumstance then meant anything to her.

After getting cleaned up, Scott went across the street and next door, asking the neighbors if Laci was over there, or if they had seen her. Scott called Laci's mother, Sharon Rocha, to tell her Laci was missing. Ron Grantski, Laci's stepfather, called police at 6 p.m., to report her missing.

Here Scott had begun demonstrating what has appeared to be off-cue behavior for what might have only been a harmless situation. Sharon Rocha later stated she thought it was odd Scott referred to Laci as "missing" so early in the game, instead of simply asking if Laci was over there. Some of the neighbors also hinted, independently of Laci's mother, that they thought Scott was behaving strangely frantic very early on, before someone might normally suspect something *is* that wrong. But in spite of these inconsistencies, his character seemed to rise above the situation, and everybody stood behind Scott. This included the Rochas, who did not know about their son-in-law's infidelity yet. They were still in a state of denial, not wanting to actually believe or consider the possibility of...the unthinkable. To them, he was still their all-American, dream son-in-law. But ever so gradually over time, reality started to materialize, showing the other more vile side of this young man to whom they had given their fullest trust.

When police arrived to take the missing person's report, the salesman/husband told the officers that he last saw his 27-year old wife, who was eight months pregnant, that morning (Tuesday, December 24, 2002) at about 9:30 a.m., before he left for his fishing trip. He told them that Laci was planning to walk the dog in the nearby park and maybe do some shopping. Scott said he tried reaching his wife on his cell phone, unsuccessfully, when he was done fishing. When asked to go down to the station for questioning, Scott made some excuse, that he was too distraught, but said he would be willing to do it at a later date. When asked to take a polygraph, he made a cell phone call, then told officers his parents didn't want him to.

At the outset of any missing persons case, high-profile or not, the immediate family members are almost always asked to submit to a polygraph exam, so that they may be cleared from suspicion, opening the path for further investigation. John Walsh and Marc Klaas were no exceptions in their children's abduction cases, in which they submitted to the test and cleared themselves paving the way to help solve their cases. Stranger abduction is considered much more rare. Family-member kidnappings are far more frequent, of course. In fact, the statistics for spousal murder are so high, that the husband is the first potential suspect police will look at when starting from scratch in any missing person investigation.

In the majority of missing person cases, police, as a general rule of thumb, don't begin searching for the subject until at least 24 hours have elapsed. This allows the majority of cases to solve themselves, because 9 times out of 10, the missing person just walks in, after having been upset the night before, or for any of a variety of reasons depending on the person's personality, lifestyle, etc. Laci's mother Sharon said, "Somebody has her. Laci would never walk away." Detective Ridenour said early on it was determined that it would be totally out of character for Laci to have voluntarily left home like that, and that family members said that she was very happy about becoming a mother.

The massive search for Laci Peterson was launched immediately that night.

The evening of Thursday, December 26, 2002, at 7:45 p.m., officers arrived at the Peterson home with a search warrant. Yellow, crime-scene tape was wrapped around the perimeter of the property that included Laci's house. The local Modesto P. D. Homicide Division was also joined by FBI crime scene investigators. At 10 p.m. that night, workers began towing two vehicles (Laci's Land Rover and Scott's Ford F-150 truck ('02, brown, lic. Plate #6T59718), as well as the 14-ft aluminum boat from Scott's warehouse) from the home to be brought to a Department of Justice lab for examination by forensic technicians. They also took 2 computers and some patio umbrellas, as well as a whole multitude of smaller miscellaneous potential evidence, such as the most recent contents of the Petersons' vacuum cleaner bag, in an attempt to find evidence of a possible crime scene cleanup. Detective Doug Ridenour said it could be as long as sixty days to receive the results.

Laci's husband, by the way, did not stay at their own home during the investigation. Police said that he was staying with friends on those nights.

It was announced that Scott had provided detectives with a parking receipt from the Berkeley Marina that verified his whereabouts the day his wife disappeared, as well as a gas receipt from his trip home. Also, the Modesto Police released photos of the two vehicles and the fishing boat, and asked the public to help corroborate the young Mr. Peterson's story on that Thursday. That way anyone who may have seen him at the Berkeley Marina, on the freeway or anywhere in and around Modesto the morning of Christmas Eve could come forward. This information would help clear him by confirming his story or it could bring other possibilities to light.

The lie detector test came up several times during this early phase of the investigation as something of public interest. How dependable is the polygraph exam? There is no simple answer to this question, but I'll try to shed some additional light on the topic. There are several different types of polygraph tests. Each of these tests are based on different assumptions and will undoubtedly have different degrees of accuracy. The basic purpose of the polygraph is, of course, to help determine whether the subject is being truthful or deceptive with more diagnostic accuracy than an interviewer could achieve without the exam. One form of the test is called the Backster and is a psychological analysis. In this test, physiological reactions are used as a basis to draw inferences about the mental state of the respondent. For example, was the subject aroused more by one question than by another. In fact, there is a field called psychophysiology which is a sub-discipline of academic psychology and directly involves the use of physiological responses as indicators of mental actions or states. But only a few polygraphers have had any actual scientific training in this field.

There are also the Keeler and Reed forms of the polygraph. These types, similarly, are based on psychological diagnosis. One aspect of this test that distinguishes it from others is that it doesn't specifically ask direct questions about actually committing the crime, such as, "Did you murder your wife Laci?" It makes use of a broader range of questions, some of which would be the control questions to determine truthfulness. One reason for bypassing the more obvious objective question is that most people involved in a crime, innocent or guilty of committing it, would naturally have a higher emotional response to it. When this happens, emotions of stress or tension for innocent respondents have shown to be similar to those of the guilty.

The polygraph field is one industry that seems to have an equal number of advocates and opponents. Most of these individuals are scientists and political lobbyists. In order to become a member of the American Polygraph Association, a person must have a college degree, have successfully completed a minimum of 300 hours of classroom training at an accredited polygraph academy, and must individually conduct at least 200 polygraph exams in the form of an internship. Once a member, each examiner is required to attend seminars annually, to keep them educated in the latest advances in diagnostic methods, testing, and instrumentation. By 1980, about half the states in the U.S. required examiners to be licensed. Since the polygraph is only an instrument that measures and records physiological reactions, it can only scribble a graph, much like an EKG reads your heart rate. The diagnosis of the graph must be interpreted by an examiner who, of course, is only human. It is on the examiner's precision and integrity that the usefulness of the polygraph evidence depends.

There are a number of reasons why polygraph exam results are not admissible as evidence in a court of law. Some states allow its use on a limited basis. One reason for its lack of use in the courts, is that there are a variety of ways to defeat it and unfortunately, it tends to be the career criminals who have and practice this knowledge more than the innocent bystanders being subjected to it. In civil litigation, for example, if both parties agree to submit to it, the results may be used as relevant evidence. More often than not, the polygraph is one mere tool out of many techniques used by detectives in their overall investigation of a case.

The loved ones of Laci Peterson could only search and wait. I'm sure they would have given anything to see that glorious smile once again. The feeling must have been terrible that, as every day passes, rescue workers became more and more pessimistic. Dennis Rocha appeared to show the deepest heartfelt sorrow out of all of them. One of the things he stated to the media was, "We don't know where she is, or what has happened, but we love her, we miss her, and we just want her home safe." After the reward amount swelled to a half million dollars, Laci's father had even directed his comments toward whoever the perpetrator might be, by saying, "Take the money. Take the money and go. Just bring back my daughter unharmed." He spoke sobbingly with his head low and covering his eyes and forehead with his hand.

Since Laci had been considered to be abducted in the nearby East La Loma Park, just off Covena Avenue where she lived, the neighbors were a bit bewildered by the whole thing. One older resident, Mary McKibben, who has lived on Highland Drive near the Petersons' street for approximately fifty years, told the media, "I'm just puzzled. Covena has never been known as a bad area."

The actual street in question is in what I would describe as a picture-perfect tree-lined neighborhood you might see in a Florida orange juice commercial, very serene and pleasant. With children riding bicycles in the street, houses and lawns are well maintained in this neighborhood. In some ways it resembles a retirement community where deer and birds will come right up to you and feel safe eating directly from your hand—very nonthreatening. Neighbors all seem to know each other very well. In fact, one neighbor said that they greet new homeowners with cards and friendly visits, something that I was accustomed, living not far away. Neighbors commonly gather for chili cook-offs, as well as Neighborhood Watch meetings. One resident commented publicly that the weirdest part about this whole thing is that she thought everybody looked out for one another in this neighborhood.

Directly across the street from the Petersons' home, approximately around the same time that Laci disappeared, and contrary to almost everything people had recently mentioned about the nature of the neighborhood, a burglary occurred. This was the home of Rudy and Susan Medina, who were away that Tuesday, Wednesday, and Thursday for the holidays. The following Thursday a person called state parole officers with a tip that directed police to two suspects in this burglary. These men were Donald Glen Pearce, 44, and Steven Wayne Todd, 35, who were taken into custody shortly thereafter; in fact, they were arrested the very same night the tip came in and were booked at Stanislaus County Jail. The two of them gave police many facts and statements that checked out, matching the burglary scene. This convinced investigators that these individuals were in fact the actual burglars and were telling the truth.

Pearce and Todd apparently broke into the home on December 26, just two days after Laci was reported missing. Todd went ahead and disclosed to authorities that he had cased out the neighborhood while he commonly frequented the area and noticed what appeared to be an empty house, the occupants of which were probably out of town for Christmas. Todd said that he and Pearce entered the home at approximately 4 a.m. the morning after Christmas and actually stayed for about 3 hours. Just the amount of time they were supposedly in the house burglarizing sounded very bold to me. Todd also said that they decided to enter the home a different way because he spotted two TV news vans nearby in the neighborhood. But nevertheless, the two burglars went ahead and carried a heavy safe out the front door and across the front lawn. The safe contained jewelry appraised at $50,000.00 and $3,000.00 in cash, among its contents. The burglars also took numerous other items of high liquid value including a Tec 9mm semiautomatic handgun, a Beretta .380 caliber handgun, power tools, a camera, a Gucci watch, and a Louis Vuitton purse.

Detective George Stough stated that none of the crews of those news-team vans ever noticed anything suspicious during the early morning hours of the burglary. Steven Todd appeared to be very concerned and said that it was a bad coincidence that their escapade coincided directly with the Laci disappearance and said he had been fearful they would become associated with it. The two men had been described as being unusually cooperative, telling the police everything. They were, indeed, very eager to distance themselves from being, in any way, shape or form, connected to the high-profile Laci Peterson case. Modesto police sergeant Ron Cloward said that there were people other than the burglars who ended up in possession of the stolen loot and that the same was true for these persons, very anxious to have nothing to do with this national spectacle.

Late one evening over the weekend after the disappearance, a shady-looking man entered the Modesto Police Department and put a large duffel bag on the counter. He said to the officer on duty that night that the bag was full of stolen property from the alleged burglary across from the Petersons. But the man ran outside and disappeared when the officer told him he would get someone to take a report. Sergeant Cloward then visited surprisingly numerous people in southeast Modesto whom he knew were in possession of some of the stolen property, as well. He informed them that they could all avoid prosecution, if they would turn in everything from the burglary that they had. He left his card with each of them, so that they could bring the articles directly to him.

By Monday, police had almost everything recovered that had been stolen in the burglary. Cloward told the media, "When you've got guys running into the Police Department, throwing stolen property on the counter and then running away, that's pretty rewarding. Really, that just doesn't happen."

The two men were summarily cleared as suspects in the search for the missing pregnant woman.

I believe the *only* reason this burglary across the street from the Peterson house was solved, is because of the "Laci" connection. I am convinced that the police, under normal circumstances, would hardly have lifted a finger in their investigation of that burglary, and it would still have gone unsolved, even now, if not for the coincidence of a high-profile media case like this being nearby. Police have tools at their disposal which, if it wasn't for the called-in tips, might still have led to the arrest and conviction of these individuals. An office I used for my business a number of years ago was broken into and burglarized. When I asked about fingerprinting, the officer taking the report just nonchalantly blew off the idea by saying it's not routine that they would do that over just a burglary. I really got the impression the officer didn't want to make more work for himself. Anyone who's been a victim of a burglary obviously knows the frustrating feeling that police simply aren't motivated enough to use their forensic resources.

I once knew an individual who was actually robbed at gunpoint in Oakland, California. Yet police, believe it or not, did nothing. He was told by the reporting officer that they would not even try to talk to any of the adjacent neighbors because, he said, Oakland residents don't talk to police—sorry. He told this guy that people might talk to police where he's from, but not there in Oakland. Now what kind of attitude is that? The normal non-media influenced way of investigating, I suppose. This victim, unfortunately, was just straight out of luck. I, however, can't say police efforts are all that bad when not scrutinized because I did, years ago, have a car stolen, and within a week of making the report, I received a call from the police. They had recovered it. I was very thankful. In that case, I felt that they did a good job.

A publication reported that one of the officer's taking the missing persons report, before leaving, happened to ask Scott what he used for bait when he went fishing. Scott, according to this information, paused a few seconds then said he didn't remember. After they left, the cop supposedly said to his partner that *he* could remember what bait he used when he went fishing with his dad at the age of 13. If this was possibly true, I thought it would make an interesting survey question, so I asked a few people what they thought of it.

The first person I asked was a retired lab-technician biologist. She said, "Well I don't think that Scott had used any bait at all, because his Christmas Eve boat ride in the bay was for another purpose, to sink bodies where they might not ever be discovered. And his answer demonstrates he hadn't considered he'd be asked this question, revealing a certain amount of deception." She then went on to ask me, "Don't boys use those worms or little fishy things when they go fishing?" I said, "Yes. Yes they do."

Another person I surveyed was a computer systems analyst. He said, "Well I think it would be logical to conclude that he didn't go fishing then. At least if he was on the bay that day, he must've been doing something else. We can only imagine what that might've been."

Then I happened to be in Berkeley one afternoon because I was down at the marina taking some pictures of the receipt machine that Scott used to help generate his alibi. Anyway, I figured that while I was there, I might as well go and get a world-famous, jumbo slice of pizza on Telegraph Avenue. For those of you who aren't familiar with the Bay Area here in California, Telegraph Avenue happens to be the boulevard that gave this city its nickname, "Berzerkley." It's always a bit of a show anytime you go there. You'll see quite a variety of street performers, panhandlers, exhibits, street vendors, an occasional topless woman dancing with a snake, trinket booths, every type of spice, candle, beads, and incense imaginable, people with long dreadlocks wearing tie-die and just a lot of psychedelic, 60's-type people, some of them living in the People's Park who look like they haven't bathed for a week. Well, you know, basically that kind of stuff. Anyway, I saw a young, homeless woman sitting there on the corner, not too far from some of the other ones. She had long, black hair and was wearing black denim and studs. Since she appeared to be by herself, I thought I'd catch one last response to my survey question.

After I explained the question to her and the reason for the survey, she responded with, "He probably used the unborn son for bait." She went on, "But he also knew this would be suicide to admit, so caught off guard and with nothing else to say, he simply said he couldn't remember."

I told her I appreciated her point of view.

2

The Search

The search started at the footpath a block and a half from the Peterson home on the night of Christmas Eve 2002. This is where Scott led Lt. Bruce Able and 6 other officers to where, it was believed at the time, Laci had walked their dog that morning. This was East La Loma Park, a part of the greater Dry Creek Regional Open Space Reserve. Dry Creek, which runs through the park, is a tributary of the Tuolumne River. Despite the fact that it was already dark at this point, the officers penetrated their way into what seemed like a vast and tangled wooded abyss.

The mission began to intensify as the Stanislaus County Sheriff's Department brought out additional troops and eventually, that evening, two pilots for the search helicopter. This was only a small sampling of what was continuing to build that night, into that following morning and next afternoon, not to mention the days and weeks that would follow. This was not only impressive simply for what it was, but also it was amazing that a preponderance of human forces were sacrificing what most people consider to be *the* two most important days of the entire year, Christmas Eve and Christmas Day. This alone demonstrates the awesome power of both Laci's character as a person and the local community as a force coming together to help one of their own.

Dry Creek itself was by no means a dry creek. It was a long meandering brook, but deep and wide at some parts, as much as 15 feet at places. The water's edge was not always easy to reach in this area. It was often difficult to reach entire segments of the creek because thick ivy, overgrown and withered from many years of age, covered the treacherously steep slopes intermingled throughout the expanse and length of its cascading formations. The color of the water was a deep brown, muddy at parts, and sluggish, gradually creeping along, while other pools were silently still and glassy like the cold midnight air. The darkness of night lay heavily shaded from the moon and stars by the deep willowy branches drooping from high above. A slightly hanging fog drifted in and around the enormous basins of the park's wooded growth, giving these late hours of the quest for Laci a gloomy atmosphere. The shadowy figures of the giant ancient oak trees hung heavily over some of the steep edges of the creek where, at times, the appearance of what seemed to be a face in the girth of their trunks could be seen hiding between the mammoth thick gnarled roots, some of which descended into the depths of the water's darkness.

Mag flashlights used by police, waved back and forth through the dense foliage, poking in and out of the heavy underbrush. The thunderous clap of the helicopter propeller was heard roaring up above in the midnight sky, as the powerful beam of its giant searchlight pierced the darkness by probing relentlessly up and down Dry Creek and between many of its gargantuan obstacles. The park itself had many of these same immense lumbering oak trees, staggered in and around the vast expanse of the East La Loma territory with enormous appendage-like branches woven in a seemingly endless convolution of decaying bark with various stages of green and brown mosses.

Aside from the jogging path, the ground was densely covered in various levels of decaying timber debris, including leaves, bark, ivy, twigs, and branches, some of it wet and decaying, while much of it was dry and brittle. There were coarse, dry, rocky areas with varying degrees of steepness in their rolling slopes. One would have to be careful in the dark, so as not to step or fall into a deep crevice or catch an ankle on a jagged edge jutting out.

During the search, between the shrouds of leaves and many twisted and intertwined branches, there were undoubtedly many sets of glowing red eyes of all shapes and sizes, peering out into the darkness. These feathered wood owls, different furry mammals, and other dry, scaly as well as slimy creatures were an embedded part of the park's eco-system, but these critters didn't stick around too long that evening. Most of them disappeared into the night. Their natural habitat was being turned upside down with a man-made fine tooth comb, as they fluttered, scurried, and slithered as far away as they could go with no place to hide.

Several horse teams of mounted patrolmen rode their mighty steeds gallantly into the darkening wooded search area. Heavy leather straps and thick buckles harnessed these heavy warhorses courtesy of the county Sheriff's department. Distant thuds could be heard from the stride of their powerful hoofs that dug at the hard earth, raising an invisible dust into the dark atmosphere. Bursts of white steam snorted and grunted from the muzzles of these beasts of burden, as their heavy breath hit the cold night air. Down through the inconceivable panorama of branches and layer upon layer of innumerable green and brown leaves, filtered the tiny, slanting, emerald rays from the miniscule stars in the dark, midnight sky, but metallic police badges woven into the fabric of their chivalrous uniforms barely reflected a shimmer of this light or that from the half-shaded moon high above. They proceeded in warlike configuration. What creatures may have dwelt in these mighty trees now poised cautiously for cover in what they could only have perceived to be—a possible encroaching danger. The ripple of broad, sinewy muscles extruding from the forms of these dark stallions was, by itself, a marvel to the eye of the observer. Together in the dark wooded La Loma night, the police search effort was a vista of such awe-inspiring magnificence as to be almost breathtaking.

Hidden deep in little, hollow pockets behind the thicker shrubbery along the creek, sometimes beneath a low, rocky overhang, were homeless encampments. An officer said many of the homeless had fled, probably because of all the activity, leaving behind what little belongings they had. Every once in a long time, I've encountered some of Modesto's homeless here and there. I've seen them in front of some of the seedier liquor stores in the lower income parts of town. These full-grown adults were, of course, dirty and smelly, wearing an assortment of torn rags for clothes. I've seen them just hanging out by the pay phones and what not, messing and playing around with each other with apparently nothing better to do like they were only kids, even though most of them appeared to be well into their fifties. Based on this, I did have an idea of what the ones living in the park may have looked like. When I heard about the police search party's brief encounter with them, I pictured how this little episode may have unfolded. You just know how these drunken buffoons must've been knocking each other over to get out of there. Some short, pot-bellied ones must've come popping out of their cozy lair, dragging moth-eaten blankets in one hand and holding their pants up with the other, stumbling away into the darkness. Tall, skinny ones with missing teeth, clutching liquor bottles with long, bony fingers, hobbling along only to catch a tree branch in one of their faces, knocking him to the ground. Tucked away in their nook, perhaps older ones with long, white beards peered out of their hole with a flickering, old, rusty lantern, before hurriedly bumbling along behind the others, then scattering in another direction away from the wooded, open space. The seedy park dwellers had all fled. I had done some fishing in various lush parts of Modesto, and you could say that there was a bit of a community of them in there.

Lt. Able said that altogether on Christmas Eve they had 30 officers searching. That same night, as well as the next morning, police and the first of the volunteers fanned out through the La Loma neighborhood, checking in back alleys and yards.

Modesto officers worked through the night in their efforts to locate Laci. The search intensified the next morning. At daybreak Wednesday, which was Christmas morning, in radiant glory the brigade formed again with reinforcements for the search. These additional officers included three more on horseback, two more on mountain bikes, several canine units, and six additional Modesto firefighters, who wore water rescue gear when navigating Dry Creek in an inflatable raft. With officers walking side-by-side through the width of the park, they searched from the El Vista Bridge downstream to Beard Brook Park, south of Yosemite Blvd. This was the most thorough of the searches and took place early that afternoon.

Friends, family members, and neighbors, after disbursing throughout the neighborhood, taped missing persons flyers they put together that morning all over utility poles. Since the first flyers went up Christmas Day, the family did not open gifts, according to relatives. They spread the word around, asking anyone who walked or rode past them if they had seen or heard of Laci Peterson. "Christmas is over for us," Brent Rocha, Laci's brother, told the media. "We all feel empty and want our sister returned." Police urged ranchers and farmers, or anyone who owned a decent amount of land, to inspect their property for signs of clothing, disturbed ground or anything amiss.

The city planners of Modesto had originally intended to name the town "Ralston," after the San Francisco banker who had founded the city in 1870. William Ralston thanked them very cordially for the honor but modestly declined. This modesty he showed stood as a founding pride and it stuck. The town was named "Modesto," the Spanish word for "modest."

I discovered an interesting piece of trivia about the founding father of Modesto, William Ralston. Many of the ventures this senior banker invested in were not so sound. Once in 1875, account holders withdrew their savings from his bank, forcing its closure. His body was later discovered floating in San Francisco Bay—he had drowned. It was speculated to be an apparent suicide resulting from his recent financial failure. Upon hearing this, I thought the defense might be able to use this tidbit of trivia as one more factor to their advantage. For example, they could say, "Even William Ralston, the founding father of Modesto, was found floating in the San Francisco Bay, exactly how Laci was found, demonstrating that coincidences do happen. That if *this* individual, of all people, was also found in identically the same place Laci was found, it is simply more common for dead bodies to end up in the San Francisco Bay, which is enormous, than what people, on the average, might think."

From its very beginnings, Modesto was a community devoted to forward progress, expansion, and general quality of life for its residents.

Modesto (for those who might not know) is the county seat of Stanislaus County in central California. It has three rivers running through it, the Tuolumne, the Stanislaus, and the San Joaquin, as well as being centered on three railroads, the Southern Pacific, the Central Pacific, and the Modesto~Empire Railroad. The city is a famed agricultural center established in the northern portion of the San Joaquin Valley, in a region irrigated by the Don Pedro Dam. The town is located on U.S. Highway 99 and is situated approximately 85 miles southeast of San Francisco. Modesto was laid out in 1870 by the Southern Pacific Railroad and incorporated in 1884. Food processing plants, dried fruit and quick-freezing plants, and meat and poultry packing houses became the principal industries of the city. Interestingly, I had a family member who'd been working for Del Monte Corporation in the 1960's. To this day, Del Monte still has major manufacturing plants located here. In fact, this person was the source who enlightened me about the economic climate of the area, before I made my decision to move here.

There was a strong flow of businesses, structures, dwellings, and people moving to this one square-mile town, once it was generally known where Modesto would be located. It was considered, to some degree, to be a barren settlement on the plains, without a lot of trees or vegetation, but was instead a profuseness of wind-blown, dry soil and was often described as just a large wheat field. On November 8, 1870, Modesto became the end of the line for the Southern Pacific Railroad, and it wasn't for two more years that the tracks were continued on to Merced. At this time, there were only about 25 buildings to speak of, when newcomers first got off the train.

In the year 1900, the town had about 2,000 residents. By 1910, the population of Modesto was estimated to be approximately 4,500 inhabitants. In 1930, when Prohibition ended, it had grown to almost 14,000 people, and today, its population stands at about 200,000. Part of the boost in population the town received after Prohibition resulted because the brothers Julio and Ernest Gallo, who had apprenticed their skills from their father's vineyard, then went on to found here in Modesto one of the most successful wine companies in the world. Still headquartered here, the Gallo Company is largely responsible for the leaps and bounds of prosperity our town has made.

Modesto was one part of the U.S. that experienced an exponential rate of growth starting in 1950, when its population was approximately 20,000 citizens. By 1960, that number doubled to about 40,000. By 1970, it tripled to 60,000. By 1980, it had more than quintupled to 107,000. Then, in 1990, the census counted close to 165,000 persons. Since then, about 35,000 more have come, mostly commuters fed up with rising Bay Area housing prices, including myself.

In 1912, the prodigious arch that reads "Water, Wealth, Contentment, Health" was built downtown between 9th and I Streets for a cost of only $1,200. It stands 25 feet high in the middle and spans 75 feet across I street with 668 built-in lights that illuminate its letters. The sign's slogan was chosen as the result of a 1911 contest. Sam Harbaugh, of the Modesto Business Men's Association, was awarded $3 for his winning entry.

Some of the founding fathers proudly referred to the town as the "most metropolitan and classy of its size in California."

Modesto eventually became known as the "Garden City" because of its well-manicured lawns and also the "Rose City" because of its plethora of rose bushes. Early on, strength was placed on education, cultural activities and the theater. The city has publicly praised both its top-of-the-line entertainment productions and the scholarly achievements of its students. In 2001, voters passed a bond to renovate the elementary schools and actually build more high schools. Bordered by low, medium, and high-income neighborhoods, the city had an impressive downtown, and suburbia eventually kicked in. There's a name-brand video store on every corner. The farther you move away from the downtown, the more modern it gets. In the 1990's, in addition to seeing a middle-class housing expansion, a market for large, opulent homes blossomed. The north and east sides of town are covered with them. In short, a good deal of variety exists here. If you want old, traditional, and modest, it's here. If you're looking new and affluent, it's here. If you want old affluence, coupled with vintage historical sites, it's here.

Because the city, county, state, and federal offices are all located downtown, they employ thousands of workers. And, since Highway 99 splits the downtown in half, Modesto makes for an ideal commuter's paradise. In fact, citizens are now debating the idea of building a cross-town expressway, to get traffic to Highway 99 more rapidly. Many private practices have their offices downtown, which, of course, helps the variety of shops and restaurants. This central area also has a high-rise hotel, hospital, and movie complex. Despite the downtown's central location, the preponderance of housing built in recent times has blossomed much more heavily on the east side of this area. About 5 miles north of downtown on the 99, lies Modesto's Vintage Faire Mall, which for those who are familiar, is about the same size as Pleasanton's Stoneridge Mall. The Vintage Faire Mall includes the typical Nordstroms and Sears, as well as dozens of other department and specialty stores. Naturally, just beyond the mall, are the large discount super stores, such as Costco, Wal-Mart, etc.

Modesto also offers quality nightlife, with a variety of bars, gourmet restaurants, and a multitude of delis and coffee shops. It has a large community college and an airport. All the neighborhoods have at least one park, some of which adjoin a school. It even has a large skate park for thrashers, and four golf courses for its yuppies.

A few days after the search began, an employee of mine made the suggestion that I get involved. He knew I had recently gotten out of a long-term relationship and said, "Hey Brad, you know, some of Laci's friends are kind of cute. You might want to go lend a hand and check this thing out." His comment was a little on the light-hearted side, of course, but I think he meant well, and sincerely did think it was a good idea. I said, "Yeah, I've been thinking about going over there."

The first three days of the search were, unfortunately, without success. Officials, also at this time, were remaining very low key about the whole investigation, being very careful not to divulge too much information when answering questions, apparently so as not to jeopardize the case. They actually declined to say what they might be looking for, at least in terms of certain leads. And, as we know, no arrests had been made, and no suspects had been identified in connection with Laci's actual disappearance, this early in the game.

Also on Thursday, just two days after Laci disappeared, at about 5 p.m., police brought in a bloodhound that actually led authorities in the opposite direction from the park. La Loma, of course, is where investigators theorized that the pregnant woman vanished some time between 10 a.m. and 6 p.m. the day before Christmas. When officers released the bloodhound in front of the Peterson home, the dog did not go to the dirt path that leads into the park. Instead, the canine led officials to properties around the corner, then south to Yosemite Boulevard, and eventually to Santa Rosa Avenue, near the E and J Gallo Winery. It was in this area the bloodhound seemed to lose his trail at some dumpsters where he simply was nosing around. The Contra Costa County sheriff deputies, who supplied the hound, climbed into the dumpster and examined it with flashlights, but didn't appear to find anything significant. It had already been emptied. They ended their day's findings from the bloodhound at this location. The determination was made by the handlers that Laci had left in a car the day she disappeared and not on foot, as was originally believed.

It had also been reported that Modesto Police had used five dogs of their own earlier in the investigation. This, I thought, could be a useful piece of information, because a clever defense attorney might, or perhaps Geragos should, use this as a point to argue. For example, if the prosecution is presenting this single hound from Contra Costa County as the only "dog" evidence, by not submitting with it any of the miscellaneous findings of the other previous five dogs...why? Perhaps because those findings are as haphazard as this animal's discoveries, but this canine gave the police a result more closely fitting the investigators' theory.

At first the family members and friends put up a $100,000.00 reward for Laci's safe return. This, very shortly, increased by $25,000.00 more from an anonymous donor, through the Carole Sund-Carrington Memorial Reward Foundation. This missing persons center located in Modesto was established after the violent death of Francis and Carole Carrington's daughter, Carole Sund, as well as their granddaughter Julie, and their friend, Silvina Pelosso, in the spring of 1999. This was also known as the Gary Staynor-Yosemite slayings case. The organization is headed by Kim Petersen (different spelling, no relation to Scott) who is currently the Executive Director. Here is their mission statement:

> The Sund/Carrington Memorial Reward Fund has been established to provide resources to families without economic means, to offer rewards for information to help law enforcement officials locate missing loved ones, and to bring violent criminals to justice. Additionally, the foundation is determined to raise public awareness surrounding the problem of missing persons and violent crime in this country.
> The foundation will act as a liaison between law enforcement, the victim's family and the media, to bring swift attention to an abduction, by offering a substantial reward for information in a timely manner. The direct, immediate attention via the media will help elevate the exposure of the missing person and details surrounding the disappearance. The reward will encourage people with information to come forth when they might otherwise stay silent.

It is our goal to bring loved ones back to their home and to secure the arrest and conviction of the criminal(s) responsible. As criminals are caught and convicted in the first instance and removed from our communities, it will ultimately protect our communities from repeat offenders.

Sharon Rocha, during several televised press conferences, praised Kim Petersen and the Sund/Carrington Foundation for doing such an extraordinary job with her daughter's case. Again, it was fortunate for Mrs. Rocha, along with the rest of Laci's family, that Modesto was so well-established and on the cutting edge of this most difficult field.

Here is a quote from Stanislaus County Sheriff Les Weidman regarding the center:

"The Foundation serves a vital role in assisting law enforcement officers tasked with the responsibility of investigating homicides which are arduous and complex. I would personally like to thank the foundation for their concern and generosity in helping make our communities a better and safer place."

This location was also used as a command center during the Yosemite slayings investigation in 1999. I should also mention a statistic regarding the area; in 2001, there were seventeen homicides in Modesto, which is high for a suburban town. There were three homicides in 2000 and five in 1999.

Then, on that Friday, only three days after Laci's disappearance, the reward for information leading to Laci's safe return grew from $125,000.00 to $500,000.00 in just one day. Altogether, Thursday's (day after Christmas 2002) search effort involved more than 50 law enforcement officials. Among those joining their Modesto police counterparts were eight mounted patrolmen from the Stanislaus County Sheriff's Department.

After the family had been using the Peterson home for the last day and a half, they moved the volunteer headquarters over to the Red Lion Hotel on Sisk Road, to help give the family more privacy. This also would offer the operation a centralized location with more phone lines, which Laci's friend, Renee, happened to mention. From there, people then began to flood in from all around California. Sharon, while still supporting her son-in-law at this time, said, "Scott was overwhelmed by the support of the community." Peterson, however, was not as vocal as the other family members had been. They said he was not speaking to reporters at this time because he was still so upset over Laci's disappearance. The Modesto Police at this time also set up a separate command center of its own in East La Loma Park.

During those first few days after the disappearance, among the inner core of volunteers helping to run the search center, were Laci's friends, Renee and Jeff Tomlinson, who currently live in Hughson, which is right next door to Modesto. This was the young couple who had planned to hold a baby shower for the Petersons a few weeks later, had Laci not disappeared, of course. Jeff, when describing her, said, "She's such a fun-loving girl, always smiling and joking with you." He was among the friends who couldn't help but get choked up when reminiscing about her. "All our families are just now getting rolling on this together," he said.

Renee said, "She's the most energetic person you could meet—spunky, happy, always has a smile on her face, and dimples you can't miss. That's the smile we want back."

Earlier that day, the officers conducted another thorough grid-pattern search in the park. This time they spaced themselves evenly and explored meticulously, while walking across fields and paths, through different parts of the water, through denser wooded areas by daylight, in the hope of finding any kind of clues. The search continued on after dark late that Thursday.

Reports had come in earlier in the investigation that several potential witnesses had possibly seen a person roughly fitting Laci's description, walking a dog that morning near the park. One avid bicyclist said that, because it was Christmas Eve, he happened to skip his morning ride in the park the day Laci disappeared, and that he was sorry he did. He thought he might've been able to provide clues, since he knew he had seen her in that location before.

On Friday, investigators expanded the search over to the Berkeley Marina, where Scott said he had gone fishing on Christmas Eve, when Laci disappeared. On this first trip to the Marina, officials were merely investigating the legitimacy of Peterson's alibi. However, this first Marina search involved not only Modesto police, but also a Contra Costa County Sheriff's Department dog team, as well. Detectives did not reveal at first what they may have found, if anything. Det. Ridenour, however, reported that it wasn't anything "conclusive" at that time, and that there didn't appear to be any evidence of foul play. Police continued to insist at this point that Peterson was not a suspect; however, they said nobody had been officially ruled out yet, either.

As more days passed, however, the police said the situation was becoming more grim. Ridenour then said, "In investigating the circumstances of her disappearance, and in view of the timing of the holiday season, it becomes more apparent that her disappearance *is* a result of foul play. The investigation is progressing forward with that main focus, but we have not ruled out any other possibilities."

Because of the high-publicity nature of the case, many of the Petersons' neighbors were interviewed extensively during these first few days of the search. Here are some of the things a few of them were saying publicly. Sabrina Hull, who lives on Highland Drive next to Covena Avenue, said she, along with friends, walked the trails in East La Loma Park regularly every day at 6 a.m. She said the park was normally filled with joggers, bike riders, and other walkers, and that she never felt any imminent danger while there, although she said out of general paranoia, she wouldn't walk there alone either.

A Covena Avenue resident, Albert Urquidez, said the only trouble he has ever known in the neighborhood was the break-in of his brother's car, and that all areas have their problems.

Amy Krigbaum, who helped search for Laci in the park on Christmas Eve, lives across the street from the Petersons. She said that her family's been more on the edge since the disappearance, and that her roommate no longer allows her 12-year old son to play outside because of concern for his safety, at least for the time being, anyway.

At the Red Lion Hotel that was being used for the makeshift volunteer center, Scott Peterson had been a visible presence, but relatives explained he'd been declining on-the-record media interviews because he supposedly didn't want to detract from the investigation. Officials mentioned at this time that Scott was continuing to cooperate "to some degree," but wouldn't elaborate any further.

That Saturday, members of the family and volunteers said they were remaining hopeful Laci would be found safe and healthy. Jackie Peterson, Scott's mother said, "We believe she was abducted. We hope somebody realizes they made a big mistake, and they let her go. We are all looking forward to the baby." She went on to say that she believes her daughter-in-law's disappearance and the burglary across the street were related. She pointed out that police notified them that the burglary might have occurred some time Christmas Eve, a time that coincided with Laci's disappearance. "There's no possibility that he (Scott) would be involved," Mrs. Peterson said. "They were like honeymooners, even after being married five years. They doted on each other. We all wanted to be like them."

The primary sweep of Saturday's search effort covered the territory where the San Joaquin River merges with the Tuolumne and the Stanislaus, near the west end of Highway 132. The day before, boat and dive teams made their way down the Tuolumne River from Modesto to the San Joaquin. Police pressed 10 miles west of Modesto, to 4,000 acres of wetlands along the Stanislaus, Tuolumne, and San Joaquin rivers, in their continued hunt for the missing woman.

It was the bloodhound's earlier findings that convinced authorities to broaden their search westward. Divers swam or walked through Dry Creek between Claus Road and the La Loma Bridge, a few miles east of downtown Modesto, on Thursday and Friday. Also, on Friday, a helicopter crew scoured the Tuolumne River from Fox Grove, near Hughson, to the San Joaquin River.

This was when Laci's brother, Brent Rocha, was asked if he thought Scott had anything to do with his sister's disappearance. "No way. Absolutely not." He said the couple had a good relationship. His opinion, of course, was to change a little later on.

On Sunday, December 29, 2002, scores of volunteers canvassed out across Modesto, as the search intensified. Since Christmas, more than 600 volunteers had emerged from the fabric of Laci's community, to post flyers, distribute leaflets, answer the recently set-up tip-lines, hike and re-hike sections of East La Loma Park, trying to find any trace of the 8-month pregnant, Covena Avenue resident. The steady stream of volunteers only continued to pour in from there. Divers and horse patrols essentially were working non-stop since the outset, and naturally, they were starting to need some rest, so they were given Sunday off. Likewise, the helicopter was scheduled for routine maintenance. Stacey Boyers, who's been one of Laci's friends since the third grade, was among the 15 to 20 persons who had staffed the family command center from its opening on December 26. She said, "It's amazing how this community has come together to help us." She had been logging in volunteers all day Sunday and said, "We've had 50 sign up today and probably more than 600 in the last few days."

Two guys brought their own horses to East La Loma Park that day, Jack Marks and John Adams. Marks said, "This is a tragedy in the community, and I'm just trying to give something back. Maybe if we get more people out here helping, she's going to turn up."

Authorities said that, at this point, about 340 calls had come in on the tip lines, none of which had resulted in a "concrete lead," and that investigators were trying to follow up on anything called in that was deemed credible.

On Monday, Sgt. Ron Cloward said that the helicopter search team, police divers, and mounted patrolmen were resuming the job that day. Helicopters then hovered over the Hetch Hetchy and California Aqueducts, searching for any trace of the now world-famous, Princess of Modesto. The Stanislaus County Sheriff's Underwater Search and Rescue Team inspected a section of the San Joaquin River about one-half mile north of the Old Fisherman's Club on Highway 132, an area that was approximately 15 miles from the Petersons' home. In addition to scanning the river, divers inspected marshes near the river, and a large pond at Mape's Ranch. The divers were there because the bloodhound made a straight path down Maze Blvd, the direction of the Berkeley Marina.

The next day was Tuesday. New Year's Eve had arrived. A candlelight vigil had been planned that night for Laci, the missing pregnant mother-to-be. Over a thousand people showed up for this tearful affair. Many passed up New Year's celebration plans, to make room for this more serious and meaningful event. Fourteen hundred glowing candles were held aloft in the cold, dark, night air, as the multitude of heart-struck masses sang songs of encouragement for the missing angel and her family. The vigil took place in an open clearing at East La Loma Park, where the search for Laci had originally begun.

A flatbed trailer had been brought in to serve as a stage for the ceremony. The damp field was bordered by television news vans, as well as the large police mobile command unit. On the platform Laci's family was joined by the Chief of Police, Roy Wasden.

One of the lady singers took the microphone and performed "Amazing Grace," as the crowd swayed back and forth together in unison, many of them wearing yellow ribbons for Laci and blue ribbons for Connor. Laci's mother, Sharon

Rocha, then took the forefront and addressed the crowd. With her voice cracking, she spoke out, "Laci would be so happy to see she has so many friends and supporters. Just keep looking for Laci. Don't give up."

Wasden joined in adding, "Wherever that search takes us, let's keep looking for Laci."

Then all the other family members rotated in, one at a time, giving their prepared remarks and thoughts between songs and prayers, to the gathered citizens. All except...Scott.

The mysterious one was again remaining low key while in the crowd, spending much of this time on his cell phone. As we found out later, one of the persons Scott was speaking to, at that time, was Amber Frey, apparently letting her know when he and she would be able to have an exclusive relationship with each other.

The people who attended the vigil represented all segments of the Modesto community, including friends, neighbors, teachers, former classmates, landowners, and local business people. Many of these persons had never met Laci, but said they came to express their support for the family and community. Laci's father, Dennis Rocha, merged his way into the crowd from the stage, shaking as many hands and giving as many hugs as he could. He proclaimed as he went, "I want to meet you all. Thank you."

Scott greeted friends and family tearfully after the ceremony, but continued to decline any on-the-record interviews with the media.

Scott Peterson's sister, Susan Peterson-Caudillo, 42, said on New Year's Eve that her brother was devastated that his wife was missing and didn't know where she was. She said, "If you knew Scott the way the rest of his friends and family know him, there's not even a remote possibility that he would be involved in anything about Laci's disappearance." She said that her family understood that it is normal procedure to look at the husband and close family members. She said, "It's unfortunate that he didn't choose to go golfing instead of fishing that day, because it would have been a lot simpler of an investigation, so that is taking more time, and time is very important here in this case."

A New Year's Day brunch at the Red Lion Hotel was scheduled for the following morning. It was basically a pajama brunch fundraiser, where customers were supposed to wear their pj's and could purchase a meal for $2.03 per person. By 8 a.m., there was already a big line waiting for the doors to open. Brad Saltzman, the general manager of the hotel, said they were expecting maybe three or four hundred people, but they ended up with over eight hundred and had to turn people away after 2 p.m., when they stopped serving. He said that during most of that time, there was at least a 45-minute wait to get a table. The proceeds went to help cover some of the search costs. They raised about $4,000.00 that morning alone.

This then served more as a day of rest, since the volunteer search center was temporarily closed for the brunch. Detectives, however, continued their investigation throughout the day. According to police, 155 parolees and registered sex offenders living in southeast Modesto alone had been questioned in connection with Laci's disappearance. To me, someone who lived in southeast Modesto near the Petersons, this sounded like a lot of individuals. However, since Modesto, within city limits, has an overall population of about 200,000, the southeast section, being about one quarter of that area, would have an approximate population of 50,000, making this percentage of the population very tiny, only about one-third of one percent. This, of course, is more consistent with the national average than what it appeared to be at first glance.

Several large shrines had formed to commemorate hope for Laci's safe return, including one in East La Loma Park and one on the front lawn of the Petersons' home. Several smaller ones were started and distributed throughout other parts of the park, as well. People would come by, add a candle, a flower, or even a teddy bear, and some would just say a prayer at the growing monoliths. Aside from attending some of the events, I and sometimes, a friend or two, came by a few times to pay our respects to Laci at these makeshift shrines. We found this was where and when we had the opportunity to meet quite a lot of family and friends of the missing woman, and to discuss many of the on-going factors in the case at the time. Another valuable source of day-to-day coverage of the investigation was the *Modesto Bee*, not only because I was a resident and this was the local paper, but also because the *Bee* had been such a longtime, established and well-organized institution. For example, the paper had somewhere around 10 separate journalists working different parts of this case alone, which allowed subscribers to read many different perspectives and angles regarding the matter, as it unfolded.

At another press conference, Laci's mother, Sharon said, "We feel Scott has nothing to do with the disappearance of Laci." She pleaded to whoever the perpetrator may be, "Have some compassion in your heart…and please bring our daughter home."

Scott's mother, Jackie, of San Diego, said the reason her son wasn't talking to the media was because he wanted to keep the focus on his wife. His father, Lee Peterson, then added, "He doesn't have to defend himself; he's looking for his wife. That's where his energies are."

Detective Doug Ridenour announced again that they were trying to clear Mr. Peterson as a potential suspect and needed anyone with information to come forward, who could in any way corroborate his story. He said, "We continue to have the desire to eliminate Scott Peterson as a suspect. We have not eliminated him, but we have not eliminated a number of folks and directions at this time."

Susan Levy, Chandra's mother, said she had dropped by the command center and contributed some time working with the volunteers, especially with Laci's mother, Sharon. She said, "It makes me very heartsick that this is happening again in this community. It is very hard for us." During the peak of *their* daughter's investigation, the Levys spent countless hours with numerous network and cable television commentators, as well as radio and print journalists, trying to maintain their daughter's case in some of the limelight. "We think that's very important—to get the word out," she mentioned.

According to Laci's doctors, her baby was due February 10, 2003.

At this point in the investigation, 1,100 calls had been made to the tip line. According to Sgt. Ed Steele, some of these leads were substantial, but he couldn't elaborate as to the specifics. He said, "They're not the type of things that are going to break the case open, but from what the investigators are saying, they believed the tips to be credible."

Sgt. Ron Cloward said, "Each day we become a little more pessimistic. The odds are working against us, but we're holding onto the same hope the family is."

Officer Matt Lengel, who was answering and sorting the police tips line, said that, out of the first 1,400 calls that came in, one hundred of those were from psychics. This can almost be expected in a case with a half-million-dollar reward, along with widespread media attention—some may be seeking financial gain, while other psychics may be seeking notoriety. Federal and local law enforcement officials, however, determined that the majority of psychic findings were either too nebulous or just merely inaccurate. Kelly Huston from the Stanislaus Sheriff's office said that psychics are right about 50 percent of the time. He said that, with the pieces of a puzzle, a good psychic can put them together without a whole lot of difference of accuracy than any experienced detective can, and that this sometimes makes the psychic appear more accurate.

Another official mentioned that law enforcement resources can be frivolously wasted on following up on psychic leads; therefore, as a general rule, they will exhaust more viable leads first, such as witnesses and statements. However, people were not discouraged from calling in, since this was the purpose of the tip line.

In other findings, some government agencies have spent millions of dollars on the use of psychics in the area of national defense and espionage. Many of the findings were deemed useful; however, most of these programs were dismantled because of the stigma associated with psychics.

Again, after a relatively light search effort on New Years Day, the continued widespread effort resumed Thursday, and volunteers were given new assignments and new areas to cover. This included divers returning to the Berkeley Marina, to continue their start of the exploration of the bottom of the San Francisco Bay.

When divers and dogs were used during the search in the marina area on Saturday, a blue tarp was discovered and taken to be examined as evidence. Modesto Police, however, said they did not think it was connected to Peterson's disappearance.

After spending several days at the Berkeley Marina, Modesto Police Sgt. Ron Cloward said that divers were aided by side-scan sonar equipment from the San Mateo County Sheriff's Department, and a small fleet of vessels returned empty about 4 p.m. Thursday, when the search that afternoon ended. Seven divers and other searchers were carried by three boats from the Berkeley Harbor Patrol and Alameda County Sheriff's Department to an area beyond the fishing pier, where they were obscured from shore by low clouds and rain. Modesto Police then made an announcement that Thursday afternoon, after having spent the day searching the floor of the bay for clues. They declared that they had found what might be a human body in the murky depths—but they said the divers were exhausted and wouldn't resume until Saturday morning.

Poor weather and diver fatigue prevented investigators from recovering the object, and the divers with their specialized sonar equipment wouldn't be able to return to the marina until Saturday. This startling development was announced shortly after 6:30 p.m. and provided officials with the first promising lead in an investigation that was frustrated by its very lack of evidence.

When investigative divers announced that they would resume searching for the body Saturday, to see if the mystery object was, in fact, a body, they did not place any markers at the spot of the discovery. They were concerned that this possible evidence might be disturbed by the media before the police could get to it. Sure, it would make sense that police wouldn't want to come back to the spot that millions in the public were anxiously awaiting the results of, only to find that some overzealous tabloid reporter was already poking and prodding away at it with a long stick.

If this had actually occurred, then here is what could've happened: When the reporter is questioned by investigators as to what he may be doing there, the reporter might have this guilty-yet-innocent look on his face, as he tries to explain away that he was only trying to help. Irritated, the police rudely shuffle him away to get on with their search.

Modesto police used a high-tech sonar apparatus, called a "side-scan sonar device," to help reveal the object which might be a human body, that was discovered near the end of the old Berkeley pier, about 2 miles from shore. This piece of equipment can locate objects as far as 300 feet below the surface and pinpoint them to within 5 feet of their position. They also used another type of unit, mainly employed by the Navy and law enforcement agencies throughout the U.S., to do everything including screening the bottom of ships coming into the bay and searching for bodies dumped in a Tuolumne County lake a year before. This device is called the "tow-fish" because of its torpedo shape and metal fins. It was brought in and operated by Jeff Baehr and his 18 divers from the San Mateo County Cliff/ Rescue Dive Team. He said that, even though divers are limited in time because of the air in their tanks, they need only to dive until they actually see something. Also, because of the bay's murky waters, sound travels better than light in this environment, which is an advantage to using this device because the crew will be able to scan a larger underwater area.

Baehr described how the "fish" works, by having five members of the dive team on board the vessel lower the 50-

pound fish slowly into the water while carefully keeping it from touching the floor of the bay. Then the boat trolls along at no more than two knots per hour, dragging the device behind it with a cable, scanning up to 150 feet sections of water at a time. The fish's sonar signal beams generate a continuous photographic image of its viewings to a personal computer on board the boat. Once the closest proximity is located, they simply dive in and retrieve it. The only downside is that the device doesn't generally work well, if the water is rough.

A couple of reasons the Alameda County Sheriff's search and rescue team discontinued efforts the prior Thursday in retrieving the located object is because they were hindered by a strong current while in depths of 25 feet of water, as well as the persistent wind and rain. Also, they wouldn't have the device yet from San Mateo County, which was used Wednesday to spot the object. The sonar device wouldn't be available until Saturday. Lt. Jim Knudsen from the Alameda County Sheriff's Dept. said, "We can't endanger divers' lives. If they say it's too dangerous, we have to pull them out." Because all of the divers were volunteers, more of them would be available Saturday. Plus, they expected better weather and would have the use of the San Mateo County sonar equipment, so investigators forewent Friday, despite the heavy public anticipation. That day, family members went on a string of network and cable talk shows expressing that they weren't upset that the search was postponed a day, out of safety concerns for the divers.

When divers returned Saturday, and the object was finally recovered, it turned out to be...only a boat anchor. All that for just a rusty old boat anchor. In fact, this came as good news to the volunteer center at the Red Lion Inn, because it also meant there was a possibility Laci was still alive. There was an uproar of cheers and applause when the announcement was made at the headquarters. The members of the Peterson family were, of course, relieved to hear this news. Investigators were frustrated by this futility, but continued forward with additional exploration of the bottom of the bay.

During the search for Laci, when one of the reporters asked why this case went national because most missing persons cases do not, Detective Doug Ridenour responded with, "It is difficult to understand why these things (media frenzies) occur, but they do." I think that what the detective was really saying was that it's difficult for *him* to understand why these things occur. For me, there was no question in my mind as to why the case went national. I think Ridenour was simply caught with a question he hadn't thought about yet and tried to give the most polished sounding answer he could without embarrassing himself.

Here is a list of what I believe to be the most significant reasons for the case going national:

1. Laci Peterson's world record-breaking smile.
2. The city of Modesto had just become a recent high-profile spectacle with the Chandra Levy/Gary Condit scandal. This, in turn, was very comfortable for the national media, since they were already familiar with the hotels, court house, coffee shops, and restaurants, etc. They could just settle right in.
3. Scott and Laci Peterson lived, by all accounts, an idyllic life; a nice house in the suburbs of sunny California, a

successful livelihood, new vehicles, fishing and golf on Sundays, they held "Melrose Place" type parties, etc.

4. Scott was good-looking, he dressed GQ, he was sporty and rugged, yet financially successful, articulate, and polite. He appeared to be an "All-American Guy."

5. Laci was good-looking; she was a former Modesto cheerleader; she dressed fashionably; she was warm, friendly, and popular; she was an avid cook, gardener, and host for her privileged get-togethers. She was an All-American young woman. She was a piece of Modesto's heart and soul.

6. Modesto was also the recent command center for another high-profile triple murder—the Yosemite sightseers slayings. This attention-grabbing multiple murder case occurred in 1999, and a man named Cary Staynor was convicted.

7. When Amber Frey came forward and disclosed her involvement, the case just absolutely exploded off the map. Amber not only was the missing puzzle piece to the case, but she fit right in with the All-American theme the case had been exemplifying thus far. She was a slender, good-looking blond, or basically, a Barbie doll. This was all the media needed. They absolutely exploded in ecstasy because they knew the public would simply love this new but similar character and would just devour it all up like a pack of hungry wolves that hadn't eaten in a week. And they did.

3

The Affair

Amber
> Angel of Justice?
>> ...or Mistress of Death?

It was the night of Monday, December 30, 2002. Detective Al Brochini said he happened to be sitting at the Modesto Police Department tip desk when an actual call from Amber Frey first came in. (Coincidentally, Al Brochini happened to be the detective who first inspected Scott's boat and found Laci's hair in the pliers underneath the seat.) He quickly picked up whatever he needed and drove all the way out to Fresno that night to interview her. It sounds to me that, with all the detective's years of experience, there was no question in his mind as to the magnitude of importance this person potentially was to the case.

It makes one ponder for a moment about whether or not Amber, for even an instant, may have been slightly touched by the fact that a man she once loved was literally willing to kill for her...and did. That Scott harbored enough passion to slay another woman...for Amber's love. That everything he did and everything he owned would now be...for Amber. Amber was a love-hungry, single mother, who'd been frustrated by frivolous love in the past. This young man was different, however. Not only was he good-looking and rugged, but he had a successful career, as well. And here he had committed the ultimate act of passion, taking another human life that stood in the way of them being together, demonstrating not frivolous love, but only what one might interpret as "true" love. Perhaps a less emotionally stable woman could have fallen for that. Or possibly a woman with not as strong a moral fiber could have been tempted into crossing over into...the dark side—by common sins of selfishness, greed, and a deep longing for true love. Or in simpler terms, was she at all charmed, just enough to make, perhaps, a wrong choice? For those who think such a possibility is too remote to become a reality, I'll cite as an example Charles Manson's groupies. A little charm goes a long way. (We, of course, learned later that Scott *did* try to prey on this young, single mother's emotions in this exact manner, as was later revealed through the telephone wiretaps.)

But Amber chose to stand with the side of right over wrong. She chose to stand with the grieving family members, the community of Modesto that was looking for Laci, and the entire nation that came forward with an interest at heart in finding the California girl with the beautiful smile, alive. Despite the fact that she would be losing her new lover and potential future husband, despite the fact that she would be hit with a relentless pounding from the media, and despite the fact that she'd be subjecting her life to scrutiny by high-profile defense lawyers, she knew it was she, and she alone, who held the key that would solve the biggest case since that of O.J. Simpson. She chose to stand with the people of the State of California and invoke the law—instead of everything Scott Peterson stood for in her life.

Amber's own brother was a deputy sheriff in San Bernardino County. Whether Scott knew this or not, is unknown. But with her strong family ties in law enforcement, this perhaps was one of the reasons why she had the courage to come forward so quickly. A more average woman also may have come forward, but possibly too late, for instance, waiting until after the trial. A high-profile example of something similar occurring was when Paula Barbieri came forward after O.J.'s criminal trial was over. The secret she was keeping to herself was that she had "broken up" with O.J. the day Nicole was murdered. This was huge, but…too late; O.J. was already acquitted. For those who don't think this really means much, one can only assume that perhaps you just haven't had the experience yourself, yet, of being "dumped" by the person you finally thought was the perfect replacement of your long-term significant other who had previously "dumped" you. You are happy that you are finally with the person you believe is the perfect replacement for your previous mate, who had previously left you, only raising your hopes high enough to be shattered into a thousand pieces yet again, when you find out that he or she ultimately doesn't feel the same. This, for anyone who's experienced it knows, could cause one to feel a tremendous amount of animosity towards one's previous mate because we as human beings tend to place the blame of our current dilemma on that person for having put us in our present situation to begin with, for which we feel so miserable.

The other compelling factor that may have succumbed Amber to come forward was the fact that, *if* Scott could bring himself to murder Laci, what would stop a man capable of this from doing it again and eventually killing Amber for, perhaps, yet another woman?

Now let's just imagine for a second what *would* have happened if Amber, say, for example, would've called the Peterson tip line instead of the Modesto Police Department, after making her momentous decision to reveal her involvement. In fact, at the very beginning of the investigation, Marc Klaas, on national television (I believe it was the Larry King Show), was asked a question and pointed out something very similar to this. He said that if anybody is calling in a tip on the case, to make sure to call the Modesto Police Department, and to definitely **not** call the Peterson tip line, because you would only be putting any information you have through a Peterson family filter before, if at all, it reaches the police. In other words, before Amber came forward, if, say, one of her friends knew about the affair and went to call it in as a tip, do you really think Scott's mother or sister, after taking the tip, would forward this information on to the police? Sure, if *Laci's* mother or sister had answered, then of course they would, but just listen to everything Scott's parents and siblings have been saying in adamant defense of their family loved one!

Here's what probably would happen if Amber called the Peterson tip line, and Scott's mother or sister happened to answer: Let's say that about three weeks after Amber "reported" the information, she's starting to wonder why no officer has contacted her regarding this startling development in the case. Instead, it is Amber's friends who had been introduced to Scott, say, at the Christmas party, who recognize him from television, and then they start pestering Amber about it, eventually forcing the situation to surface from several different angles. The police, at first, may be more suspicious of Amber because when they ask what was her reason for not coming forward immediately and if this is what she knew, she, at some point in her efforts to justify her legitimacy when confronted with the issue, would say, "But I did. I did call...less than a week after the disappearance!" She would probably become adamant in her assertions, which would lead to her naming the person who picked up the tip line. Eventually the police would confront whoever the family member was—let's just say it was his sister. When the police say, "Hey, this woman says she called three weeks ago! Why didn't you report it to us?"

The sister would probably respond with, "What woman? We answered hundreds, if not thousands, of calls. I don't know who you're talking about."

Using investigative skill, the detective further pounds into the relative, eventually getting a more revealing response. For example, he could say, "Well, according to our records, we show here that the person monitoring the tip line on the night of Monday, December 30, 2002, was...you?"

In a very soft, slow, and dismissive kind of voice she might've responded, "Ohhh, thaaaat woman...Well, she was just one of Scott's old girlfriends. What would she have to do with our search for Laci?"

The detectives must have been thanking God that this didn't happen, because if it had, it would have been nothing less than disastrous to the case. If several more weeks after the disappearance were allowed to elapse, the recorded telephone conversations between Scott and Amber during these crucial fresh moments and days that Scott thought Amber was still in the dark about his involvement, may never have been revealed.

The call came in about six days after Laci went missing. The detective immediately dropped what he was doing and just drove straight down there, he even left his burrito in the microwave. Brochini wouldn't have to worry about getting a speeding ticket on the way to Fresno, because if he did get pulled over, he could always flash his badge and continue on his way. When the detective finally *did* get there, the first thing Amber said before he could open his notebook was that she had been having sex with Scott Peterson for a month before Laci disappeared. When Brochini asked her if she knew that Scott was married, she responded that she suspected the possibility, that she had confronted him on December 9 about it, and that he had responded to her with what must have later sent chills down her spine. When she saw Scott in the news involved with the disappearance of his wife a few weeks later, Amber had remembered him telling her that he had "lost his wife," and that this would be "his first holidays without her." Or, in other words, Scott seemed to know in advance, before his wife disappeared, that he wouldn't be spending *this* holiday season with her.

Of course, at the time, Amber apparently accepted at face value what Scott had told her, probably because of nothing more than the fact that she simply *wanted* to believe him from deep within her heart, even though there may still have been a tiny amount of uncertainty still lingering in the back of her mind. Plus, the term he used, "lost," might have raised even more suspicion in any person's mind, unless of course he specified, say, "cancer" as the *cause* of the loss.

Starting right away, Brochini explained to Amber how imperative her cooperation in this investigation would be toward solving the greatest whodunit in the last decade and, perhaps, of all time. She said that she understood, and then she agreed to do everything she possibly could to help. He started her out immediately on the case by explaining how they would wire-tap her phone, in case the prime suspect, Scott Peterson, who might have thought that Amber was still in the dark about who he really was, might make the fatal telltale call.

Here is a key portion of the recorded transcript of one such call:

With Amber being used as a decoy, the call was made on January 6, 2003; it was 23 minutes long and was being recorded by police without Scott's knowledge.

Scott: I am so sorry I hurt you in this way...it's the worst thing. I'm sorry, Amber. I'll just tell you.

Amber: OK.

Scott: Uh, you haven't been watching the news, obviously?

Amber: No.

Scott: I have lied to you...I haven't been traveling.

(He then tells her that he's been in Modesto, looking for Laci...his wife.)

Amber: You told me you lost your wife. What was that about?

Scott: She...she's alive.

Amber: Where? She's alive? Where?

Scott: In Modesto...The media has been telling everyone that I had something to do with her disappearance. So the past two weeks I've been hunted by the media...You deserve so much better.

Amber: I deserve to understand an explanation of why you told me you lost your wife, and this was the first holidays you'd spend without her. That was December 9th you told me this, and now all of a sudden your wife's missing. Are you kidding me?

(Scott stammers and says he cannot explain it now. He repeatedly says he needs to protect "all of us.")

Amber: So, where is she?

Scott: That's what we are trying to find out...I'm so sorry. You should be *so* angry at me, and, God, I hope you are.

(Pause)

Amber: You sat here (Dec. 9) in front of me and cried and broke down. I sat here and held your hand, Scott, and comforted you, and you were lying to me.

Scott: Yeah. (Pause) If you think I had something to do with her disappearance...er, it, that is so wrong.

Amber: And you still have the audacity to call me "sweetie," right now?

(Pause)

Scott: I know you can't trust me.

Amber: Didn't you say, "Amber, I will do anything for you. To trust me, oh baby, we have...I feel we have a future together." What was that about?

(Pause)

Scott: I never cheated on you.

Amber: Ha, ha, ha.

Scott: I never did.

Amber: You're married! How do you figure you never cheated on me? Explain that one to me?

(Peterson says he can't explain it to her at this time, a refrain throughout the conversation.)
(Pause)

Amber: How did you lose her then, before she was lost? Explain that.

Scott: There's different kinds of loss.

Amber: Then explain *your* loss.

Scott: I can't.

(Pause)

Amber: How would you explain your baby to me?

Scott: Sweetie, you don't know everything.

(Pause)

I want to tell you everything, but I can't.

Amber: Why should I not go to the police with this?

Scott: It's your decision.

Amber: Really?

Scott: Of course.

Amber: What stopped you from telling me this?

Scott: It was probably just weakness and hoping that I could hold onto you.

Amber: Just a weakness and…holding on to me?

Scott: Longing to hold on to you.

Source: Transcript admitted into evidence in the case of People v. Scott Lee Peterson in Stanislaus County Superior Court.

Let's talk about Scott claiming here that he had never cheated on Amber. When he first said that, Amber laughed at him and reminded him that he had a wife. Then he turned around again and adamantly claimed that he had never cheated on Amber. What could Scott have possibly meant by this? *One,* he was either testing his control level over Amber, by seeing if he could still pull her back into dreamland again with how much hypnotic control he still may have had over her, and seeing if he couldn't subliminally block Laci's image from Amber's mind. Or, *two*, he was simply trying to tell Amber he hadn't actually had sex with Laci (even though they were still married) since November 20, 2002, when he and Amber met. I suppose it could be one, the other, or both.

In another recorded conversation, Scott responded to Amber's question about his involvement with Laci's disappearance this way—he said that, no, he didn't do it, but he knew who did. This response perhaps gives a hint of the upcoming "Nazi Low Rider, murder-for-hire" revelation. I probably shouldn't say this, but I will anyway: if Scott were smart, he could always say that, what he really meant by his statement was that, they were investigating a brown van that was parked on the street that day, and that he possibly believed that these burglars, or whoever they were, abducted Laci on her way to the park and left her dog behind, so as to eliminate her as a witness, or possibly these satanic cultists who wanted her baby, or whatever. In other words, he simply could have claimed that he only *thought* he knew who did it—again, possibly the burglars, or the cultists who were being investigated as a side lead. Again, I'm probably helping a guilty man by saying that, but like I said in the beginning, I was going to try, at least, to be reasonably fair to both sides (families). I suppose the whole purpose of asking the defendant questions such as this, if he ever takes the stand would, of course, be to determine what he really meant by that, and how seemingly honest an answer he would give. However, I do get a little frustrated sometimes when a person is too blind to see the obvious answer right in front of his or her face.

Detectives arranged a meeting with Laci's side of the family for the evening of Wednesday, January 15, 2003. They would be disclosing some good news and some bad news about the disappearance of their daughter. The good news, of course, was that they believed they had finally solved the case of their missing girl. The bad news *and* the purpose of this meeting was to explain why the investigation team believed their son-in-law was responsible for their daughter's disappearance. This was something that, yes, on the one hand the family *did*, deep down inside, suspect. However, I'm sure they were hoping, praying, and probably just wanting it not to be true.

According to some of the information they knew at the time, the police let the family know that Scott had taken out a $250,000 life insurance policy as recently as the previous summer, which was *after* Laci became pregnant. (Scott, by the way, adamantly denied this allegation later on, calling it and the affair with Amber a "bunch of lies." He said the life insurance policy was purchased much earlier than that. We, of course, would have this discrepancy either confirmed or refuted at the time of the trial.) The other items they revealed to Sharon Rocha, Ron Grantski, Dennis Rocha, Amy Rocha, and Brent Rocha, were the photos taken of Scott with his girlfriend the month before, which Amber herself furnished to the detectives.

One of Laci's family members stepped forward and agreed to some interviews, but at this juncture in the investigation, he wanted to remain anonymous. He said, "I don't think she ever saw it coming. As to exactly what happened to her, I don't really know. If he's innocent, fine, then take a lie detector test, like we all did. At first he told us he was willing to, but then he said he talked to his parents, and they told him not to." He went on further to say, "There were no signs. They never fought. They were never abusive to each other. He's a cold and calculating type guy. This is a guy who has to have all the nice stuff. He wanted his Del Rio Country Club membership."

For the very first time since Laci's disappearance, the family and friends did not open the volunteer search center the following morning, which was Thursday, January 16, 2003. The volunteer staging area at the Red Lion Inn is where Scott had been a visible presence since its inception when Laci first disappeared. I don't think the family members could bear to look this person in the face, after what had been revealed to them, and what they now knew. One of Laci's friends who worked the center said that day, "Obviously it was hard to close it down. Everybody's numb right now. It's hard to hear that Scott Peterson is not the person we all thought he was."

Kim Petersen of the Sund/Carrington Foundation also stepped forward and announced, "Due to recent developments and the incredible media attention, we felt the volunteers would not be able to get any work done, if the volunteer center was left open. We have accomplished the goal of letting people know about Laci." She went on to note that the center was planning to close the following week anyway, since the majority of assignments covering the search, etc., were completed.

All the boxes, chairs, and computers were moved out of the hotel Monday morning.

Scott had planned to lead a number of volunteers all the way to Los Angeles for a one-day search that Sunday. By that Friday, however, this mission too had been abandoned. It must have all seemed like a big, disgraceful waste of everybody's time that, during this entire period since his wife's mysterious disappearance, Scott was leading these sacrificing individuals on wild goose chases all over California, when it had been *he*, and he alone, who had all along held the key of knowledge as to the location of Laci's and Connor's whereabouts. The thought of these in-depth, misleading actions could only have been considered reprehensible, adding insult to injury.

Although Scott apparently took hardly anyone local from Modesto with him, he did, in fact, leave for Los Angeles on Thursday morning, after all. There wasn't a lot of information reported on the nature of this expanded effort, but officials with the Double Tree Hotel in Westwood, Los Angeles, said on Monday that there was some backlash from the volunteer event hosted there Sunday. Several people apparently called to threaten a boycott of the hotel chain for helping Scott Peterson, according to Joe Titizian, the hotel's general manager. But, he said, "The event took place with the blessings of both families. The hotel stands behind both families and is not taking sides."

Scott returned home the evening of Sunday, January 19, to find that his home had been burglarized. Peterson reported the break-in at 7:46 p.m. Police said that a window had been broken to gain entry. Detective Doug Ridenour refused to comment on what exact items were missing, but did say that it wasn't that much stuff.

Another detective, Sgt. Michael Zahr, said, "We are currently investigating this break-in, and we are not prepared to release much information. Detectives are working on leads which may solve this case (the burglary) soon, and we don't want to interfere with identifying the suspects."

Then, early that Monday morning, Scott put a padlock on his front gate.

Neighbors said that the burglary added to the feeling that their street was under siege. Since Laci's disappearance, hundreds of cars had driven past the home in the 500 block of Covena Avenue. (Perhaps they could have set up a toll entrance in the neighborhood, requiring a $2 donation per car toward the

Laci Peterson Fund. In fact, I actually had seen an effort like this organized once in a neighborhood where award winning Christmas decorations were built by neighbors competing to build the most impressive displays. Naturally, this attracted multitudes of observing motorists nightly, who gladly paid the donation.) Reporters had camped out along the street, and at least one other home was burglarized.

"Can anything more happen to these people?" one Covena Avenue neighbor asked. "Isn't it enough what they are going through, and then to have this added?" She said she believed the home was burglarized because anyone with a television knew that Peterson would be in Los Angeles that weekend.

Three days later, police reported that they had identified a suspect whom they described only as someone known to the Petersons. Police then said the stolen property was returned. The suspect's name had not been released, and no arrest has been made. Doug Ridenour said, "We will forward it to the district attorney's office and see if they want to file a criminal complaint."

Occasionally, I get a question or two from people regarding reasons for various biases that certain family members have, depending on *how* they are attached to a case. People who work in law enforcement and the legal profession understand these biases, and, I believe, most of the general public *does*, as well. But, as I mentioned, every once in a while someone throws a question my way about this. For example, someone, believe it or not, asked me about the investigator's meeting, in which they disclosed the affair photos to the family—why were Lee and Jackie Peterson not there, or even invited?

I hate to say it, but that was kind of like asking, "Gee, I wonder why one presidential candidate will say such negative things about his opponent during their campaigns, especially while debating?" This wouldn't happen to be because they both want to win the election or anything, now, would it? Or even a better example is this: During the California Governor recall election, only days before the vote, a reporter asked Governor Davis what he thought should be done to Arnold Schwarzenegger regarding the sexual harassment allegations, and Davis responded with, "Well, I believe he should be brought up on charges for this." He paused for a second, and then he said, "Immediately." To me, he almost sounded credible, until he said, "immediately," but then, I kind of laughed because it was almost like he was saying, "Quickly...before the election, so that Arnold doesn't get a chance to kick my butt." The point is, the Petersons wanted to win the case, too.

Well, of course, the majority of us already know why the Petersons were not invited to this meeting; for the most part, it's just common sense, but for the sake of full disclosure, I'll explain it. As I illustrated in my tip-line example, it would have been nothing but disastrous for the investigation, if a member of Scott's family answered the phone, instead of a member of *Laci's* family, when Amber called.

Here are a couple ways to look at it. Jackie Peterson is the mother of the man who murdered Sharon Rocha's daughter. Sharon Rocha is the mother of the girl whom Jackie Peterson's son killed. In fact, we'll see a little later on how Jackie made an attempt to fool Sharon into forgetting who she *really* is, by sending her an innocuous, yet questionable, e-mail. In it, Jackie suggested that the Rochas should postpone Laci's memorial service so that, in her view, Scott could be exonerated and all of them could mourn together. Jackie systematically received correspondence back from the Rocha's attorney, warning her not to attempt any more subtle, yet loaded, communications with the Rochas, due to the unethical nature of this activity. Of course, if she had continued this behavior, ultimately, a restraining order would have been filed.

The detectives know that, unfortunately, in most investigations, a lot of "secret keeping" is involved among its participants, in order for it to be effectively conducted. In other words, if any of the wrong individuals got a hold of the right information, say, too early in the probe, these people with predetermined biases could possibly thwart the efforts of the detectives, eventually making the case run cold, and perhaps, to a point where it may never be solved.

So, getting back to the question of why Scott's parents were *not* at this meeting—just imagine if they had been. The police would hardly be able to expose a thing, without Jackie throwing buckets of cold water on anything remotely pointing to her son's guilt. The police don't need that crap. Straight up, they need to get the right information out to the right people, at the right time, for the right reasons, without interference.

At a later date, Jackie tried to take revenge on these detectives by confronting them outside the courtroom. (See Chapter 10, Into the Realm of Nightmare)

Janey Peterson, Scott's sister-in-law (she's married to Scott's brother, **not** Laci's brother), had adamantly defended Scott on national television since day one. Moments before Amber went nationwide with her special press conference, Janey told CNN's Connie Chung, "There is absolutely no way Scott had anything to do with Laci's disappearance. I'm unaware of any affair and frankly, it wouldn't matter. It's a distraction from what our primary focus needs to be, and that's to bring Laci home." Gee, *she's* really credible. Quite frankly, I think that, even if Scott had confided a murder confession to his sister-in-law and told her where Laci's body was, she *still* would have made this same grandiose statement of Scott's innocence at the time that she did, despite all moral and ethical longings to do her duty and come forward with the truth. I hope I've illustrated the permanence of immediate-family-member biases.

Also on Friday, January 24, 2003, just before Amber was to go before the public, the Rocha family gave a preliminary press conference at the Red Lion Inn. Several family members held notes for the prepared statements they were about to make. Police, of course, had already informed the family of the mistress's planned appearance. Showing teary eyes and withdrawn expressions, they looked drained from all the exhaustive work and exposure of the last month.

Approaching the podium first was Amy Rocha, Laci's younger half-sister. "This last month has been the most painful time I've ever experienced." Tears began to flow. She tried to say more, but the words simply didn't come.

Brent Rocha, Laci's older brother, stepped up to console his sister, and to continue with the family's statements. He said, "Laci, the last month has been the most disturbing and emotional time of my life. Your disappearance has completely changed my life as I once knew it. I miss your beautiful smile and your fun-loving personality." His voice trembled as he struggled to maintain control. "We talked about our children growing up together, spending summers at each other's house. Family and events will be very lonely without you and Connor. As your older brother, I only wish that I had the opportunity to be there to defend you from the person that decided to take you away from me. Wherever you may be, I hope you know how much I love you, and how important you are to me. My search for you will never end." He then shifted gears and began addressing the issue of his brother-in-law. "Scott Peterson did admit to me that he was having an affair with a Fresno woman. (This, by the way, referred to a call that Brent had made to Scott on January 16, 2003.) I would like Scott to know that I trusted him and stood by him in the initial phases of my sister's disappearance. However, Scott has not been forthcoming with information regarding my sister's disappearance, and I am only left to question what else he may be hiding. Since Scott is no longer communicating with anyone in Laci's family, and because we have so many questions that he has not answered, I am no longer supporting him." Brent then folded his piece of paper and stepped back down to rejoin the rest of his family.

Sharon Rocha, Laci's mother, then approached the mass of microphones at the podium. She stood silent for a moment collecting herself before she spoke. "Since Christmas Eve, our one and only focus is to find Laci, and to bring her home to us. I love my daughter so much. I miss her every minute of every day. I miss listening to the excitement in her voice when she talks to me about her baby. I miss listening to her talk about her future with her husband and her baby. There are no words that can possibly describe the ache in my heart or the emptiness in my life. I know that someone knows where Laci is. I'm pleading with you to please, please let her come home. You can send an anonymous letter to the police department, or make an anonymous phone call."

Even though Amy Rocha's composure crumbled to the point where she couldn't go on speaking, what she had written in preparation to speak was that she was pleading with Scott to cooperate with police and to tell them *everything* he knows. She also had written that she believed that he had *lied* to her family.

The family chose not to answer any of the questions afterwards from the conglomeration of reporters.

The time had finally arrived that the family and the rest of the world had all been waiting for. They were now going to see the woman who may very well be the largest missing puzzle piece so far in the investigation of the Laci Peterson disappearance. There are three main segments of an investigative "pie" that DA offices around the country look to fullfill when deciding to prosecute a particular defendant. The segments of that "pie" are as follows—<u>motive</u>, <u>opportunity,</u> and <u>physical evidence</u>. We'll discuss more about the other two segments a little later, but Amber Frey, now very compellingly, began to fit the first third of this pie, given the stunning factor of the "recentness" of her affair with Scott Peterson. The timing of the romance was considered to be "hot-on-the-pan." The whole country knew Amber Frey potentially was the ultimate reason for the worldwide search for Laci Peterson.

Now the focus shifted, as everyone made their way from the Red Lion Hotel to the Modesto Police Department, for the other, even more globally captivating press conference of the day. The amassed horde of reporters swayed and pushed for position in anticipation of the arrival of the currently most famous mistress in the world. A silence took over the crowd, and the tension was so thick that you could cut it with a knife. The demigoddess had arrived.

A slender, but tall, young woman suddenly emerged from between several escorts, climbed the few short steps, and rose to take the adorned podium. She was conservatively dressed in a dark blazer, with a white-collared blouse beneath it. It appeared that her hair was only haphazardly thrown up at the last minute before her first and most important grand public appearance, because wisps of the blond strands sprouted down awkwardly from either side of her ears and out of the twisted bun on the rear of her head. She appeared frazzled and tense. Amber Frey now stood before the viewing world in her entirety for the very first time.

> **Amber:** "Okay, first of all, I met Scott Peterson November 20, 2002. I was introduced to him. I was told he was <u>un</u>married. Scott told me he was not married. We did have a romantic relationship. When I discovered he was involved in the Laci Peterson disappearance case, I immediately contacted the Modesto Police Department. Although I could have sold the photos of Scott and I to tabloids, I knew this was not the right thing to do. For fear of jeopardizing the case or the police investigation, I will not comment further." (She hesitates here then continues) "I am sorry for Laci's family, and the pain that this has caused them, and I pray for her safe return, as well. I would appreciate my friends and acquaintances to refrain from talking about me to the media for profit. I am a single mother with a twenty-three month old child, and I ask you to respect my privacy. Thank you."

She then stepped down and slipped her way out the back. Detective Doug Ridenour then took the podium. His prepared statement went as follows: "Amber Frey had contacted the Modesto Police Department on Monday, December 30, 2002. She met with detectives and gave the information about the relationship with Scott Peterson. This information was verified by a variety of means, and Amber Frey has been cooperative in the investigation and has been eliminated as a suspect in Laci Peterson's disappearance. For the near future, we have asked Miss Frey not to make any statements to the media. It is her desire that you respect her privacy. Please don't follow, harass, or make any other attempts to interview her during the investigation. This concludes the press conference. Just a reminder again, as we have in the past, we'll notify you if there's a significant event. We'll give you ample time to respond for a presser. I will try to answer some questions, but I am still limited, as I have been for the last month, in my response."

The facility then burst forth with a loud uproar from the sea of reporters. The detective and his superior, Chief of Police Roy Wasden, tried their best for the next twenty or thirty minutes to answer what questions they could from the crowd. However, almost every single question asked by the reporters was answered with an apology because they simply couldn't elaborate on those issues. This, I thought, made the two officials appear a bit unprofessional because, again, they stood there for perhaps thirty minutes answering questions, by saying that they couldn't answer questions. It seemed almost a little odd that they would do this because, if they couldn't answer any more questions, then they should have just said so and left. But no, they just stood there repeating themselves over and over again that they couldn't answer these types of questions. Well then, to save time, maybe they should've instructed the reporters on what kinds of questions they *could* answer, or perhaps they didn't really know, anyway. Again, I think that most of us who attended this conference got the impression that the investigators' answers steered a bit into the redundancy zone. The only logical reason that I could see for them doing this was simply to feed the mad and starving frenzy of journalists, so that perhaps, in the near future, the reporters would back down a little regarding their questions about the events, places, and people associated with the case. Again, this was the obvious purpose for the press conference, for reporters, networks, publications, etc., to let off a certain amount of steam in a specifically allocated forum.

Right after Amber went public, Scott immediately came out of hiding and started talking to the media. For example, right away he agreed to a full-blown interview with Diane Sawyer on *Good Morning America*. He said that the reason he didn't come out sooner was because he wanted the focus to remain on Laci. I've never heard a bigger bunch of bullshit in all my life. If a person really wants to keep the focus on their missing family member, then they'll be in front of that microphone on the very first day! He obviously had not wanted Amber to recognize him on TV. Even more so, what he really wanted was to keep the focus *off* Laci. The reason I earnestly believe this to be true is because Scott's not stupid; he knew that if Laci just simply passed into obscurity, like any other missing person whose photo was on a milk carton, like just more water under a bridge, then the investigation would go cold, as did the Evelyn Hernandez case, and then *he* could now go on with the rest of his new life, which was the sole, yet compelling, incentive for his investment in this monumental amount of risk.

His coming out, especially the *Diane Sawyer* interview, was a 180-degree shift from his previous stance. I believe this demonstrated two prominent factors. *One*, Scott had no more reason to hide now because at this point, he knew Amber had seen him on television—the cat was out of the bag. And *two*, he realized how suspicious skirting the media must have looked when he was supposed to be the next of kin in a case as big as the Polly Klaas kidnapping. Of course, at the time, he didn't feel that he had a choice because he simply didn't expect the onslaught of coverage, and naturally, he knew that he couldn't let Amber find out. But now that she *did* know, and there was no stopping the growth of the case (its expansion was absolute), I believe that he instantly tried to make up for that "guilty-looking" behavior that he exhibited earlier, by opening himself up to public cross-examination in a weak and half-hearted attempt at trying to look like a spouse of a victim of an abduction. At this point, when he had been hiding throughout the first few weeks after Laci's disappearance, and everything became publicly disclosed about Scott, to think that he was actually audacious enough *now* to try to fool the populace into believing he was just another respectable advocate, as was Elizabeth Smart's dad, is almost laughable.

Scott's lies were as obvious as the nose on his face, it just kept growing and growing like Pinnochio.

I remember seeing the very first news footage of Scott on television Christmas Eve night. He was sitting on a couch in a sideways position. He appeared to have one leg up on the furniture and one foot on the floor. It was his left profile that was visible from this camera angle. He had one finger poised against his temple, and he was just looking straight ahead with as serious and unflinching an expression as he could muster, while the camera remained focused on him for a few seconds. This, of course, was quite some time before I had decided to write about the case, which naturally would deepen my interest in the investigation. However, despite my only passing interest in the case, this very first image I saw of Scott stuck with me throughout the entire project. Why? Because I knew his type. I knew the type very well. He reminded me, right off the bat, of a roommate I had in college—he was the egotistical, selfish, cold, calculating type. Anyway, getting back to Scott: the look on his face suggested one thing, and one thing only, to me. It said, "Come on, hurry up and take your picture, so that we can get this damned thing over with, and I can get on with my new life." From day one, every time the media got footage of Scott that we could see him trying to avoid, I knew he was going to try to "poker face" his way through this entire investigation. You know, a look that said, "Hey, even if I am guilty, you can't prove anything anyway."

The media correspondents weren't stupid; they picked up on this right away. When Scott's "bizarre" behavior was pointed out on national television, Sue Caudillo Peterson (married to Scott's brother)was a guest on the show, reacted just as I said Scott's mother would have reacted had she been invited to the "affair disclosure" meeting. She immediately snapped to the defense of her brother-in-law. She slammed her foot down, insisting that there is no way one could say that any one type of behavior is "proper." The media backed off. She was right, and that's why they gave her that respect, but what she didn't realize is that these are seasoned reporters, whose gut instincts, honed from years of experience, tell them a lot more than she would like to realize or ever admit. For example, the media didn't treat Scott any differently than they did the family members of Dru Shodin, before her abductor was caught. The family's behavior all seemed very natural to the reporters at the scene of that crime. Scott, however, for a person of his supposed character, was acting oddly defensive and elusive towards the media for a "legitimate" family member of a victim of an abduction. This did, in fact, raise a bit of a red flag to many individuals from all walks of life. Right away people were calling in to the programs and pointing out Scott's behavior, which typically is something that is quite rare for the next of kin in an abduction case.

One of the things Scott had said on *Good Morning America* was that he had told investigators about his affair on the night of Laci's disappearance. If and when Scott testifies, *how* will he explain that he told this to the cops, when they claim they didn't know about the affair until Amber called six nights later?

Very easily. He could always *say* that he told them about the affair, and whether or not the officer wrote it down, is a different story. Or, whether or not the officer was listening, is the officer's problem. Scott could say, "What was I supposed to do?...Remind the officer a few days later about the affair, just in case he forgot? That was his job."

The only problem with Scott testifying like this is: what if the reporting officer specifically asked Peterson if he had a girlfriend, and Scott's response was recorded as, "no"? Then the jury would have to decide which of the two is lying. Chances are, the jury would believe the officer over Scott.

These facts on how Scott and Amber met, is based on public information from Amber's friend, Shawn Sibley, the one who made the connection between Scott and Amber.

Shawn had more or less said that she met Scott Peterson at a fertilizer conference late in October 2002. He had apparently shown some interest in her, but she informed him that she was already engaged. He then politely (or smoothly, depending on how you look at it) asked her if she had any available friends that might be interested in going out with him. Apparently, she then asked him if he was really interested in a serious relationship, or was he just having fun. He assured her that he was serious. She then gave him Amber's phone number. (Obviously, Scott had removed his wedding ring from his finger *that* day.)

In November, when Scott called Amber, who by now was expecting his call, they arranged to meet for their first blind date at the Elephant Bar in Fresno.

Amber Frey is the youngest of three children. Her older brother, Jason, 33, is a San Bernardino County Sheriff's Deputy. He served in the Iraq War with his Army Reserve unit and has since been stationed at Fort Bragg, North Carolina. Her older sister Ava, is 31 and is a Shiatsu massage therapist in Fresno. Amber grew up in the Fresno area and stayed at times with each of her parents, who divorced when she was only five. Her mother, Brenda, 51, is a hospital supervisor, and her father is a general contractor.

Amber worked as a clerk in a jewelry store after she graduated from high school. She decided to get a two-year degree in child development at Fresno City College. While she attended there, she worked at a child daycare center, and after completing her junior college credential, she then went on to attend a vocational school, to study massage therapy. More recently, she's been treating elderly people and athletes recovering from injuries at a physical therapy center in Fresno, called American Bodyworks. She's been enhancing her career there lately by taking skin care classes, as well.

After the Amber Frey Press Conference on Friday, January 24, 2003, nearly everyone associated with Amber in any way, was requested by both Amber and the police not to do any interviews about her, which in turn, might jeopardize the case. The only person who might have been immune to this request was Amber's father, Ron Frey, because he had conducted a number of media interviews starting as soon as the very next day after his daughter's public announcement.

"Amber really believed he was the real thing," said the young woman's father, Ron Frey. He said his daughter was really devastated when she found out her "genuine" prince charming was in reality...a fraud. She felt she should have known better, that when it seems too good to be true, it usually is. Mr. Frey, who is a successful general contractor, went on to say that his daughter's life has been turned upside down. "I keep telling her that she didn't do anything wrong. He not only fooled her, but he fooled the nation for a month," the father said during an interview at his home in Fresno that Saturday night after the press conference. "She really thought he was truly a fine person. She had no clue in the world that he was married. She was proud to be with him. She's single, she met someone she liked, and she really thought he was the real thing. She never meant to hurt anyone." He explained that if his daughter had known Peterson had a wife, she never would have struck up a romantic relationship with him. He said, "Instead, she became a victim of someone she trusted and now feels embarrassed and shattered."

Amber's father went on to say that Amber was hurt that Scott wouldn't be around for Christmas. "He told her he was going to Paris. Nobody leaves his girlfriend alone on Christmas. He told her that because of his job, he had to travel all over the country, and that it was not unusual for him to be gone from home for up to 30 days at a time." Mr. Frey said that it wasn't easy for his daughter to come forward and contact the Modesto Police about her relationship with Scott Peterson. He said, "It was very important for the public to know right away that my daughter is also a victim in this thing. Right now, she does not know what is going to happen. Because of all the publicity, she does not know when or if she will return to her job in Fresno. Right now, she just wants everything to go away. How do you make this go away?"

A friend of hers also confided that, even weeks after Laci's disappearance, and despite Amber's growing suspicions of him, she continued to nurse feelings for Peterson. The two shared multiple phone conversations over a few months. "You don't get over something like what she thought they had in a split second, even if the guy is possibly a murderer," the friend said.

Amber's father attributes his daughter's life-long interest in fitness to a baby sitter she had when she was a teen. He had a woman who was a body builder come over and babysit Amber. I'll stop right here and make a side note: I thought it was interesting that a teenage female needed to be babysat. Isn't it usually the other way around? Doesn't, normally, a teenage female do the babysitting for younger kids? Why would Amber need a babysitter when she was already a teenager? And why would she need such a strong, impressive, and influential a babysitter as a body builder? Possibly to control Amber from misbehaving in some way? Maybe, it's just a coincidence. Or, perhaps these questions may be answered this way: I realize that this is a rather "ball park" possibility but, perhaps, his daughter demonstrated wild promiscuity at this age. I've heard of cases like this, where the girl, after going through puberty, must be watched constantly, or she'll almost automatically get herself into trouble, if left on her own, due to a strong sexual appetite. I had an older employee a few years back, who had told me about a situation like this in his family. He said that he had a niece who was only thirteen years old whom her family apparently had some difficulty controlling. After it had become apparent that his niece had tendency, it had evidently gotten a little out of hand. He said that they couldn't watch her all the time because she would quite often sneak off after school and apparently would go behind the warehouses in the industrial areas, looking for any men who were willing. Evidently some of these men turned out to be just good Samaritans and felt obligated out of concern to inform the parents about what was really going on, and what their daughter had allegedly been offering. My employee said that, after a while it had become such an embarrassment, that they had to put his niece on a plane and send her back to Hawaii, to stay with her stepmother. Cases such as this are normally kept very discreet for obvious reasons. This may even be something the defense might pick up on.

Amber's father did mention that he chooses never to speak about Peterson with his daughter. He concluded, "We don't open those doors and it makes it a lot better."

As an excuse for Scott's infidelity, one of his brothers had supposedly commented publicly that Scott is a sex addict. I think this was a lame excuse. That's like saying someone is addicted to food. Or, addicted to sleeping at night. Scott's an adult; if the guy doesn't have enough discipline to control it, then that's his problem.

If there is any sufficient merit to this claim, perhaps, in Scott's case, this would chalk up a few points for an early American pioneer religion, which remains one of the largest and strongest faiths here in the country, even today. (And certainly, no disrespect is intended toward this religion; in fact. I'll keep the denomination anonymous. I only bring it up to illustrate another point.) This particular faith was founded on the premise of condoning the marital arrangement of polygamy.

However, today this is no longer practiced with the exception of a few offshoot cults. If Scott were to give up his current religion and join one of these followings, he could have the 2 or 3 wives that he needs to keep up with his habit. It appeared that he might have been in a high enough economic class to afford more than one wife. I recently read several articles from a very reputable publication in which a woman had gotten out of one of these old-fashioned marriages as recently as the late 1980's. She was one of three wives and decided to break this nuptial bond for her 2 daughters whom she wanted to raise elsewhere. This American pioneer religion is perhaps what Scott needed, so that his lifestyle wouldn't ultimately result in something worse.

In my research of Amber, one prominent circumstance that stood out to me, even though it was merely brushed over as no big deal by most of the media, was the fact that Amber actually *owned* her own house. The home is located in Maderas Ranchos in Madera County. I think that, to almost any young bachelor, this really would mean something, especially to someone like the financial hustler that Scott turned out to be.

From what I understand, Amber didn't have any roommates either, who, of course, could have helped with her mortgage payment. She had been staying with friends instead during the weeks after her notorious press conference. Apparently she was only living at her house with her small daughter, which, in my opinion, demonstrates quite a bit of independent resourcefulness from such a young, single mother. (Of course, we don't know the behind-the-scenes working of this factor. For example, her father, for all we know, may be helping her out quite a bit.) Let's assume that she earned enough on her own to purchase her own home at the age of 28 or younger. We all know Laci was only working as a substitute schoolteacher, which we also know hardly makes anything, certainly not enough to purchase a home anyway. Perhaps Amber's demonstration of success through her own personal fortitude impressed Scott as to Amber's level of character, which ultimately added to his already growing motive.

After some time had elapsed since the Amber press conference, there were a few other people who felt a little less inhibited about talking to the media about Amber. One of them was Dean Hoffinger, an ex-boyfriend of hers. He's a party promoter from Fresno and dated Amber from 1999 to 2000; since then, he's remained on amiable terms with her. He basically described her as always having been a little reserved, but never formal or stiff. He said, "She's always been a fun girl. Always into different things. Not prudish, kind of hippie-ish."

Amber introduced Dean to Scott at the notorious Christmas party we've seen so many photos of. When he was asked his opinion of Scott, he said, "He seemed like a player."

Here's a quote from someone speaking to the media shortly after Amber's press conference. "She said she didn't know he was married. That seems hard to believe." He then acknowledges that Peterson probably had something to do with his wife's disappearance. Then he continued, "I don't rule that guy's girlfriend out either. I don't rule anybody out." The person who said this was Art Scheuch, a 74-year old retiree in the La Loma neighborhood. As soon as I heard he was a senior citizen, this immediately explained the reason for his opinion, which by the way, I totally disagree with. I, myself, happen to be in Laci, Scott, and Amber's generation. "Generation-X" they call us, which was right after the "Baby-boom Generation." Naturally, someone like this gentleman, who was from the World War II generation, was most certainly failing to realize that this is the "age of the cell phone." In Mr. Scheuch's generation, for example, most women didn't even have sex with men before they got married, let alone have a cell phone. Therefore, in those days, a woman would not have been able to call a man at home, since this could have resulted in her discovering that there was a wife at home, etc., because, of course, all telephones up until a few years back were exclusively land lines.

Not only did Scott have a separate cell phone he used when away from home, but let's not forget who Scott was, a salesman! Do you really think a guy with this type of skill doesn't know what to tell a female he's hot for? Even though Scott used his cell phone for work, I'm sure his voicemail greeting probably said nothing more than, "Hi, this is Scott. I'm away from the phone right now, but please leave a message after the tone, and I'll get back to you as soon as I can." Laci couldn't answer Scott's cell phone. Scott answers Scott's cell phone. Scott could've told Amber anything! For example, Amber might have asked Scott (being the smart cookie that she is) if she could have his *home* phone number, in addition to just his cell phone. A skilled salesman who's out to "get some" could simply respond with, "Currently this *is* my home phone, Sweetie. Since I travel away from home with my job so often, I figure this is the best way to get all my messages right away." Or, another response might be, "Well, I'm currently using this for my home phone right now because I've got my house partially under construction" (you know, fixing up Connor's room). Which, by the way, is also the perfect excuse, temporarily anyway, to keep Amber from coming over to his house, so they can make love over there, or just so, you know, she could check it out and have it proved to her that the salesman really did own his own home. All he's really doing is basically slappin' down some game, and you know, just straight throwin' some spin. That's all it is. Thought it wasn't?

Just as Dean Hoffinger (Amber's ex) said, he could tell his boy Scott was a true player at heart.

I don't know this for sure, but it certainly wouldn't surprise me if Mr. Scheuch doesn't even have a cell phone of his own yet, even though *I've* had one, and most people I know have had one, for over ten years. As you can tell, when I first heard this elder fellow's reaction, I thought, "Boy, this guy is way off." Not only that, but just look at the kind of behavior Amber's exhibiting, heavy loads of anger, fury, and resentment towards the salesman who suckered her. Especially someone like Amber, who prides herself on the attitude of, "Nobody's gonna dupe me and get away with it!"

Speaking of players, where I come from originally, the East Bay suburbs, we always considered a "player" to be just a guy who goes around trying to have sex with as many girls as possible, by using whatever lies he can get away with. But, boy, I sure learned an entirely different expanded version of this definition from a young man whom I temporarily employed for a month at my business a few years back (he, by the way, grew up in a more "urban" area). His definition went like this: "A player is a dude who tries to impregnate as many young women as he possibly can, by spinning lies of love and seduction. That way he develops a whole portfolio of walking, talking trophies he can boast about." He also went on to say that "players" only stay at one job long enough before the wage garnishment of child support catches up with them, then they ditch to find employment elsewhere in their quest to feed only their own selfish pleasures.

If you ask me, this sounds like the makings of the criminally irresponsible "dead beat dads" of America.

I happened to be dating a schoolteacher like Laci at the time I heard this, so I went ahead and told *her* about it, to see what she thought. This girl straight hit the roof. She said, "What?! Walking, talking trophies?! Brad, I think you better have a talk with some of your men and explain to them that this is not right. These girls are probably going around struggling to make ends meet with these kids."

Of course, I explained to her that this was only one guy who said this, as shocking as it may have been, and that, to the best of my knowledge, this type of activity was certainly not pervasive within my company. Otherwise I'd, of course, be receiving wage garnishment packages from the government on some of these individuals, if that were the case. After hearing this "new" definition though, I can understand why they also have persons out there who are known as "player haters."

Also, not too long after Amber's national press conference, the media staked out Scott Peterson's house in full force, hoping to get a glimpse of him if he had to go in or out. It was convenient for me. I just lived a few streets over. I had it easy where most of these individuals and crews were either staying in their vans or at the downtown hotels.

Still, with no bodies yet discovered, but with a full motive now revealed, the media were having difficulty controlling themselves. On one of these days, along with many news stations, commentators, and the usual crowd, a typical crew of media couldn't hold it back. Scott Peterson momentarily came out of his house, to stack some wood in the back of his truck, and the conglomeration made a surge. A boisterous man took the lead of his crew, with large rolling camera equipment following behind him, and started making a straight bee line for the fertilizer salesman, while blurting out through a megaphone, "Scott, nobody believes your story!"

Scott looked like he was partially startled and bewildered at first.

Right then, a woman went up to the man, saying she was with the *San Francisco Examiner*, and that she thought this was bad journalism.

The man defiantly responded in his megaphone, "I'm a talk show host! Not a pompous journalist!" He went on, "Besides, I don't see *you* getting any answers out of him!" He then walked with his crew to the foot of Scott's driveway and continued, "Oh, Scott, I apologize. Did we disturb you or something?" Again, his tone was extremely sarcastic and boisterous. Scott just continued to act like he was ignoring them, then he went back in the house.

All these little things add up. Perhaps, Geragos was taking notes, so he'll have some grounds for appeal.

More recently, since Amber's press conference, she attended a church bible retreat in the mountains near her Fresno home with a few of her friends. Among the activities the girls participated in were bingo, bible study, prayer groups, and just casual talk sessions. One of the girls who also attended this weekend getaway made only a few brief comments about Amber. She said Amber was surprisingly relaxed.

It apparently was assumed among all the participants, that naturally the last subject Amber would want to discuss would be Scott or Laci Peterson. According to this young woman, the topic never surfaced all weekend. It was a good opportunity that Amber attended, since it allowed her a breath of fresh air from all the high-pressure investigation she had been so instrumental to. It provided a chance to touch base with herself and reflect about the more positive things of her life in general.

Amber had done a session of nude modeling in 1999 that she later came to regret. Within a month or so of Amber Frey's notoriety being established, a porn broker named David Hans Schmidt managed to get custody of the photos. He published them on the Internet, provoking Ms. Frey to file a $6-million lawsuit, charging she never gave her authorization to do this. Schmidt claimed that this was all legal because, not only did he have a signed release from the photographer, but also the photographer had a signed contract from Amber releasing any rights to this pornographic property over to him entirely, as part of her acceptance of monetary compensation for the session.

As we know, Amber had another relationship in 2000 that yielded a daughter. The girl was born in February of 2001, and Frey has refused to identify the father for some reason—his name does not appear on the birth certificate.

If Geragos and the defense are capable of being truly sleazy, they might even try to portray Amber as a dark and sinister temptress of the night. Think about it. They've got all the tools to do it with, a job in the massage industry, nude modeling, or what some call pornography. Amber was an unwed mother, and the father's name mysteriously doesn't appear on her daughter's birth certificate. In the 1950's, being an unwed mother was called being "knocked-up" and this label was reserved for only the most hardcore of women. Just prior to her affair with Scott, she was in a bizarre relationship, in which she was living with a married man, Josh Hart, who was a male stripper, and who was having a baby with his wife, who lived at a separate location. To illustrate how crackpot this relationship was, it was Amber who set up a surprise baby shower for this "boyfriend" of hers and his wife.

I realize that it would be pretty low for the defense to go, if they were to claim that Amber was the one who talked Scott into killing Laci, so that they could share the proceeds of the house together. From the looks of him, the defense's Kirk McAllister seems like an old-school veteran. Maybe he could take these circumstances and exploit them to the hilt. Just a possibility.

If I were now to choose between whether Amber is an "Angel of Justice" or a "Mistress of Death," after reviewing evidence that came from either court testimony or recorded police statements, which were publicly announced through *these* agencies (I'm trying to avoid here the concept of someone being tried in the media), I would most definitely choose…"Angel of Justice."

I believe her heart was in the right place all along.

4

Murder in the Air

By the end of January, the police had still not returned Scott's Ford F-150 truck, but they *had* returned Laci's Land Rover. Undoubtedly, authorities believed that Peterson had used the F-150 in the commission of murdering his wife and were simply holding it as evidence. Either that, or the cops were playing the basic leveraging game with Scott, who was their prime suspect in the biggest who-done-it case of the new millennium. What I mean is that Scott casually inconvenienced detectives when he nonchalantly refused the interrogation and, likewise, disregarded their request for a polygraph. So it naturally makes sense that experienced homicide detectives would do everything in their power to casually and nonchalantly *inconvenience* their "non-cooperating" prime suspect in any way *they* could. The detectives could at least make sure that he didn't get his vehicle back, while knowing full well that what Scott did now for transportation would be his *own* problem. If he couldn't go to work or get around, oh well, he could always bum rides, use the buses, expensive taxis, or of course, rent cars. After Scott did an interview with Gloria Gomez of KOVR Sacramento, he drove Laci's Land Rover into Robert's Auto Sales on McHenry Avenue. He traded in the green, 1996 SUV towards the purchase price of a new, white 2002 Dodge Dakota 4x4. (For those who aren't familiar with Dodge trucks, the "Dakota" is the mid-size pick-up, whereas the Ram is the full-size one). The 1996 Land Rover blue books from $9,000 to $16,000, depending on its condition, although the actual dollar amount Peterson was reimbursed for it was not mentioned.

At the beginning of February 2003, Ron Grantski noticed the new truck parked in Peterson's driveway and that Laci's Land Rover was gone. It didn't take long for the Rochas, with their far-reaching network of resources, to pinpoint the exact roots of this unannounced change. According to one report, once they were informed about this barter that was transacted without their consent, Ron Grantski went into a rage. It said that he was stomping his feet, clenching his fists, and yelling in the driveway. Surrounded by a small group of officials, Sharon and Ron immediately stormed into Robert's Auto Sales on McHenry Avenue. There was no argument. The owner had already given it some thought and realized that it would be in everyone's best interest, if he simply donated the car back to the family. He indicated that he wanted this to be his business's community contribution to the Laci cause, which, of course, so many local businesses had sponsored in some way. He knew, of course, that the national and local attention his company would receive by the media would probably serve more in his best interest, if it were *positive* rather than negative publicity. He also cited that, in this way, if Laci were found, she would have something to drive, when she returned.

Shortly after Sharon and Ron had gotten Laci's car back, they called a press conference. Ron Granstki announced, "We know that the cars were in Scott's name, but thanks to Mr. Roberts, it's in the family's hands now. We thought that, until we find out differently, the car should be here for Laci, so she has something to drive." He also indicated that Scott was trying to sell the house, too. He said, "The house is in both names, Laci's and Scott's. I find it hard to believe that he thought he could sell it without Laci's signature. Of course, we find it hard to understand a lot of things Scott has done, so why should this be any different?"

Detectives went ahead and took the liberty of confiscating Scott's new truck as well, so that he wouldn't be able to use that one, either. Detective Doug Ridenour announced, "We will hold onto his truck for the length of time that we need it for the investigation. We will turn it back to him, when we can no longer justify having it, but that's a decision that will be made through the courts."

Tuesday night, February 4, 2003, Dennis Rocha stored the Land Rover on his property in Escalon.

I wanted to mention something regarding the two computers taken as evidence from the Peterson home. There was a certain amount of suspicion raised about these computers, because it was discovered that Scott had been checking the tide reports for San Francisco Bay, specifically in the Richmond area, which led investigators to check more actively in this area during the search for the bodies. Interestingly, I've only heard a one-sided argument being reported about this circumstance: that Scott, of course, was using this information to help him cover-up the disposing of Laci and Connor's bodies, perhaps in an attempt to see if he felt police could locate her with the type of equipment they were using. As I continued to hear this hype over and over again, I never once heard the other side of the argument. And that would be that Scott *said* he went fishing, which explains why he needed to check the tide reports. All good fisherman check the tide reports before going out, especially when sturgeon fishing in the bay. Why do people think these tide reports are printed in the paper and on the Internet?

Also, toward the end of January, another interesting perk in the investigation occurred. A woman came forward in Longview, Washington, to report that she may have seen Laci only a few days after she was abducted. The woman was working as a convenience store clerk at the time and later told police a pregnant woman, whom she described as a "classic beauty" with sleek brown hair, came into the Market Place store. The 45-year-old clerk said the woman appeared to be in her twenties and in a later stage of pregnancy. She also said the woman was accompanied by an older man with a ruddy complexion and "strong features." When the man had stepped out of line to get something he apparently forgot, the woman allegedly informed the clerk that she had been kidnapped, but not until the clerk had mentioned to the pregnant woman that she should be wearing a coat on such a chilly day. The woman responded that she didn't have time to get a coat because the man had kidnapped her, and also that he had a weapon. The clerk told the police that she didn't know whether to take the woman seriously or not. When the man returned, she said that he asked what the two had talked about while he was gone. The clerk responded, "She said you kidnapped her."

According to the report, this remark agitated the man, so the woman teasingly added that her husband always kidnaps her for dinner. The man relaxed and laughed. He said, "Yeah, I guess I kidnapped her."

After the couple left, the clerk tried looking for a phone book, but got distracted by other customers and, apparently, kept putting it off until almost a week went by, before she saw the report on television about Laci. She said that she feels terrible about it now. In the report, the clerk quoted the woman as saying, "This is serious. I was kidnapped. Call the authorities when I leave." Police reviewed surveillance tapes from the grocery store. Unfortunately the tapes from the previous week had already been reused.

This incident struck many people as uncanny because it seems hard to believe that anyone would not notify police immediately, if there were any question at all about a possible kidnapping. Nothing ever came of it.

Monday, February 10, 2003, was Laci's expected due date to have Connor. In honor of her and her unborn baby, Laci's friends and family planned to gather, say prayers, light some candles, and read a poem. Terry Western, a family friend, said that they planned to keep the group to about twenty persons. She said that they wanted to keep the gathering low key and private. She said, "We aren't prepared to handle thousands of people and a rush of media. It's something that Laci's friends really wanted to do." Meanwhile, relatives vowed to keep up the search for the 27-year-old mother-to-be who had vanished in Modesto on Christmas Eve. People looking for Laci began to concentrate the search toward medical clinics, in the hope that there was a chance she, or whoever had her, could make it to one of these facilities for the birth of Connor. Volunteers worked to notify hotels, clinics, birthing centers, and hospitals. The California Registered Nurses Association instructed via e-mail all of their members to view Laci's website and noted the urgency of the delivery date.

The ceremony was held in East La Loma Park just after sunset. Laci's friend, Heather Sutton, led the poem reading and prayer. She stood at the center of a small crowd of about 25 people, mostly Laci's friends and family. The group was surrounded by at least two dozen reporters and camera crews. After several speakers made prepared statements, the group broke into the song, "I'm With You." At the end of the hour-long service, the participants released a bouquet of blue and yellow balloons for Laci and her son.

The husband, who was under suspicion, stayed home that day and did not participate in the park observance. Although it wouldn't surprise me if they deliberately had not invited him.

Since returning from his Los Angeles volunteer effort, Scott Peterson hadn't been by his warehouse for almost two weeks. Somebody had bashed in the front door of his business, evidently by backing some kind of a vehicle into it. After Scott called authorities to report the vandalism, a Stanislaus County spokesperson confirmed that the damage appeared to have been deliberate, perhaps caused by someone driving a vehicle into the door. This latest vandalism report went to the Sheriff's Department because Peterson's office-warehouse is in county territory, which is located on Emerald Avenue off Kansas Avenue in west Modesto.

Kelly Huston of the Sheriff's Department said that authorities do not know when the vandalism occurred, and she reconfirmed that Peterson told officials that he hadn't been there in two weeks. Huston noted, "Nothing was taken. Peterson reported that he removed everything of value about two weeks ago. It looks like someone took a car and rammed it into the walk-in door." Then, Huston went on to say that deputies believed that the damage was intentional because of the angle at which the vehicle hit the door. Parking spaces in the complex are perpendicular to the buildings, but the damage to the warehouse door did not come from a vehicle going straight, as if pulling into a parking space. "There's also a large space between the parking and the door, so it would be pretty difficult to hit the door," Huston said.

The small warehouse is in a complex that includes a custom cabinet design business, a sign company, and an automotive glass company. The impact put a gaping dent in the metal door and bent it, so that it no longer fit the frame properly. It also cracked the frame and shattered some of the wall next to the door. That Tuesday, sheets of wood were nailed across the door, to keep anyone from getting inside.

Forrest Aarvig, who owns the warehouse property, said that Peterson would most likely be moving out shortly thereafter, but that Tradecorp had the property leased through the following October. Aarvig added that another company manages the property for him. He reflected, "When I opened the newspaper a few days after Christmas and saw police searching my unit, I thought to myself that I was going to have a vacancy soon."

One of the searches I went on was held on a Saturday in February—around 150 people showed up. Brent Rocha was there, as well as some other friends and family members, and he was going around, organizing and explaining what the goals were for that particular day. After being given our assignment, a friend and I were teamed up with two nice, young women who had just arrived for their first Laci search. One of them was a shorter, brown-haired girl who was a dental assistant and said she'd been wanting to get out and join the searches for a while and seemed a little excited to be there. The other girl was a taller friend of hers, who was still a student. Since I had the biggest vehicle, I drove the four of us out to our section of the Don Pedro Reservoir area. Then, from there, we mostly just hiked around. We didn't search in a formal gridlock pattern, as was conducted during the earlier police searches; however, we spaced ourselves apart adequately, so as not to waste efforts retracing already covered ground.

As we continued to comb through brush and waterways, an occasional mountain bike rider would stop and talk with us. Some of us had backpacks containing water and snacks.

Well, we didn't find Laci that day, but one of the girls with us happened to give me her phone number. Well actually, I had asked her for her e-mail, but she went ahead and volunteered her phone number anyway.

Without any warning to Scott Peterson, the police converged on his home at 8:10 a.m., the morning of Tuesday, February 18, 2003, serving him with a second search warrant. (Again, the first warrant was served on December 26 and 27, right after Laci's disappearance.) When detectives turned onto Covena Avenue, they saw the prime suspect coming towards them from the opposite direction in his shiny, new truck. They stopped him, had him turn around and go back home. Officers served him the warrant to search his house, the yard, and the truck. Doug Ridenour said that Peterson was cooperative with investigators. Peterson then left in a car driven by someone else.

Scott returned approximately 45 minutes later in a rented Chevrolet Tahoe. During the next hour, detectives spoke with him on his driveway several different times, while they took notes on a yellow, legal pad. Apparently, officers were not allowing Peterson to re-enter his home at all, while they were inside exploring it. Peterson occupied some of this time by rotating between sitting on the brick wall, standing and pacing in the driveway, and sitting in the Tahoe with the unknown person. At about 10:15 a.m., while talking to several of the detectives on the driveway, Scott threw his arms in the air in apparent frustration and went into the backyard with them.

Scott left the house again at about 10:30 a.m., carrying two duffel bags and a white plastic bag stuffed with clothes, which police proceeded to search, of course, before he was allowed to leave. Ridenour said that these were only personal and work related items that they allowed him to take. Peterson refused to speak to reporters on his way out, and he left in the rented Tahoe driven by the unknown individual.

Detectives brought Laci's 21-year-old sister, Amy Rocha, to the house. She entered the home with them at 12:30 p.m. and came out approximately two hours later with a distressed look on her face. Perhaps she was hoping to find something that wasn't there or, maybe after the search, became even more convinced that her older sister was murdered by her no-longer-seemingly-perfect brother-in-law. It wasn't clear what role she actually took that day during this second warrant search. Not willing to jeopardize the investigation in any way, Amy did not make a statement.

Detective Ridenour said, "Amy was asked to come here today to assist detectives. This isn't unusual, if there's something that a relative would know that detectives wouldn't." He would not say specifically what they asked her to do.

At approximately 11:30 a.m., one of the police officers on the scene drove Scott's new, white 2002 Dodge Dakota away. Since the police originally had taken Laci's Land Rover, but returned it, I'm sure that Scott figured out later that he would have been better off had he never traded in the SUV, because chances are, since they had already inspected it, they would not have confiscated it a second time, but since they hadn't looked at the new truck yet, they had the perfect excuse just to take it, rendering Peterson without a vehicle. Police still had Scott's Ford F-150 pick-up, of course, which they had seized on December 27, 2002, along with his boat. (Although, the more I think about it, since Scott didn't purchase the new truck until a full month after the alleged crime, I don't see what evidence in the world the police could have actually expected to find in it at that point.)

Police started out by removing several brown paper bags, filled with potential evidence, from the house. Wearing surgical gloves, a dozen investigators and crime scene technicians hauled away about 50 more bags of evidence by 6 p.m. on the first day of the second search of the Peterson home. That number later escalated to 90 or 95 bags by the following day, Wednesday.

At noon, still on that Tuesday, officers closed off both ends of the 500 block of Covena Avenue, because of the excessive number of spectators driving down the street. Dozens of curious people parked their cars nearby and walked down the street toward the house, to come check out the action. Especially after many of these local people had been watching live news coverage of the event right from home, these numbers just continued to grow and grow all day. At approximately 1:30 p.m., Turlock police detective Kipp Loving took about twelve brown paper grocery bags, apparently full of evidence, into his vehicle, and proceeded to the headquarters of the Hi-Tech Crimes Task Force of Sacramento Valley. At about 3:30 p.m., police, interestingly, returned Scott's new truck to the house after inspecting it for only about four hours.

Throughout the day, Scott came back to the house more than once. When he first returned, Peterson handed a detective a bag of cat food. The second time, he had returned with some items that the officers apparently had requested. When asked, Ridenour would not specify what these articles were.

Somehow, despite the roadblocks, a UPS deliveryman made it to the edge of the yellow, crime scene tape anyway, with a package addressed to Laci from the wine-of-the-month-club. Authorities summarily turned him away. I guess that they kind of figured that this guy *really* should have known that Laci would not have been there at that time, despite his authorized delivery stop.

That Tuesday's search was concluded at about 6 p.m., when they sealed up the home. They returned the next day for more evidence collection.

On Wednesday, the second day of this significant inspection, officers arrived at the home about 9:30 a.m. and routinely cordoned off the property, as well as part of the street, with yellow, police tape. The purpose of the tape was to keep some distance between investigators going through the house and the dozens of reporters outside. Authorities with Modesto Police and the County DA's office spent about seven hours measuring the outside of the Peterson home, the driveway, and back yard. Ridenour, who had been the main police spokesperson throughout the investigation, said, "Part of the search warrant requires you take measurements, so you can figure out where you got the items from. That's so you can put items back where they came from during a court trial, or any other situations that may arise." Ridenour listed representatives from Modesto Police, Sacramento Valley Hi-Tech Crimes Task Force, the state Department of Justice, and the Stanislaus County District Attorney's office as participants in the two-day search.

Since the white pick-up truck the police had seized and returned the day before was still just sitting there in Scott's driveway, one of the officers got into it and apparently took it to another location so that Peterson, who was staying with friends during the inspection, could reclaim it.

After being loaded, the police evidence truck finally was driven away at 3:30 p.m. on Wednesday. Then, at 5 p.m., Ridenour announced that the inspection had been completed, and that the house would be returned to Peterson.

Mark Geragos, who eventually was hired by the Petersons, had said on cable television around this time, "It is clear from detectives' actions, that they are taking a hard look at Peterson. By taking measurements of the house, investigators are preparing for a criminal trial. That to me is a telltale sign they think this is a crime scene, and they are mapping it out. Clearly there is some kind of focus on Scott Peterson. I can't think of a better time to have a lawyer."

Well, we all know what Geragos was implying here, but let's not forget that Peterson already had a lawyer at this time, Kirk McAllister, who had been working on his defense all along.

This last search warrant was believed to be the eighth so far in the investigation. Other search warrants had been issued for Peterson's warehouse, phone records, vehicles, and even his "person," according to legal records (this would presumably mean they could legally strip search Scott, if they wanted). Any warrant for his "person" also means the gathering of any hair and bodily fluids (semen, blood, and saliva).

Court records indicate the issuance of all the warrants in the case; however, all of them have been sealed by judges' orders. Ridenour stated, "As far as I know, all the warrants have been sealed. We are not going to try this case in public." Under state law, a search warrant must be returned to the authorizing court within ten days after being issued. Each warrant must include a roster of articles collected as potential evidence and an explanation for why investigators believed the warrant was necessary. Unless a magistrate seals them, warrant documents automatically become public record. The California Public Records Act states: Records are public, unless the disclosure would endanger the safety of a witness or other person involved in the investigation, or unless disclosure would endanger the successful completion of the investigation.

Detective Craig Crogan, lead investigator in the Peterson case, read a prepared statement. He announced, "The position of the Modesto Police Department has been, and remains, that no details about this investigation will be released."

Scott's mother, Jackie Peterson, told reporters in San Diego (where she lives) that the sole purpose for this new, two-day search of the house was simply an effort by Modesto Police to harass her son. She said that this was all it was really for. However, Mrs. Peterson did not find a single person, besides her own family members, who actually agreed with her.

Jackie did have at least a small point, and that's the fact that the police seemingly unnecessarily confiscated her son's new truck, which, having been purchased a whole month after Laci's disappearance, couldn't logically produce any kind of meaningful or tangible evidence at this juncture. But since police held it for only a short period of time, perhaps it actually was a justifiable routine inspection, given the overall magnitude of the Laci case.

One of the items seized during this second search, which was revealed a few days later in a court hearing was, of all things, an envelope found in Scott's new truck. This envelope led detectives to another self-storage unit Peterson was apparently renting without the investigator's knowledge. He had evidently not revealed its existence to them, and they had not inadvertently discovered it until this time.

When asked by reporters, a manager at the Security Public Storage, where the storage unit was located, said that she did not know whether police searched Peterson's unit there as part of the investigation. The storage facility is several blocks from the office/warehouse (which police had already searched during the first warrant, back in December) that Scott Peterson had used for his fertilizer sales business.

This was the same week that the previous owner of the boat—who had sold it to Scott on December 10, 2002—was asked by police to come by and inspect the craft for any noticeable changes. The previous owner is Bruce Peterson (no relation to Scott), he is from Fresno, and the boat is a 1991 Sears aluminum Gamefisher, for which Scott paid the man $1,400 in cash. This price, by the way, also included the trailer.

Bruce Peterson told television reporters, "I saw what looked like cement residue, powdery stuff that would come out of a bag. I just know it wasn't that way, when I sold it to him."

After this interview, Jackie Peterson was asked by journalists for her opinion of the man's findings. She stated that she was not surprised at all that they found cement residue in the bottom of her son's boat. "The residue was likely there because of the boat's concrete anchor," she said. "It was mentioned long ago that Scott had a cement anchor."

Eyebrows already were being raised about several oddities regarding Scott's new boat. One, most people considered the day he chose for christening the vessel with its maiden voyage to be significantly strange, Christmas Eve, which, of course, was also the day that his wife disappeared. Two, he told investigators that he was fishing for sturgeon that day. Well, the boat is only 14 feet long, which common sense says, is way too small to be pulling in a kind of fish that averages 6 feet in length. Furthermore, a small, aluminum boat such as that is made for lake fishing, and to take it out on the vast and severely choppy San Francisco Bay is a bit extreme, unless, of course, he needed a much larger and deeper body of water in which to sink a body where it would be less likely to be recovered than it would in a lake. Three, he had just gotten the boat very recently before his wife's disappearance, and he had hidden it over at his warehouse, with nobody in the family having any knowledge of the boat until after Laci vanished.

Perhaps leaving the pliers under one of the boat's seat cushions, with a strand of Laci's hair in them, was the one fatal mistake Scott overlooked when he attempted to carry out a perfect murder.

December 10, 2002, when Scott purchased the boat, was just three weeks after he met Amber Frey at the Elephant Bar in Fresno. Interestingly, this was same day that Amber asked him if he'd ever been married—he responded with a sob story about having "lost" his wife. Prosecutors, no doubt, would say that this was no coincidence. It makes sense that the young man, who was obsessed with his new lover by this point, had to come up with a serious plan of action to cover his colossal lie.

An older lady, who was in her seventies, had believed she saw, from her kitchen window, Laci walking her dog on the morning of Christmas Eve 2002. Her name was Vivian Mitchell, the wife of former three-term Modesto city councilman, Bill Mitchell. Vivian said that she was washing dishes at her sink on December 24, when she saw someone, who she thought was Laci, walk by the front of her house. The Mitchell home is located at Buena Vista and La Sombra Avenues, approximately 10 blocks from the Peterson house on Covena Avenue.

I thought 10 blocks away was a bit too far for Laci actually to walk when she was eight months pregnant. I mean, I could see a woman eight months pregnant maybe walking her dog 2 or 3 blocks away from her own home, and maybe even 4 or 5 blocks at the very most, in that state of health, but 10 blocks just seems a bit much to me.

Mrs. Mitchell said, "I had glanced out the window, and the sun had come out, and it was a very nice day. It had been raining recently, so the sunshine brought out all the dog walkers. I had seen Laci walk by the house several times before." Vivian went on, "When she walked by on Christmas Eve, I hollered to Bill, 'Oh look, it's the lady with the golden retriever.' She must have come from Kewin Park. The dog wanted to head toward Yosemite Boulevard. She circled the dog around, and they headed the other way. She looked very happy and smiling, and they were having a nice walk. It made me feel bad that she disappeared then."

Based on Mrs. Mitchell's descriptions, Laci appeared to be headed south on Buena Vista, toward La Sombra Avenue.

Her husband Bill, said he had gotten to the window just in time to see the dog go around the corner. Then, he said, "It looked like the dog wanted to go one way, and she was going another."

Mrs. Mitchell said that she didn't report the sighting right away. She said that she waited a week to call it in because she said she figured other people had also seen Laci walking her dog that morning. Then, after her husband and friends had encouraged her to do so, she tried to make the report. Vivian said it was about 10 or 10:15 a.m. when she saw Laci Peterson on

Christmas Eve morning. This time, according to police records, would be approximately 45 minutes after Scott said he left for his fishing trip. She didn't say anything about remembering whether or not the woman was pregnant, but she *did* say that she believed that the woman was wearing black and white clothes.

The day Laci disappeared, a neighbor later reported finding the dog running loose in the neighborhood about 10:30 a.m., at which time she returned the dog to the Peterson's backyard. Two days later, police used bloodhounds trained to track people's scent. This is usually done by letting the dogs sniff an article of the victim's recently worn clothing. These dogs led their handlers toward Yosemite Boulevard, rather than the other way, toward East La Loma Park, where Scott originally directed searchers.

When Mrs. Mitchell finally did call in the sighting a week later, she said police didn't call back. Then, apparently a week or so later, her husband, Councilman Mitchell, called City Manager Jack Crist to inform him that police had not followed up, and only then did the department have someone call her back. "Shortly after talking to the city manager, a police captain called us," Bill Mitchell remarked.

Scott's father, Lee Peterson, reacted to hearing about the way this lead was handled. "How do you follow up on a lead, if you don't return someone's calls?" He asserted to reporters by telephone, "It makes me wonder about their competency. Here's an eyewitness account of my daughter-in-law, and they don't follow up on it."

When Detective Ridenour was asked about this lead, he responded that his department had received the tip, and that,

"It was appropriately handled during our investigation, but we have 8,000 tips, and the majority we haven't called back."

Mrs. Mitchell had mentioned that she had seen Laci walk by on several different occasions, although in this interview, she appeared fairly certain that this time had been, in fact, on Christmas Eve. This undoubtedly would've become a point prosecutors would cross-examine her on, if the defense were to call her as a witness to testify during the trial. For example, a clever prosecutor could lead up with some questions about her age and memory, before hitting her on the subject of her having seen Laci on other mornings. This type of "cross" could possibly provoke the witness into admitting that, perhaps she's "not sure" about the exact date. The prosecutor could then go on to exploit this opportunity during his closing arguments.

However, something unfortunate occurred later, rendering this possibility null and void; Vivian Mitchell died in January 2004, several months before the trial start date.

Bill Garcia, the private investigator, who put the team of volunteers together that found the body of Danielle Van Dam the year before, had done some free-lance searching here in the Laci case and made what he thought was a decent discovery. After finding what he thought was freshly laid cement near the Delta-Mendota Canal, he videotaped the scene.

"The spot, which looks to be less than three months old, looks like a half bag of concrete mix was spilled from the back of a trailer or truck that was backed up against the canal," he said. "The spot, on the edge of the canal, about 20 feet off the road, has a track in it, that looks like it's from a trailer tire."

Several media outlets reported Garcia's findings, which of course, later turned out to be insignificant.

On Wednesday, March 5, 2003, about one month before the bodies actually turned up, but a little over six weeks after the affair was publicized, the police called another press conference. The investigation had taken a significant turn, and the case was reclassified as "homicide" from its original status of "missing person." Modesto officials announced that they believed that Laci Peterson was the victim of murder.

Several of Laci's family members stood off to the side behind the podium as the detectives addressed the afternoon crowd of reporters. The family held hands and listened intently, as the officials spoke.

The lead investigator on the case, Detective Craig Grogan, announced, "As the investigation has progressed, we have increasingly come to believe that Laci Peterson is the victim of a violent crime. This investigation began as a missing person case, and we were all hopeful that Laci would return home safely. However, we have come to consider this a homicide case."

Kim Peterson, Director of the Sund/Carrington Foundation, said that the reward of $500,000 had been reconfigured to a $50,000 reward for information leading directly to the location and recovery of Laci's body. However, she also pointed out that the $500,000 reward still remained available should Laci be found alive. She then read a statement from Sharon, Ron, Dennis, Brent, and Amy: "Our family desperately needs to know where she is and what has happened to her. We plead to the person or persons responsible for Laci's disappearance to dig deep within yourself, find the compassion for our family and provide the information necessary for her recovery."

Then Detective Ridenour took the podium. He wouldn't elaborate on why or when the missing person case became a homicide investigation. "This hasn't really changed anything for us," he said. It has only changed for the media." He continued, "Investigators told me yesterday that the investigation is going well. We're confident this case will be resolved, and we're continuing in that direction."

When reporters starting asking Ridenour questions, the family began exiting the building.

After this announcement was made at the press conference, Scott's mother, Jackie, said that she believed that the police department's choice to reclassify the case as a homicide would stop people from looking for Laci. She remarked, "I would hope that, if I were missing for a month or two, people wouldn't stop looking for me. Laci was reported missing Christmas Eve, slightly more than 10 weeks ago—not enough time to assume that she has been killed." She went on, "It's sad they made the announcement because it takes away hope." She said that she was afraid that thousands of fliers around the state would be torn down, now that police had said publicly that they believe Laci is dead. "Please don't stop looking for her," she said.

I believe that, not only was Mrs. Peterson's opinion obviously skewed in favor of her son (as, of course, all her opinions in the case have been), but I also believe that her opinion is largely irrelevant. But not entirely so—here's why: Anytime you have a missing person case, if you do not simultaneously investigate the possibility of homicide and then, it ultimately turns out to *be* homicide, you'll be sorry you hadn't, because all the timeliness of the fresh evidence goes right out the window. So, Mrs. Peterson's discouragement of any homicide investigation is grossly wrong and mischaracterized. However, as I mentioned, there is some validity to her argument, and that's the fact that Elizabeth Smart was found *alive* many months after investigators believed her to be dead. Naturally, after that many months had elapsed in the Smart case, officials could determine, if nothing else, at least by the laws of statistical probability, it was extremely unlikely that she could possibly still be alive. Even though the Smart investigation was obviously an abduction case, the circumstances were so significantly different, that people have even claimed that it had many of the markings of, and could at least partially be considered, a runaway case.

Right around this time, a majority of the media were shifting their focus onto President Bush and the emerging war with Iraq, which, perhaps to some degree, allowed the investigators to go about their searches and investigation into Laci's disappearance with a little more peace and privacy than usual for this case. However, on the other hand, this created a galactic-size distraction from the overall focus on the Laci search and investigation.

However, one of the main news reporting agencies following the case from day one, actually maintained their intense focus on the Laci investigation. Around this time, this major media outlet filed a petition asking the courts to unseal the Peterson search warrants. One of the highest executives within this organization argued that the court failed to follow proper procedure, as required by law, when sealing these warrants. He said that both the press and the public, on whose behalf the press acts, were denied their guaranteed right to argue against keeping the documents from public view.

This press organization's petition, which cites earlier cases and state law, indicated that, unless "specific on the record findings are made," public records couldn't legally be sealed. The petition read that the burden to provide evidence that "closing them is necessary," is on the party seeking to seal these public records, and not the other way around.

Without holding hearings on the matter, judges sealed eight search warrants in the Peterson case. Detectives, of course, used the warrants to search the missing woman's home, husband Scott's warehouse, and the couple's vehicles. Police also obtained search warrants on Scott's phone records and his person.

Deputy DA David Harris (who, by the way, was later appointed a lead prosecutor in the case against Peterson) responded only briefly on this matter. He said that there were state and federal precedents to seal search warrants without holding a hearing. "There is no authority to have a hearing prior to documents being sealed," Harris stated, "period."

In my own opinion of this matter, I could see very clearly that both sides had strong and valid arguments. I could especially understand the position of the press since current legislation appeared to be more weighted in their favor. However, the question that came to my mind was: should the judge have to explain to the media that, in a low-profile case, as opposed to a high-profile one, if the warrants are unsealed, then there still won't be enough exposure to jeopardize how many impartial jurors would still remain if the case is tried? So again, by unsealing the warrants in a low-profile case, there would still be plenty of fair and impartial jurors from which to choose, but in a high-profile case, if you unseal the warrants, good luck! This is only a big picture view of the situation, but nevertheless, it remains very true.

During the week of Wednesday, March 12, 2003, police continued in their search of San Francisco Bay. This time they were more specifically looking in the waters off the Richmond shoreline. Investigators with Modesto Police and the Tuolumne County Sheriff's departments were continuing to explore in this area. Apparently, they felt tipped off by the tide charts that Peterson had on his computer, which showed that he was researching the tide activity in this particular region. Three vessels from the Tuolumne County Sheriff's Department were exploring the offshore expanse at Point Richmond, a few miles north of the Berkeley Marina. Joining them were units from the San Francisco Police, as well as other divers. The effort involved four other boats as well, some carrying dogs. During previous exploration of the bay, police had used cadaver dogs trained to pick up scents from human corpses in the water.

On this day of the bay search, police centered their efforts in the area northeast of Brooks Island, off Richmond, where they said that Scott Peterson told them that he went fishing around that island on December 24, the day Laci disappeared. Detective Ridenour said at this time that he only commented on this aspect of the search because, apparently, reporters had spotted the operation from shore. In regards to why investigators chose this particular area, he only said, "It's another logical area in their investigation that they need to search."

Sgt. Ron Cloward was in charge of this particular search, and he said, "Police have covered an area from Berkeley to Angel Island." He happened to mention as well, "Authorities also continue to search rural areas of Tuolumne and Calaveras counties." Despite the police announcement of the investigation shifting into "homicide" gear the week before, he reiterated, "We still hold the hope of finding her alive."

Police, to help in the search, hired Gene Ralston, of Ralston & Associates of Idaho. In the previous bay searches, police had used sonar equipment from San Mateo County. However, the sonar equipment that they were now using from Ralston's company was the same used to successfully recover bodies that had been dumped in New Melones Reservoir, on the Tuolumne-Calaveras county border, in an alleged kidnap-for-ransom scheme reaching from Los Angeles to Russia.

One of the units that this company provided was a high-tech sonar device that hung from the side of one the four boats they were using. This device, which could scan for anything that might resemble a body, was used for nine hours that day, in about 40 feet of water.

Using this sonar, Modesto Police evidently detected something of interest later that afternoon.

According to Gene Ralston, "Whatever the sonar detected had not been retrieved and investigators did not know what it was. There's all kinds of stuff at the bottom. I don't know if it's anything to get excited about."

On the one hand, I could understand their apparent apprehension. The last time a big announcement had been made about a possible discovery at the bottom of the bay, it turned out to only be a boat anchor. High-profile reporters, such as Geraldo Rivera, were all standing out there, only to realize that it appeared that investigators had almost "cried a type of wolf." The national television reporters all went home empty-handed and with their high expectations shattered.

But, on the other hand, could this mysterious object of interest that they discovered be the actual bodies that did, in fact, turn up in this exact area about a month later? Perhaps, if it hadn't been for that previous boat anchor fiasco, investigators might have taken a closer look here. And if, in fact, it did turn out to be Laci and Connor, they would have possibly saved the prosecution against Peterson the burden of explaining why *they*—the police—didn't find the remains, but, instead, a couple of dog walkers did.

Wind rocked the search boats late that afternoon of the discovery, forcing the search team to return to the Richmond Marina. The next day, Thursday, March 13, 2003, high wind and choppy water halted law enforcement officials who had gathered to continue their exploration off Brooks Island, where the latest object of interest had been discovered. Modesto Police had planned to use the new sonar equipment and divers, but cancelled the search at approximately 10:30 a.m.

"The weather conditions required us to discontinue the search," announced Sgt. Ron Cloward. "The wind came with the front of a storm that, forecasters said, would bring rain for five days."

A woman by the name of Connie Fleeman said she had a random encounter with Scott Peterson on the morning of Christmas Eve 2002. Apparently having become frustrated in waiting for Modesto Police to return her call regarding this tip, she contacted the local and national media, who gladly publicized her story.

Ms. Fleeman said on that morning, between 9:15 and 9:45 a.m., at the Crescent Food Market on Coffee Road near Floyd Avenue, in north Modesto, she noticed a boat in the parking lot, which momentarily made her think of her son, who fishes religiously. So, she said that she took a look, but didn't see any fishing gear in the aluminum craft. She said that it was a brown, pick-up truck that had the boat in tow on a trailer. The woman also said that she noticed a green storage box, sitting at an angle in the truck bed. Connie said, "The curious thing was the big, green thing in the back of the truck. It looked like it had been thrown in there, and there was something hanging out of it. There was nothing in the inside of the truck, or even inside the bed of the truck, besides the big, green thing." She said, "There was a white, or light gray, blanket that was hanging out."

As she made her way into the store, she said that someone pushed the door open from the inside, and the door tapped her lightly. She observed, sure enough, that it was the man she now believes to be none other than Scott Peterson. She said, "He had a big grin on his face and looked very happy. I told him that he almost killed an old lady." She said that Scott apologized to her then, and that she wished him a Merry Christmas. She said he was wearing a clean, white shirt, the type a golfer might wear, and twill pants.

After buying her cigarettes, she left the store and began driving north on Coffee Road. She said that the guy with the boat was going the same way. The woman said that she then pulled into the left-turn lane at East Rumble Road, and Peterson also stopped for the red light right beside her because he was going straight. Then, she rolled down her window, to let him know that something might be coming loose from his truck bed, that the box back there was slightly open. Connie Fleeman said, "He looked out his side window and gave me a look that was the most horrifying, scary look I have ever seen in my life." She went on, "As I'm trying to tell him that stuff is hanging out, the light turned green, he floored that truck, and he took off so fast, you would not believe it."

This incident, which remains unsubstantiated by police, would have occurred Christmas Eve, the morning Peterson said he went fishing, the day that he later claimed Laci had gone missing. Yet, Fleeman said that she had not received any response back yet from investigators after she tried to report the tip, not once, but twice in January. This, along with Vivian Mitchell, the wife of the former city council member, was the second known publicly reported lead that Modesto Police refused, for some reason, to respond to. The store manager said that officials never contacted him either, but he admitted that his surveillance videotape from that morning had been taped over. Connie Fleeman had said that she goes to Crescent Food every morning, to buy two packs of cigarettes. Fred Hanna, the father of the storeowner, said that he did not recognize Peterson, but he added, "Connie said he came in, and I believe her."

Maybe again, it's simply a legitimate matter of police having their hands full with the 8,000 tips, as to why they can't always get back to these people.

Media conglomerates made continuing efforts to get a judge to rescind previous rulings on the search warrants that remained sealed. Stanislaus County Superior Court Judge Roger M. Beauchesne ruled on Thursday, April 10, 2003, that he would not release information from search warrants in the case of Laci Peterson's disappearance, citing this as a potential death penalty case as the reason. He wrote, "It is paramount that the investigation be thorough and unhampered, in part because of the potential penalty of death." He also stated, "Investigation techniques, clues and focus on future avenues of inquiry by law enforcement personnel would unduly alert any potential suspect and unsealing any of the documents in issue would likely impair any suspect's rights to a fair trial." He also indicated that any potential defendant could face the death penalty, because Laci was about eight months pregnant when she was reported missing on December 24. State law defines murder as the unlawful killing of a human being or a fetus with malice aforethought. The unborn child must have grown passed the embryonic stage, which is usually between 6 and 8 weeks. For anyone convicted of multiple murders, California law allows for the death penalty.

Judge Beauchesne ruled the week before that the judges acted improperly when they secretly sealed the documents. The judges acted at the request of law enforcement officials, without allowing a proper hearing. These documents included search warrants, lists of items found, and affidavits explaining why investigators needed the warrants.

The judge conducted a closed hearing that week and determined that all documents related to the warrants in the Peterson investigation would remain sealed.

After the search that Saturday, my friend, Ross, and I invited the girls we had met back to my house later that afternoon, for lemonade and crackers. I've got a nice, circular, wood bench with an umbrella on my back porch, and it was such a nice, warm day out, so we just figured—why not? As we served them drinks, one of the girls, in an attempt to break an awkward silence, said, "I really like to go on museum tours."

I commented, "Oh, is that right?" And I thought to myself, I wonder what else she really likes to do?

PART II

5

Bodies Are Found

On Sunday, April 13, 2003, a full-term infant washed up from San Francisco Bay on the shore of south Richmond, which was discovered by a couple walking their dog near the water's edge. Richmond police and fire officials responded at approximately 4:45 p.m. to the call from the dog walkers. The next day, Monday, April 14, at 11:43 a.m., a woman, also walking her dog, found the body of an adult, human female lodged in the rocks at Point Isabel Regional Shoreline, about a mile south from where the baby's body was found the day before. The remains were found in marshy wetlands about 15 feet from the waterline. This area is surrounded by both condominiums and industrial warehouses.

The infant, to whom authorities referred as a "full-term, male child," was mostly intact but had a deep scratch along its upper torso. The umbilical cord was still attached, according to a Richmond Fire Department official. The find came just hours after storm-driven waves had washed the infant ashore a mile northwest of the woman. The adult female was found front-side down in a more decomposed state than the infant—mostly a torso with some limbs, missing the head, the feet, and both hands.

Law enforcement sources told reporters that investigators were focusing on the maternity undergarments found on what was left of the woman's body. Contra Costa County Sheriff's spokesman Jimmy Lee disputed that maternity clothing was found on the body. "There was only a standard woman's bra," he said.

After the discovery, East Bay Regional Park District police notified Modesto detectives. Modesto Police got the call at 12:15 p.m. and flew investigators to the scene by helicopter arriving at about 5 p.m. Detectives, who had been putting the finishing touches on a "non-body" homicide case, landed at the scene. They arrived that afternoon, but didn't finish their work until about 2 a.m. Tuesday. Detective Doug Ridenour announced, "At this point, we have no information, nor has the recovered body been identified as that of Laci Peterson. Until such time as our department has been notified, and it has been confirmed that the East Bay body is related to the Modesto case, this is an East Bay Regional Park District Police Department case."

Nevertheless, Stanislaus County and Modesto Police sent five individuals, including someone representing the district attorney's office. The Contra Costa County Sheriff's Department dispatched canine teams trained to detect human remains. Monday afternoon, the five Modesto police investigators watched Contra Costa officials remove the woman's body from Point Isabel Regional Shoreline. Authorities carried the body bag that contained the woman's remains, to the coroner's van. At one point, a total of twenty investigators had converged at the location. At the Contra Costa County Coroner's office in Martinez, the autopsy on the woman's body began shortly after 6 p.m., Monday evening, April 14, 2003. The Modesto investigators witnessed the autopsy that night. It would take several days for forensic testing to identify the bodies. Genetic factors, of course, would be used in the process.

Chief of Police Roy Wasden's pager went off when he was sitting at the Familia Juarez restaurant in Modesto that Monday afternoon. Taking a quick glance down at the pager, he noticed the message had been sent from Assistant Chief Dave Young. It simply said, "Call the office as soon as you can." When Wasden called Young, he was told that the head of the East Bay Regional Park District had phoned and notified them of the woman's body discovery in Richmond and, likewise, the infant's body from the day before.

After a search of nearly four months, this break certainly appeared to be what authorities had been waiting for. "My first thoughts were that I hoped it would bring us some answers," Chief Wasden said. "I would have liked for us to have been wrong in declaring this case a homicide."

Jackie Peterson, Scott's mother, said that she called Modesto Police in the afternoon on the day of the discoveries, after hearing media reports about the findings. Police told her what they knew, which had not been confirmed because investigators hadn't arrived in Richmond yet. She told the detectives by phone, "We, of course, feel bad for whoever it is. We pray for Laci's sake, because we still don't want to give up."

Jackie mentioned she then called her son Scott and told him, "We're praying that it's not Laci."

Sharon Rocha also called Scott that afternoon on his cell phone, to ask him if he would come up to Richmond, to help identify the bodies. Scott, who was living down in San Diego at his parent's house at the time, apparently told his mother-in-law he had something else to do and wouldn't be able to make the trip up. His response only helped further the "separation" between himself and the Rochas (which had already been made clear since the public disclosure of the affair), and strengthened their suspicion of him.

Richmond Police spokesman Sgt. Enos Johnson said, "Right now we're just trying to determine what the cause of death is, how long the child has been in the water, and how long it had been up on land. We've had some high tides recently with the stormy weather, and believe that it washed ashore."

The autopsies were completed within a day of the discovery, only to reveal no obvious cause of death for either the female or the baby boy. Officials immediately turned to DNA testing for more conclusive identification. To expedite the DNA tests, Modesto Police called on the state Department of Justice forensic laboratory. Tissue and bone samples from both bodies were sent to this agency.

There was a news conference held in Modesto that Tuesday afternoon. Roy Wasden, Modesto Chief of Police, announced, "It is top priority of the lab that they do the DNA tests as quick as they can."

Detective Doug Ridenour said, "Investigators are still hopeful of finding Laci alive." But he added, "If it is her, it will be a relief to the department, a relief to the family and a relief to the community." Then he continued, "But for now, and until and if there is an identification of Peterson and her baby, the case remains the responsibility of authorities in Contra Costa County."

Also, Kim Petersen, the Rocha family spokesperson, read a statement from the family. Here is that statement:

Obviously this is a very difficult time for our family, as we await the results of the DNA testing. These past 3 months have been a constant nightmare for us. From the beginning, we have done all we can do to find Laci and will continue to do so until she's found. This waiting is the worst. While in the news reports these are two bodies that have been found, to us they could potentially be our daughter and grandson, our sister and nephew, loving members of our family, or possibly someone else's family who is experiencing our same pain. Please be considerate of that fact. We believe that, if this is Laci, God has allowed her to be found because our family needs to know where she is and what has happened to her. If this turns out to be Laci, we want the animal responsible for this heinous act to pay. We will do all we can to pursue justice for Laci and Connor. We ask for your thoughts and prayers, as we wait. We would like to thank all the people who have been so supportive of us during these past months. Your prayers, hugs, cards, and e-mails mean more than you know. We don't know how we would have made it through each day without all of you. During this time of waiting, we ask that you respect our privacy and our need to be together as a family. We will not be conducting any interviews prior to the test results.
Thank you,
Laci's Family

James Brazelton, Stanislaus County District Attorney, announced the next day that he believed the two bodies found were, in fact, those of Laci and her unborn son. He stated, "I feel pretty strongly it is her. It's too much of a coincidence to have a female and a baby found close to each other a day apart, and no others were reported missing. If I were a betting man, I'd put money on it." He went on, "The big question mark now in my mind is whether they have good DNA material. Let's hope they do."

A few hours after the DA made his announcement, he then stated his office would no longer make any public comments on the Peterson case until, and if, the identifications were made.

Later that same day, lab technicians determined that samples from the baby's body contained enough intact DNA to be used for testing. Technicians were working with a tibia, the larger of the two bones between the knee and ankle from the woman's body, and a femur, or thighbone, from the infant's body. Lab technicians would be comparing DNA from the bodies with a hair sample from Laci Peterson (taken from one of her hair brushes) and inner-cheek swabs from her parents. A forensic anthropologist who specializes in submerged bodies also examined the corpses for about 4 hours that same Wednesday in Martinez. One of the things the specialist was trying to determine was how long the bodies were submerged.

A few days after the discovery, and a few days prior to the DNA test results confirming the identities of the deceased, Dr. Michael Baden, the high-profile, forensic scientist, provided some public insight regarding these human remains. He said, "One should be careful speculating about some horrible murder, when it sounds like natural expulsion." Here, he was talking about the natural phenomenon known as coffin birth. He went on, "Natural expulsion can occur several weeks or months after the death of an unembalmed pregnant woman, when the gases of decomposition push the fetus from the womb."

Regarding the possible reasons why the female was missing the head, Dr. Baden remarked, "That is simply because bodies often do not remain intact, especially in the ocean."

Dr. Gregory Schmunk, the Santa Clara County coroner, said, "One of the first things to fall off in decomposition is the head, and fingertips fade within a week or two, making identification from prints impossible." He went on, "Even homicide victims weighted down can surface eventually. Their feet, for example, can naturally separate from legs, or legs from torsos. A lot depends on whether she was submerged or floating. My guess is she was not floating very long, or she would have been seen. It's much more likely she was submerged for a time, then washed to the surface."

Dr. Michael Baden then went on to explain, "Absent fingerprints and comparing teeth with dental records, the most common means of identification is X-raying a body. The X-rays can easily be compared to, say, a known chest X-ray of a missing person." He said, "April is a common month to recover bodies that entered water during winter months. That is because bacteria begin to thrive as water temperatures rise to 40 degrees, producing decomposition gases that float bodies to the surface. Although limbs naturally separate in time, it is extremely rare for all to disappear, unless the person fell victim to a crime."

Baden believed that authorities should be able to tell immediately if a head was severed, as opposed to separation resulting from decomposition or tidal activity.

Other forensic scientists who officially spoke on the case observed, "It is possible for a pregnant woman's baby to be found relatively intact and separated from the mother a few months after the woman's death. Babies generally are fairly sterilized when they're inside the mom, so very often babies don't decompose in the same way as an adult. Variations in San Francisco Bay could make it difficult to tell by a body's appearance if it had been underwater for one month or four. It all depends on the water temperature, where they are, whether the marine life got to the person."

It sounded like it was very fortunate, at least for the family's sake anyway, that it was a high-profile case because so many departments under these highly-scrutinized conditions throw a lot of resources out, to make sure that, if they solve any case of this nature, that surely they'll try to make it this one.

With the news of the discoveries and the possibility of Scott being a flight risk, the police immediately began tracking his whereabouts. The detectives had determined that Peterson was a flight risk because he occasionally worked outside the country for his fertilizer business, he was currently living near the Mexican border in his hometown of San Diego, and the probability of the bodies of an adult female and infant child being found in the same region where Scott Peterson had taken his peculiar Christmas Eve fishing trip on the same day that his pregnant wife mysteriously disappeared was just too remote a possibility to be a mere coincidence. Even though the final DNA results were not quite in yet, the police moved in for the capture.

As Scott Peterson made his rounds of different friends and family members whom he was staying with, he became aware that police were tailing him.

Modesto Police Chief Roy Wasden told the media, "Starting with the discoveries of the bodies, it became our desire to know where he was at all times. We were very worried he might flee. He did work outside the country. He knows other countries. So, yes, we wanted to make sure he was in our grasp." He went on, "The State Department of Justice and several Southern California agencies formed surveillance teams that began following Peterson's every move. At one point, Peterson pulled his vehicle over, got out, and walked back to talk to the agents. He asked them why they were following him." Wasden continued, but he did not mention how the agents responded to Peterson's question. "It was relayed to me that his behavior was unusual at times. He was driving erratically, sometimes looking around for surveillance. The lack of cooperation was a frustration in the case. There was an arrogance on Scott's part, and maybe that was fear, I don't know."

Investigators spent Tuesday, April 15, 2003, in and out of meetings, discussing jurisdictions and timelines, as they awaited results on DNA samples from the state laboratory in Richmond. Likewise, the next day they continued to do much of the same. Then on Thursday, the 17th, police got the news that they were hoping for: the DNA samples proved viable, and the results were in. However, they would not be revealed until the following day. So, that afternoon, a group of investigators and deputy DA's were seen entering and later exiting the chambers of Judge Wray Ladine. They had just obtained a warrant for the arrest of Scott Peterson.

Without wasting any time, Detectives Craig Crogan, Jon Buehler, Al Brochini, and Sgt. Al Carter drove off that same afternoon, headed for San Diego, in two, unmarked police vehicles. By early Friday morning, they had arrived. State Attorney General Bill Lockyer said that, regarding police tracking of Peterson on Friday, "He was waving at them and being, you know, kind of a smart aleck. So, they finally decided that they ought to just pull him in."

San Diego area law enforcement officers and state agents stopped the purple Mercedes-Benz that Scott Peterson was driving on Callan Road, in La Jolla, as he was pulling into the Torrey Pines Golf Course. It was at 11:10 a.m. on Friday, April 18, 2003, just days after Scott's wife and unborn son were found, but just prior to the identifications of the bodies being finalized, that authorities arrested Scott Peterson. Upon apprehending him, police found that he was in possession of about $10,000.00 cash, as well as his brother's driver's license.

Friday night, two, white, unmarked police cars headed north on Highway 5, bound for Modesto. Grogan and Buehler rode in the front seat of one car, while Brochini and Carter went in the other. In the back seat of the second car, sat a young man who the world had become familiar with during those past four months. Peterson was wearing a white, knit polo shirt and beige shorts. He had been growing a goatee since the time of Laci's disappearance, and just prior to his arrest, this facial hair had been highlighted, giving it a rugged shade of orange. As funny as the color "orange" may sound, for those who saw all the photos of Peterson's arrest, it was apparent that the colorations of the young man's beard and eyebrows did, in fact, look somewhat natural; many women were quoted as having said he looked even more attractive this way.

According to the detectives, Scott stayed quiet for the entire ride with his hands cuffed behind him.

Headquarters reached Detective Jon Buehler at approximately 10 p.m. Responding on his cell phone, he told them that Scott Peterson was to be booked at Stanislaus County Jail on charges of two counts of murder early that morning. "We're in Bakersfield right now," he said. "We're making our last stop of the night. We've got the package with us."

Several hours after officers made the arrest, the department got word that the DNA results conclusively showed that the bodies found were, in fact, those of Laci and her son, Connor.

At 5:30 p.m., Wasden and Captain Greg Savelli arrived at the home of Laci's mother and stepfather, Sharon Rocha and Ron Grantski, to tell them the unfortunate yet, resolving news. That evening, state Attorney General Bill Lockyer announced that DNA tests had positively identified the two bodies found earlier that week along the Richmond shoreline of San Francisco Bay as those of Laci and Connor Peterson.

An incited crowd of about 200 people, mostly local Modesto residents, had swarmed into downtown Modesto, to witness detectives delivering Scott Peterson to the jail. Many of them carried homemade signs with various statements such as, "Murderer." Stanislaus County Sheriff's Deputy Kelly Huston said the magnitude of the crowd was a surprise. He noted, "We were considering doing a last minute booking change. Our number-one goal was to make sure he was booked safely, and that included that he didn't get lynched when he came in the driveway. There were people out there screaming, 'Murderer.'"

Police had blocked off the street just outside the jailhouse. The officers had blocked off 12th Street between H and I Streets and had parked their patrol cars in the roadway, to make a lane for the officials to get to the jail driveway. Then, only minutes before Peterson's arrival, about twelve, uniformed officers started moving people back, to make room for the detectives' cars to get down the ramps to the back entrance of the jail. Officers said they had never observed so many people turn out to watch a suspect being escorted to jail. One woman said that the reason why she showed up here was because she waited so long for the cops to arrest Scott and thought this event would go down as a piece of history.

As the two-car convoy approached, the crowd started to erupt into cheers and applause. At this point, some of the people held up their homemade signs, while others aimed their cameras into the vehicle window, to get a shot of the murder suspect. Scott was seated in the back of the car driven by Detective Jon Buehler, and sitting next to Peterson was Detective Craig Grogan, the lead investigator in the homicide case. The suspect showed no response to the cheering crowd and was soon out of sight within the walls of Stanislaus County Jail.

Scott Peterson was booked into Stanislaus County Jail at 12:09 a.m., on Saturday, April 19, 2003, on two counts of murder.

The evening of the arrest, Modesto Police Chief Wasden and Attorney General Bill Lockyer held back-to-back news conferences. At the state DNA lab in Richmond, Lockyer went first. The DNA samples that technicians were testing included bone and muscle tissue from the two bodies that washed ashore, which would be compared to DNA samples from both of Laci's parents, as well as a blood sample from Scott Peterson. Lockyer announced, "Using DNA taken from the shin bone of the female body, and from a blood sample taken from Scott Peterson by law enforcement officials, serologists in the state forensics lab in Richmond determined that the infant was the child of the female and Scott Peterson." He said that the statistic was 1 to 18 billion, meaning that only one out of every 18 billion persons would also test positive to be the child's parents. Lockyer went on, "Law code assumes paternity when the code exceeds the hundreds, and this is in the billions. There is no question in our mind the unidentified female is Laci Peterson, and the unidentified infant is the child of Scott and Laci Peterson."

Likewise, the supervisor at the lab, John Tonkyn, said that it was more than a billion times likely that the woman's body was Laci's. He then gave a similar positive identification of the infant being hers and her husband's. The current population in the world is just over 6 billion. Using cheek swabs from Laci's parents, Sharon and Dennis Rocha, the Richmond lab determined that there was one chance in 1.9 billion that Sharon and Dennis Rocha were not the parents of the adult female. John Tonkyn also explained that the DNA samples taken from the remains were additionally compared with random DNA samples, to see if any positive matches could be found. There were none.

Technicians at the state crime lab in Ripon explained the DNA identifying process this way: After a sample is retrieved, the DNA is replicated into larger copies of itself, through a process called polymerase chain reaction. Then the DNA is broken up into pieces, sorted according to size, and compared with other samples, as well as control samples. The results are printed out in a format that looks like a long bar code. The width of the bars indicates the presence of certain sequences in the DNA strands, combinations that are passed from parents to their offspring.

Peterson had been trying to stay low profile in the three months before his arrest, but law enforcement was able to keep tabs on him. Lockyer said, "Wiretaps on phones, tracking vehicles, all of the technology available." The Attorney General revealed that investigators attached a tracking device underneath Scott Peterson's new, white Dodge Dakota pick-up truck. "We were careful about that information," he relayed. The desire to keep that information hidden from the public was one reason why prosecutors and police worked so hard to successfully keep all the search warrants sealed.

Attorney General Bill Lockyer made a rather controversial statement that night. He stated, "This is a compellingly strong case. I would call the odds slam-dunk that he is going to be convicted."

Then, just prior to the news conference at the Modesto Police headquarters, hundreds of people swarmed around the Police Department at 10th and G Streets. A multitude of electric cords snaked from the news vans, parked wherever they could fit, some halfway up the curb. Rolling camera crews and news personnel staged equipment and scattered through the front of the building, down the hallways and into the auditorium. Inside, the crews from 25 network and cable news stations pointed cameras toward a podium amassed with a conglomeration of colorful microphones sprouting from it like mushrooms, in anticipation of the explosive announcement to come.

Standing before the cameras and microphones that sent his statements across the nation, Chief Roy Wasden announced, "Scott Peterson has been arrested. He is in the custody of the Modesto Police Department detectives. We've really tried for, hoped for, prayed for a different outcome than the one that has occurred. While it's happy to have a conclusion, it's truly sad to have that conclusion." He went on, "This is just a tragedy. Modesto's lost a beautiful, young mother, a schoolteacher, a daughter, a sister. Not to mention her unborn son. And it's a tragedy on the Petersons' side: a son charged with the murder of his wife and unborn son. There are no winners here."

"Police believe the killings occurred in Stanislaus County," Wasden said. However, he wouldn't go into details that might inadvertently jeopardize the case.

"This is a tragedy that is affecting many lives," he insisted. "Lee and Jackie Peterson are Scott's parents, and they'll have to deal with that. They wanted to believe in their son, and they chose to do that. We went through with our investigation."

Officials said the white polo shirt and khaki shorts Scott wore Friday were replaced by a red jumpsuit designated for maximum-security inmates. They noted that Peterson spent his first night behind bars, sleeping on a 2-inch thick mattress in a single-person 6 by 9-foot cell. Sheriff Department spokesman Kelly Huston said, "His cell is within eyeshot of a deputy pretty much all of the time, but he was not placed on suicide watch. A television set is within view. Peterson made several phone calls Saturday and requested a haircut." Houston observed, "He was booked into jail, sporting a full goatee, and his dark hair had been dyed a lighter shade. Haircuts are given once a month, on a rotating basis, by cell block."

Lieutenant Janet Rasmussen, the overseer of the downtown Modesto Jail, said, "We absolutely do not want to treat this gentleman any differently than we do anyone else. He's being treated exactly as we would anybody else." The fact that Janet Rasmussen already called Mr. Peterson a "gentleman" implies that they *were*, in fact, treating him differently than they did other inmates. Maybe she should've referred to Peterson as a "scumbag," instead; otherwise, in a way, she has contradicted herself.

Officials were prompted to segregate the high-profile suspect from the rest of the jail population, by the nature of the allegations against him, and the national media attention the case was given.

Kelly Huston, of the Sheriff's Department, stated, "There are inmates in the jail who definitely have some unfavorable opinions of him, and they have expressed that. He is in the highest security area, so he does not have access to other inmates, nor do they have access to him." The reason that other prisoners had "unfavorable" opinions of Peterson, according to this spokesperson, perhaps initially could have been because it was known that Scott had money. According to some guards, this factor triggers more initial animosity from other inmates, than many other circumstances do.

For his first breakfast behind bars, Scott, along with the other inmates, had a cheese omelette with milk and bread. For lunch, they had beef and vegetable soup, bread, and a cherry dessert. The dinner menu listed rice, chicken soup, green beans, and milk.

District Attorney James Brazelton announced that prosecutors planned to charge Peterson with two counts of murder in the first degree, for the deaths of his wife, Laci, and their unborn son, Connor. Under California law, this would make him eligible for the death penalty, because he was being charged with more than one homicide. If it hadn't been for Connor, and the charge was only *one* homicide, rather than two, then Scott would only qualify for "life without parole." Sometimes the term "special circumstances" is tossed around in cases like this. All this term really means is that, because of the unique factor (special circumstances) of the defendant being charged with "multiple" murders, he then automatically (under California law) becomes eligible for the death penalty (the same was true with O.J. Simpson). Brazelton also indicated that prosecutors would consult with Laci's immediate family, to get their input before ultimately deciding whether to seek capital punishment.

My first reaction to hearing the identification results was actually more similar to that of a defense lawyer. For months the police were combing the bottom of the bay with high-tech sonar equipment, and they never found the bodies? (Modesto Police Sgt. Ron Cloward said that police had previously searched the waters in the area where the bodies were discovered. "We spent a whole day hovering over that area in helicopters," he said. "The water there is about 5 or 6 feet deep. It was too shallow there to use the kind of boats and equipment we were using.") But lo and behold, when police ended the search, and everyone was distracted by the Iraq war, the bodies then mysteriously washed ashore. These bodies were not found by police searchers, but instead, by just common passers-by. When were these bodies actually deposited in the bay? From one perspective, it almost looked as if someone had deliberately planted the bodies in the bay as an obvious attempt to frame Scott. Since this was my first reaction, and I'm not a defense lawyer, you would think that such a high-profile defense attorney as Mark Geragos at least would have thought of that. But, no, he got in front of the cameras and said only what any average sheep would say after watching this on TV. He said that it would be pretty hard to find a prosecutor who couldn't get a conviction in this case. Then, without much more to say, he remarked that, when you put all of it together, there are more people sitting in state prison right now who were convicted on less evidence than this. Then the News showed Geragos just walking away. In other words, Geragos was saying that, at this point, he believed that Peterson was guilty beyond a reasonable doubt. Well, this sounds a lot more like a prosecutor giving his opening statements at trial, than it does a defense lawyer trying to get hired onto the case.

Here, Geragos had been going on all these national, prime-time shows, speaking out for the defense, dogging what the prosecutors had to say, and all he could think to say about the body discoveries was *that*?! Incredible. What's even more astonishing is that, right after Geragos made this statement, the Peterson family hired him on as their lead attorney. (I'm sure the Petersons' decision to hire Geragos was finalized prior to this specific announcement, of course, but they simply didn't offer the deal until after his blunderous statement was already made.) In fact, I'm sure that Geragos, when asked by the Petersons about this statement, said that he simply reacted the same as everyone else did at the time and didn't want to sound stupid or naïve about what probably really happened. In other words, what he possibly said to justify it was that he had given up hope of ever being hired by the Petersons, at that point, because the case was so far lost. If it weren't for his surprise appointment, he'd probably not want to take on another losing case, even if it was high profile, as he did with Winona Ryder (who, by the way, was on a store surveillance video for the world to see, stuffing away the goods she was shoplifting, before making her getaway).

I remember seeing Geragos on the news after the Petersons decided to hire him. At first, he had a look of total surprise on his face, especially after his most recent comment regarding the body discoveries, it was a look of utter dumbfoundedness. But then that quickly changed. Raising one finger in the air, and with a smug look on his face, he said, "Yes, I will accept."

The police had millions of dollars worth of naval search equipment, not to mention the tens of thousands of dollars in overtime to cover a force this size, but despite all that, there simply were no bodies in the bay they could find. Even though it's a remote chance that there was another killer *unlinked* to Scott, let's just say for a minute that there was, since this is the only argument the defense can present. Now, while the world was watching the search for Laci near the Berkeley Marina, on major networks during primetime every night, doesn't it make sense that this "other" killer might also have been watching this coverage? Doesn't it make sense that, when the search ended and the entire world shifted their focus to the Iraqi war, that this would be the most inconspicuous time for an experienced killer to plant the remains where the publicly known location of the publicly known prime suspect's alibi is? The real killer, as well as the rest of the world knew that the police were searching San Francisco Bay for only one reason: Scott Peterson had said that he went fishing there on the day Laci disappeared. So, if the "real killer" simply managed somehow to get the bodies over there, where they would simply wash up on their own, the investigation for the "real killer" ends. The investigation would have ended because the real killer would have known that, once the police unmistakenly did find Laci and Connor's remains, which were the actual missing puzzle pieces that the cops had been hoping for in the first place, at the spot they were looking in, only because it was the location of the husband's peculiar alibi, then *that* man goes down, not Scott. This, the killer would have known, by matching the bodies to the other man's alibi, would lock in the public's overwhelming suspicion of the current prime suspect, the unfortunate bystanding husband of the victim. Therefore, the killer, if he were to exhibit any common sense at all, could see that this would be a sure-fire way to permanently close any further investigation into Laci and Connor's murder, because it irrefutably nails another guy about whom the killer couldn't care less. Because of the unique, high-publicity nature of this case, the "real killer" would have had an easy, yet golden, opportunity to permanently pin the murder rap on an unfortunate bystander who just happened to have a fishy alibi. Ladies and gentlemen, this was the reasonable doubt that the defense team would have been concocting had they had enough sense to think of it.

If I were in Geragos' shoes, I'd be all over this—like a fly on squat.

I should point out that many defense lawyers have been highly critical of Geragos for a number of reasons. The obvious criticism we've heard the most are the satanic cult theories that he was trying to float about Laci's murder (to no avail; hardly anyone I know bought that one). But the other criticism about which we haven't heard as much is the fact that he *lost* his high-profile, claim-to-fame case. Winona Ryder's jury came back with a "guilty" verdict. This, however, is not always an indication of a poor-quality lawyer. As we know, there was overwhelming evidence against Winona Ryder, as well as the fact that this was one of Geragos' first high-profile trials, and if he is only 45 years old while on the Peterson case, he must have only been 43 while trying the Ryder one.

The Petersons may have been wise to understand that any skilled professional also learns from his mistakes. Geragos, even though he lost the Ryder case, gained enormous insight through experience in another high-profile trial. In other words, the Peterson's could look at Winona Ryder as having been one of Geragos's experimental guinea pigs before he moved on to the more important case of representing their son, who possibly faces execution. Also, the Petersons may have realized that it is probably better to hire an average lawyer who *has* valuable experience than a better lawyer with little or no experience.

I'd be concerned that the Petersons didn't quite realize how bad a chess move Geragos had made upon making his public announcement about the bodies, or even worse yet, how they used poor judgement when they made the decision to hire Geragos, after he had made such a "prosecutorial" public statement. Let me explain. What the Petersons probably did *not* know was that now the prosecutors could actually quote word for word what Geragos had said publicly, during their *closing arguments* at trial. If nothing else, the prosecutors would score some huge points by proving Geragos a hypocrite.

Well, so much for my defense-angled views. Here are some prosecutorial views I have regarding the bodies washing up. It seems to me that Scott had made the final decision regarding his future—that it would be in his best interest for Laci to get a late-term abortion. Except in Scott's case, the abortion not only included Connor, but Laci, too. How would she not get in the way in Scott's new life with Amber? Oh no, Laci wouldn't be mad about Scott leading her on all the way right up until the birth of Connor, and then saying, "I want out." As if there's no such thing as alimony or child support. Scott gave into the temptations of selfishness and greed. He felt he had the disposal skills and charisma to get away with it. He wasn't expecting national media attention, so he figured Amber would have no way of finding out who he *really* was. He was confident enough in his ability to dispose of these bodies quickly and permanently, but obviously he didn't expect the remains ever to surface. But Amber did find out and came forward. The bodies did eventually surface, showing both Scott's hastiness and lack of experience at body disposal. Scott, during the police-recorded conversation with Amber, even tried, as a last attempt, to persuade her not to go to authorities, by using charm and romance to prey on her previous love for him, all to no avail. When the police, at one point, discovered a mystery object in the bay that might be a body, Scott must've been defecating cement anchors upon hearing this news. When it was determined to be a boat anchor, Scott's confidence and ego must have skyrocketed a mile high once more, only to plummet again a month later, when the bodies did, in fact, wash up. But I suspect the callousness he had built up because this mystery object turned out to be something else probably gave him increased fortitude when he heard that Laci and Connor's remains were verified.

Monday afternoon, April 21, 2003, Scott Peterson made his very first appearance in court for his arraignment, only days after his arrest. The night before, police blocked off 11th Street, between H and I Streets, in front of the courthouse. These streets were expected to remain closed most of that day. The magistrate appointed was Judge Nancy Ashley, whose courtroom seats 56 people. Several of the courtroom seats were reserved for the families of Laci and Scott. Most of the remaining seats were assigned to the media. Ten to fifteen of those seats were reserved for the general public on a lottery as well as first-come, first-served basis. Cameras were not allowed in the hallway outside of the courtroom because of fire and safety issues.

The first of the family members to enter the courtroom that day were Lee and Jackie Peterson, Scott's parents. Sharon Rocha then entered the court, and something uniquely interesting was seen that would only happen this one time. Jackie Peterson approached her, and the two women embraced with tears in their eyes and then took seats, at the opposite ends of the courtroom, with the rest of their respective families. Perhaps it was this emotional episode that gave Jackie the audacity to try later to stay in amiable contact with Sharon, despite Laci's mother's pursuit of the death penalty against Jackie's son.

Bailiffs escorted Scott Peterson, who was still wearing the Stanislaus County-issued red jumpsuit, into the courtroom. His wrists and ankles were shackled. In jail, his hair had been cut recently, and his goatee had been shaved clean from his face. Although his dyed hair was shorter, its highlights were still visible. Upon her son-in-law's entrance, Laci's mother began to cry. Ron Grantski, her husband, comforted her.

Just outside the courthouse was the first sample of media-frenzy crowd control that the authorities in Modesto would now be dealing with for the remainder of the Peterson hearings. Ty Phillips of the *Modesto Bee* reported virtually the same incident I had witnessed that fateful Monday afternoon. Scott's prominent, local attorney, Kirk McAllister, made it to the block of 11th and I Streets before being noticed. Whether or not he could see the anxious crowd of reporters and camera people gathered just outside the courthouse was unknown. But one journalist was able to recognize the lawyer from a block away. The reporter tried to be sly by tucking his camera under his armpit before quietly making a mad dash for the corner, in the hope of being the first to photograph and question the attorney who had represented Peterson up until the time of this arraignment. But it didn't take more than a second before another journalist saw what was happening and quickly followed chase. Then another and another. One reporter yelled out to his fleeing colleague, "Where are you going?"

"There he is," the media associate replied, while speaking and sprinting in full stride.

"Who?"
"It's him!"
"Who is he?!"
"It's McAllister!"

The reporter caught up. Within seconds, the entire pack had crossed 11th Street and swarmed, in a mob-like frenzy around the older, gray-haired lawyer, who maintained a stoic face. He did try to answer a few of the reporters questions only briefly, but was mainly trying to make his way to the entrance of the courthouse. The mass moved like molasses south on 11th, with McAllister as the nucleus, which only further impeded his progress. One couple who witnessed the excitement recounted later to Phillips that they were almost swallowed up by the advancing swarm when they exited a restaurant where they had just had lunch. The lady said, "All of a sudden, everybody was running towards us. We had to back up to get out of the way. We stood under the awning, until it all went by."

It rained on and off that day, but when it cleared, the observers outside court numbered in the hundreds. Some came to get a glimpse at the participants making their way in and out of the courthouse, others hoped for answers or breaking new developments in the case, and some just simply wanted to witness with their own eyes what it's like when a national media circus comes to their town.

Peterson showed little emotion throughout most of the proceedings that afternoon. His face remained apathetic as the charges in the death of his wife were read aloud to him. He did appear, however, to demonstrate some distress when the judge read the charges against him in the death of his son, Conner. Scott squeezed his eyes shut tightly and gently shook his head.

The case, having garnered national media attention, prompted authorities to take extraordinary measures to organize and control the arraignment hearing. Seven deputies moved in and out of the courtroom, occasionally escorting family members and high-profile journalists to their assigned seats.

In the packed Stanislaus County Superior Court, when asked to give his plea, Scott Peterson uttered, "I am not guilty."

During the proceeding, the accused told the judge that he could not afford a defense attorney and asked for a court appointed public defender. Judge Ashley appointed Public Defender Tim Bazar to represent him. Bazar had already met with Peterson earlier that day at the jail, even though he hadn't been officially assigned to the case yet. Kirk McAllister attended the arraignment hearing, but Bazar actually represented Scott. Before the hearing, McAllister cited the attorney-client privilege for not discussing his reason for no longer representing Peterson. My impression at the time of hearing this information about Scott requesting the public defender was that perhaps McAllister had previously indicated to Peterson that, if Scott were to be officially charged in the murder of his wife, then McAllister would need a retainer fee of a magnitude that initially may have soured the prime suspect. There was quite a bit of debate on the cable networks about this particular factor, which was somewhat surprising to many analysts. For example, there were those who scoffed at the notion of a guy, who had a Del Rio Country Club membership, saying that he couldn't afford his own attorney. I didn't see it this way, at all. I recognized right off the bat that Scott, who is only thirty years old, would go bankrupt in a fairly short time in this situation. Perhaps the parents and Scott himself were still holding out a little hope that the case might not actually make it to court, due to a lack of sufficient evidence, before they forked out a trainload of non-refundable, retainer fee cash. The DA's office, the evening of the arraignment, announced that the evidence against this defendant was "voluminous." Once this legal status was made clear, I believe that the parents then felt financially obligated to enter the scene. Again, because Scott was over eighteen, he needed only to declare to the court *his* personal finances. Of course, as we know, the parents did get involved, not only by eventually hiring Mark Geragos, but retaining Kirk McAllister, as well.

Superior Court Judge Nancy Ashley ordered Peterson held without bail, pending a May 6, 2003, bail hearing.

When the hearing concluded, the families were required to remain seated until all the media had been ushered out of the courtroom. Then, both families were escorted out separately by the bailiffs.

That evening, a press conference was scheduled for the family, along with the district attorney, to speak about this, eventful, juncture in the case. Kim Peterson, of the Sund/Carrington Foundation, who was representing the Rochas as their family spokesperson, was the first to take the podium. She spoke briefly, introducing the family and friends who would be speaking that evening: Dennis Rocha, Laci's father; Ron Grantski, Laci's stepfather; Renee Tomlinson, Laci's best friend; Sharon Rocha, Laci's mother; a police spokesperson; and James Brazelton, the district attorney. With a prepared statement Dennis Rocha was the first of the family members to address the reporters. His accent was somewhat thick, and he kept his remarks relatively brief.

Dennis Rocha—I would like to start by thanking Modesto Police Department, attorney general, Department of Justice (he starts to lose composure here) and the Sheriff's Department, for your continuing efforts in finding my daughter. Now we can move forward. And now justice can be done. And now I'd also like to thank my family and friends and thousands of people I don't even know. Thank you for searching and praying for my daughter and grandson. Your support has been overwhelming. Thank you. (He then took his seat.)
Ron Grantski—The last four months have been the worst times in our lives. I watched our family and friends change, both physically and mentally. But one thing that has never changed, was that we'll do anything to get Laci back. Hundreds of people worked day and night, Christmas, New Years, Easter, whatever it took, weekends, holidays, to find Laci. Our local businesswomen and men donated lodging, food, posters, whatever was needed to help find Laci. The local police, as well as law enforcement throughout the state, worked day and night to find Laci. The press got the word out to the whole nation. People everywhere got involved through the prayer cards, e-mail, donations. Our family wants to thank you so much. Without all of you, who knows. We would like to thank all the people who helped us with our extensive search efforts. Those who searched by plane, on horseback, boat, divers, and cars, on foot. They searched lakes, rivers, all over the valley and different counties everywhere. We tried to find Laci. We did our best. Kim Petersen and the Sund/Carrington Foundation has been a God-send to us. She was able to provide advice, guidance, support on so many things. She's now a big part of our lives. I know all of you would like for us to say something about Scott. But we're not going to do that. We owe it to Laci to let the courts bring the facts out. I'm not going to say anything that's gonna jeopardize all the hard work of so many young men and women. I hope I

don't have to say that too many times. We started this nightmare with one purpose in mind, to find Laci and bring her home. While this is not the way we wanted to bring her home, it will help us to begin a long process of healing. While we understand there are many people who would like to hear from us in the very near future, we have two very tough days ahead of us. Laci's birthday is May 4 and we have to start thinking about funeral services. We realize that we have a very long and difficult road ahead of us. And our primary concern...is working and helping each other in this family. All the cards, flowers, candles, stuffed animals and pictures left at Laci's house mean so much to us. We spend time each day reading the notes and cards left at the house, as well as the guest book entries. We have seen video and pictures of many of you stopping by Laci's house to show your support for our families and your love for our Laci and Conner. Our family has chosen to donate the stuffed animals to the Children's Crisis Center and the M.D.I.C. program for abused children in Laci's name. I feel sorry for Jackie and Lee and their family. They don't deserve this. But Laci and our family didn't either. Thank you.

Renee Tomlinson—On behalf of Laci and Conner's friends, we would like to thank the volunteers, the community and the entire nation for your continued thoughts and prayers. Please know that we read your postings, especially when we need encouragement. It is comforting to know that so many people have come to love that same smile that we'll miss each and every day. We have so many memories of Laci that we will cherish and hold very close to our hearts. (Pause) Laci brought so much to each of us. Her love of good food, fine wine, gardening, entertaining and always having a good time in any situation. Laci not only taught us proper etiquette, but how to laugh and not just giggle, but to laugh loud and often. For every one of our birthdays, she made sure to make it special. Whether it was a beautifully baked cake, a few hours of pampering, or a special gift waiting on your porch. She wanted to be sure each and every time we were all together that we would have fun and unfortunately it is now that we realize how incredibly blessed we are to have those memories of her. Laci's most recent passion was her baby boy. We all know how much she wanted a baby. She was so excited, nervous and anxious to be having Conner. As any new mom, she had lots of questions, and we all reassured her that we would be there to help. Now we will never know his face, never see his smile and never hear his cry. We will miss the chance for our children to grow up together. We can only find comfort knowing that they will always be together, and that Laci is with her son that she loved so much. We feel we'll never truly have closure, because each day there'll always be one phone call that we can't make, one funny story untold, one conversation unspoken with our best friend.

Sharon Rocha—Words alone are not enough to express our sincere gratitude and appreciation to every person and entity that helped in our search for Laci and Conner. We are very fortunate to live in a community that has come together and supported us from the very beginning of our nightmare and continues to do so. We thank the media for your help and your support. Through you we've been given an opportunity to share our Laci and Conner with people all around the world. We want to give thanks to all the law enforcement agencies, the fire department and Coast Guard involved in the search for Laci. The Red Lion Hotel and Brad Saltzman for donating the rooms for our volunteer center. The volunteers, who donated their personal time, spent many, many hours helping at the center. Those who helped with the search. The people who came to the center, to pick up flyers, to post in various locations all over the state. The businesses that donated supplies and food. Jonathon Smith, who established and continues to oversee the

Laci Peterson website. The thousands and thousands of people who've posted their message on the website...and to all of those who prayed for us, for the safe return of Laci and Conner. We especially would like to thank the Modesto Police Department and everyone affiliated with them. We cannot thank you enough for giving up your personal lives, for all the long hours, days and weeks you've spent searching for answers to Laci's disappearance. For your kindness and patience with us. For your understanding of our desperation to find Laci. We would also like thank your families, many of whom may have spent the Christmas holidays without you, because of your dedication to your department and your tireless efforts to find Laci and Conner. We're grateful to you for sharing your loved ones with us during our time of need. We'd like to thank Kim Petersen and the entire staff of the Sund/Carrington Foundation. They've worked diligently to inform the public, both locally and nationally, of Laci's disappearance, in order to solicit their help in locating her. Due to Kim's experience with situations such as ours, she's familiar with the ups and downs, the highs and lows and the many different emotions we are experiencing. She's made herself available to us in providing guidance and support, to help us get through some of our darkest hours. I consider her a very dear friend and offer my sincere gratitude. I highly recommend the Carole Sund/Carrington Foundation to anyone seeking help in finding missing loved ones. We are so grateful for the thoughtfulness and amazing generosity, for all the donors who donated to the reward and the search fund established to help bring Laci home. We thank you from the bottom of our hearts. To our family and our friends and to all Laci's friends. You've been with us from the beginning of our long walk down this devastating road. You've offered yourselves to us to lean on and help carry the weight of our burden. You've been here to support us, give us strength, and to help ease the pain. You gave up your own personal lives to be here with us because you know we need you. Without your love and devotion, we would never be able to face what lies ahead. We're eternally grateful to all of you, and we thank you. If Laci were here now, she'd be absolutely amazed at the outpouring of love and concern for her and Conner. I know in my heart, she is fully aware of the love we have for her. (Pause) On December 24, 2002, shortly after 5:15 p.m., I received a phone call and heard the devastating words that forever changed my life, "Laci's missing." I knew in my heart something terrible had happened to my daughter and my grandson. My world collapsed around me. Since receiving that phone call, we've been living a terrible nightmare. The search for Laci began that night. The questions were always there, "What happened to Laci? Where is she? Is she safe? And who took her from me? I made a plea to the person or persons who took her to please, please let her go and bring her home to us. We heard nothing. As the days passed, I made more pleas to take her to a hospital or fire/police station, or tell us where she is, so we could come to her and bring her and her baby home safely. Still we heard nothing. We searched and searched and searched, and still no Laci. I love my daughter so much. I miss her every minute of every day. My heart aches for her and Conner. Without them, there's a huge void in my life. I *literally* get sick to my stomach, when I allow myself to think about what may have happened to them. No parent should ever have to think about the way their child was murdered. In my mind I keep hearing Laci saying to me, "Mom, please find me and Conner, and bring us home. I'm scared. Please don't leave us out here all alone. I want to come home. Please don't stop looking for us." I feel Laci and Conner can no longer wait to be found. The last week they came to us. Laci and Conner left us on Christmas Eve. I know that God has been watching over them. He sent them back to us on Good Friday. Now we can bring them home, where they belong. Laci and her unborn child did not deserve to die. (Crying) They certainly did not deserve to be dumped in the bay and sent to a watery grave, as though their lives were meaningless. Laci meant the world to me. She was my only daughter. She was my best friend. We miss her beautiful smile, her laughter, her love, and her kind and loving ways. I miss seeing her, talking to her and hugging her. We've been deprived of meeting and knowing Laci's son, our grandson and nephew. We will miss them and mourn them for the rest of our lives. Soon after Laci went missing I made a promise to her, that if she's been harmed, we will seek justice for her and Conner and make sure that *that* person responsible for their deaths, will be punished. I can only hope that the sound of Laci's voice begging for her life and begging for the life of her unborn child, is heard over and over and over again in the mind of that person every day for the rest of his life. The person responsible should be held accountable and punished for the tragedy and devastation forced upon so many of us.

Sharon Rocha then took her seat, crying. The family members consoled her. Kim Petersen again took the podium and indicated that, because of the difficult time the family was going through, they would not be conducting any interviews in the near future. A spokesperson for the Modesto PD took the stand and began directing secondary family members and friends in leaving the auditorium. The media remained in the building, and within a few minutes, District Attorney James Brazelton took the microphone, to briefly announce that the goal of his office would be to see that both Scott Peterson and the citizens of this community receive a fair trial, and that justice would be done. He then allowed reporters to ask some questions. The first question was regarding whether his department was ready, at that time, to go to trial. His response was, "Are you ready to take a flight to the moon tomorrow, sir?" Then, he went on to say that he didn't want to be so facetious, but that with the magnitude of a case like this, it could be a very long time before it would make it to trial. However, his department, after sifting through the necessary reports, material, and information, would be ready to try the case as early as several months later, if necessary. There were several more minutes of questions and answers, much of which the DA wasn't at liberty to discuss, then the most significant press conference so far in the Laci disappearance case concluded.

In response to this press conference, Scott's parents, Lee and Jackie Peterson, gave an exclusive interview to *Time Magazine's* Jill Underwood, to share their thoughts on their son's arrest. Here are key excerpts from that conversation.

Lee Peterson: We're grieving for the loss of Scott's wife and the baby. Our family is just devastated, and we feel an equal amount of pain for the Rocha family. But...our son is innocent. We know that. We've known it from day one.

Jackie Peterson: They know it, too. They supported him fully, until the police misled them, and that was to divide and separate him from them. He was their support. They were his support.

Lee Peterson: We're just very critical of the way the Modesto Police has handled this investigation. They worked strictly on a theory that was dreamt up by this lead detective within the first eight hours, and they've pursued it backwards from there, and they have neglected so many good leads. Chief Wasden made a comment during this news conference that, on the evening before Christmas Eve, Laci's mother had spoken to Laci at 8:15, and that's the last time anyone saw Laci. Not true. There are several people who saw Laci.

Jackie Peterson: Several people who the police immediately tried to discredit the minute they came forward, so they're not coming forward.

Lee Peterson: And one of these gentlemen—and they are prominent people—he's a three-term council member up there and an attorney, and they saw her, and they know her, and the police have disregarded this. If it doesn't fit their theory, by God, they don't want to investigate it. I just can't be any more emphatic than that. And we're gonna pursue this thing.

Jackie Peterson: I would like people to use their common sense and look at the big picture, not just one incident, that for three months the police have been telling them Scott did not go fishing. Now, conveniently, the body has been found where he told them he went fishing. Why would he go 80 miles fishing, come home with a receipt and buy gas and food along the way, have a receipt of the dock, and tell police exactly where he went fishing—and the body would be there! That does not make sense. It's too damn convenient for that.

Lee Peterson: I would ask everyone to consider Scott's family. We're a good family. We don't have a record of anything.

Jackie Peterson: He doesn't either. You can look.

Lee Peterson: He doesn't. There was no domestic violence.

Jackie Peterson: No drugs. No financial problems. He worked three jobs to put himself through college and put his wife through college. They both worked hard to get everything they had, and they were enjoying it to the hilt. And they adored each other.

Lee Peterson: We were with them the week before Christmas, and you never saw a more loving couple.

Jackie Peterson: Laci's mother stated the same thing, prior to the police going to them. All her family talked about how much they loved each other. How happy they were.

How happily married people they were. And how we all wished we were like that. And then it all changed, when the police went to them. And with what we know now, now they're bragging about their technique of deception that they learned to be detectives. And that means they can lie to you, but if you say anything in the same sentence different, you've committed perjury. But they can say anything they want and tell their parents anything they want, and they're grieving, and they're looking to them for help.

TIME: **What has Scott told you?**

Lee Peterson: We haven't been able to speak to him. Again, we're grieving for the baby, as Scott is for Laci. And we'd like to extend our best to the Rocha family. But I think if they search their hearts and really position themselves where they were before the police deceived them, and look at this thing in the wide context, they'll see the police have just bungled this investigation from day one. They can come after me. That's fine. But they've bungled this case.

Jackie Peterson: I think it's inappropriate for the police to be preening and patting themselves on the back for a good job of four months, when they've done a cheap shot...is what they've performed. Not only that, but they were preening and patting themselves when the announcement of who those bodies were. That's totally inappropriate. If they want to pat themselves on the back, they should have a party somewhere else. I'm just appalled at that, that our public people are like that. You have a district attorney calling this a slam-dunk before there's even an arraignment. I'm feeling like I'm living in Nazi-Germany or the Soviet Union. I'm just sick of this. (Her eyes teared up.) I think every man out there should be in fear, if this is the way the police worked. If a crime happens to your wife, you'd better know you're with six people, and they weren't drunk, and they are good friends who are going to be able to put up with this. If they have any kind of shady character, the police will dismiss them, and you'll be ruined.

TIME: **What about the police saying that Scott tried to sell the house and her car?**

Lee Peterson: You can take this thing from the very beginning. There's no motive. That $250,000 life insurance policy they had

	for two years, and it was on each of them. They did that when they bought the home.
Jackie Peterson:	It's not a policy. It was a retirement policy that has insurance attached. The police lied to Laci's mother about that.
Lee Peterson:	He did not try to sell the house.
Jackie Peterson:	We were looking at new cars the week before in Carmel. Laci wanted a safer car for her baby. The police took his car. He's making a payment on a truck that they've had now for four months. He's not a rich man. He works, and they live the way they want to live, but they budgeted, and they do it on their own, and they never ask for anything.
Lee Peterson:	They made it sound like Laci loved that car. Laci hated that car.
Jackie Peterson:	She called it a piece of shit. The only time I ever heard a bad word out of her mouth.
Lee Peterson:	We talked a lot, driving on the Carmel trip the week before this happened, and they were gonna trade that car and get her a better car. Because the car would quit running...As for the home, one of the ladies who ran our volunteer center in Modesto is in the real estate business. And she was one of favorites...And

Scott was talking to her as a side remark and said "What do you think I could get for it?"

Jackie Peterson: That's not what he said. He said he didn't want to live there anymore. He said he didn't want to bring Laci home to that, and what would they get out of it. He did not sign a listing. He did not go to a realtor.

Lee Peterson: Did you folks know there's another pregnant lady that was floating in that bay in January? Another torso and two other pregnant women missing in that area. And that place is polluted with parolees.

TIME: **What about the fear that police had that he would run to Mexico?**

Jackie Peterson: I will tell you exactly what happened. He sold his car because his job had changed. He doesn't have to haul stuff anymore. And he couldn't afford it. He was making a payment, and we loaned him a car to drive instead. Apparently, from what we now hear, the police had a device attached to it. His attorney knew where he was at all times.

Lee Peterson: He went to Mexico, as you'll recall, maybe six weeks ago, on a business trip, came back and the police knew where he was.

Jackie Peterson: He's not going to leave his family and his life, and besides, he's innocent.

Lee Peterson: It's another smear on him that he was going to run into Mexico. And how ridiculous. The kid lives here. They ran him out of Modesto. He can't use his home. They've got his car. Where's he supposed to go? He came to us, and he was not running.

I was among several thousand or so late-comers to the colossal Laci Memorial Service. A few hundred others and I were detoured to one of the nearby, side locations where they were showing the live coverage of the service by big screen.

Scott Peterson had made a last minute request to attend Laci's memorial service. This appeared to be a last minute attempt at trying to look innocent, as if he really were a grieving husband. The authorities were at first momentarily puzzled by Peterson's request, but quickly realized his ploy and said, "No way."

Likewise, another person central to the case had also wanted to attend, as well as speak, at Laci's memorial service. This person, interestingly enough, was none other than Amber Frey. However, she was advised not to attend by both *her* own friends and *Laci's* friends, as well. This, of course, was for obvious reasons of proper social etiquette—it simply would have been inappropriate for her to attend. She was the other woman. Unfortunately, there was no avoiding that, no matter how innocent she was of Scott's conniving, or how much of a victim she herself was. Technically, if it hadn't been for Amber's loose morals, Laci might still be alive. So, from an indirect standpoint, Amber Frey was the whole cause of why there was a memorial service at all. Thus, her presence at the memorial service might have created some ill feelings among many of the participants. Again, this event was all about Laci, in her honor. Either Amber or Scott's presence would have only created an adverse distraction.

Additionally, Scott's parents, who were, of course, Laci's in-laws, wanted to attend. Their invitation likewise was denied for similar reasons, their irrevocable bias in favor of their own son, regardless of his guilt or innocence, might have caused a certain degree of ill sentiment among the masses of passionate Laci supporters. Jackie Peterson, Scott's mother, later remarked that nothing offended her more in this whole fiasco than the Rochas "not welcoming" them to attend Laci's funeral.

The day that the service was held also would have been Laci's 28th birthday. The day was Sunday, May 4, 2003. The First Baptist Church, the largest facility in Modesto, held the event. The service started with music, and the choir continued singing several hymns, as people finished taking their seats. After a few more songs, several speakers took the stand, to give a few opening statements, as well as lead the congregation in prayer. Brent Rocha, Laci's brother, then took the podium.

> **Brent Rocha:** Today is a good day. All of us are given an opportunity to come here and remember Laci and Conner. Laci would be very grateful and just astounded that she would get this kind of attention. I think, with all of us here, we're sending a very powerful message and I know Laci and Conner can hear us now. And know that we love them, the friends and family, the community and everyone that

helped try to find them. On the way over here, my mom wanted me to mention that Laci's probably saying, "Nuh uh" right now. (Some laughter from the crowd.) She would not believe all this is happening for her, and I think, when my mom said that, it was perfect because Laci would be just amazed and grateful. We're grateful, and we thank all of you for taking your time to come out today. Just a little story about my sister, I wanted to talk about how she fit in with our family dynamics. I think all families tend to have one person in your family who you always have a good time with, or is so outgoing and fun to be around. And that was Laci. She was the one we always had a good time with. She was so vivacious and outgoing. She loved to have events at her house, and to just have a good time. She will be dearly missed. It's hard to lose anyone in your family, but when it's one who plays that role, it's even that much more difficult to deal with why they may not be around now. The reason I chose to speak was to send a message to everyone here, and this message came from Laci. About three years ago, at a funeral for our grandmother, she mentioned, "Well, you know, when I die I don't want people to be sad. I don't want people to be missing me. I want people to be happy. So, I'm up here to convey that message to all of you, that she would want all of us to have happiness in our hearts for her, and that we were given the opportunity to know her. Thanks. (Applause.)

The next person to take the podium was a lady who was one of Laci's older cousins, Addie Hansberry. She spoke for several minutes, telling a number of stories about Laci. I remember one of the more memorable comments she made of Laci was about one of her character traits—she said that Laci had "pizzazz."

After Ms. Hansberry took her seat, the choir sang a few more songs. Then Terri Western, the mother of one of Laci's best friends, took the podium. Among several stories about her daughter growing up with Laci, she mentioned that they both got a dual nomination for homecoming queen their senior year. Then a young boy took the stand, T.J. Vasquez, Laci's thirteen-year-old cousin. Sandy Rickard, a friend, spoke next. The service then rolled into a video tribute to Laci, showing many photos of her growing up—along with some wedding photos; however, Scott's image was conspicuously removed from these pictures.

After the video tribute, several of Laci's best friends went to the front to take turns speaking. The first was Renee Tomlinson. The others included Stacey Boyers, Lori Ellesworth, and Renee Garza, as well as a few others. After a few of Laci's friends spoke, another one of her friends took the podium. I remember that when she spoke, part of the crowd at this one location had a somewhat different reaction to her eulogy, than the larger congregation at the main church did. After barely getting out a few sentences, the young woman appeared to be struggling with her nervousness in front of the entire world. One of the other friends came up to comfort her, in an attempt to help her to continue to speak. The girl struggled a few more minutes, but nothing seemed to be coming out, then she broke into tears and sat down with a red face.

At this point, someone in the crowd where I was, couldn't hold it back, let loose and emitted some laughter. Then it spread through about a third of the people. I didn't laugh, but I smiled a little, because I knew why they were laughing. Evidently, the part of the crowd that laughed must have thought the girl and her friend were at least partially trying to play off the overwhelming nervousness as cries of grief for her lost friend, Laci. True, the nervousness did play a part in her expression; however, I believe her crying *was* legitimately for the loss of her good friend. On the other hand, the people who couldn't hold back their snickers were doing so because they saw something else happening there, as well. For whatever it's worth, this little triste was something the crowd specifically reacted to. What these individuals must have read into the speaker was that this was the moment of a lifetime for the girl, probably the only chance she'd ever get actually to say something when the entire world of four billion people were momentarily listening to her, and a chance to be someone by having enough importance to be at these public microphones. Despite her practicing at home in the mirror, despite her desperate longing to say what she had planned to say, unfortunately her central nervous system took over and overcame the girl's personal will power to speak. She broke into tears in realization of this fact and knew at this point she had no other choice but to sit down in utter humiliation. As personally ashamed as she may have been, she did have the perfect excuse for those tears, which was mourning for her friend. Although *I* believe those tears really were for Laci, more than anything else.

I guess that, as far as this particular section of viewers was concerned, during those few, long minutes when the girl struggled and tried to speak, it gave a few of those people just enough time to think that they had figured out what was *really* happening at that moment. This, and perhaps, the girl partially trying to hide it with the "mourning" factor, struck these individuals in a humorous enough way that, even as mature and disciplined as they may have been, even they (just like the girl they unfortunately were making fun of) could not control their own physiological reactions at that moment.

As the girls made their way back to their seats, the pastor thanked them for their kind words, and the song, "Brown Eyed Girl," began to play. Right at this time, a woman in the upper section of seats stood up and tried to yell some statement that she obviously wanted to be broadcasted nationally, but by the time any cameras reached her, she had finished speaking and was standing there confused, not knowing what to do. Then, the gentleman sitting next to her tugged at her sleeve, and she sat down. I don't believe that anybody really heard what she said; it was drowned out by the music. The family members simply ignored her, as did everybody else.

186   *LACI PETERSON The Whole Story*

Now Entering Modesto at 9th and I Streets.
(B. Knight)

The Home of Laci & Scott Peterson at 523 Covena Avenue,
Modesto, California.
(B. Knight)

The Entrance to East La Loma Park one block from Laci & Scott's house.
(B. Knight)

It's not hard to see where Laci inherited her award winning smile.
(General media)

Detective Al Brochini exiting the Stanislaus County Court House.
(B. Knight)

Chief Deputy DA John Goold speaking to reporters outside the Modesto Courthouse.
(B. Knight)

Amber Frey's attorney Gloria Allred speaking to the media
outside Stanislaus County Courthouse.
(B. Knight)

Amber Frey, the modern world's most famous mistress.
(AP/Wide World Photo)

Ron Grantski, Laci's stepfather, entering the courthouse.
(B. Knight)

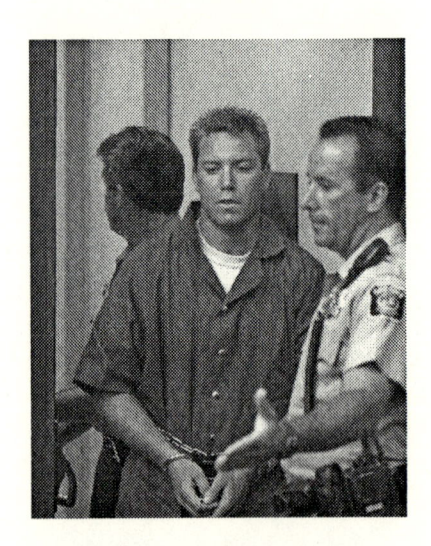

Scott Peterson being transported in his county
issued jumpsuit.
(AP/Wide World Photo)

Peterson home front driveway.
(B. Knight)

Shrine for Laci & Conner on the Peterson front lawn at the time of the searches.
(B. Knight)

The launch ramp receipt machine by which Scott Peterson
generated his alibi at the Berkeley Marina.
(B. Knight)

The Modesto hotel where the volunteer command center
ran for several months.
(B. Knight)

Front entrance and lobby of the volunteer headquarters during the searches for Laci.
(B. Knight)

The media circus in full force settling in outside the Modesto Courthouse.
(B. Knight)

A fleet of major cable and network news crews with satellite dishes, poised outside the Modesto Courthouse.
(B. Knight)

Lee & Jackie Peterson entering the courthouse.
(B. Knight)

Bodies Are Found 195

The mad rush of reporters as they scramble for a shot at Jackie Peterson.
(B. Knight)

Kim Petersen, Ron Grantski and Sharon Rocha entering the courthouse.
(B. Knight)

6

Riding On Laci's Coattails

In the beginning, I was among the neighbors in the searches, but later on, I transcended into one of the journalists among the reporters. I, for one, can attest that this case was big enough to sweep even *me* off my feet. It was like I was riding on a hurricane, just barefoot water-skiing the air currents under my heels, wherever they took me.

Starting within the first two days of the Laci Peterson investigation, many other cases began riding on Laci's coattails, as well, by getting increased publicity that they might not have otherwise received. One such case, as we know, was the burglary that occurred across the street from the Petersons' home around the same approximate time that Laci disappeared. It was cracked open wide and solved almost instantly, due to the titanic pressure of the national media in the Peterson case. Likewise, there had been several other missing persons cases that, over time, were growing cold. Some of these investigations included pregnant females found floating in San Francisco Bay. Another one involved a student at Cal Poly, San Luis Obispo, who went missing while Scott Peterson was attending school there, and Scott, coincidentally, happened to be on a list of potential suspects from that investigation, but ironically, he was never interviewed.

The girl's name was Kristin Smart—she was 19 years old. Kristin was from Stockton, California, and it was her first year of college. She went missing on May 25, 1996, and has never been found. No arrests have ever been made in this case. The campus was California Polytechnic State University in San Luis Obispo. Scott Peterson was 24 at the time and was majoring in agriculture there. After attending a fraternity party, Smart was last seen at approximately 2 a.m., walking back to her dorm room with another student, Paul Flores.

San Luis Obispo Lt. Sheriff Steve Bolts said, "We are looking at Peterson's class schedules to determine if they crossed paths at all. We have discussed the case with Modesto detectives, as well. We both are familiar with each other's case."

Lt. Bolts said that Scott Peterson's name turned up on a list of hundreds whom investigators had started questioning in connection with the Kristin Smart disappearance, but they found no indication that Peterson had ever been interviewed. One media source reported that detectives had approached Scott where he was staying back in 1996, but he denied any involvement and declined to speak to them. Another report simply said that he was among a few hundred people who were mailed a letter requesting any information he may have had regarding her disappearance, which he ignored and never returned. Well, regardless of the scenario seven years ago, I thought it was uniquely interesting that Scott Peterson would have even made it on a list of hundreds of people investigators were looking into, out of a campus of thousands of enrolled students. Regarding this apparent list, Lt. Bolts went on to say that, although Peterson was on it, his name did not appear among the few that investigators intended to take a closer look at. Maybe it *was* just a coincidence. But if it was, Scott again fell into the approximate 10 percent of students to be questioned, and not the 90 percent who were unlinked to Kristin Smart. The pressing question here remains—why was Scott on this list? Certainly whoever put Scott Peterson on this list must have had a reason to do so. This many years after the fact, though, whoever organized the list of a few hundred individuals may not realistically be able to remember the reason why Scott Peterson was chosen.

Besides cases I've worked on, I've never known anyone personally to be randomly involved in a murder investigation. But if this information stands true, then, within the short span of six years, Scott Peterson happened to be questioned in two separate but similar disappearances of young, beautiful females, both of whom attended this college at about the same time with none other than…Mr. Perfect, the world's most innocent man. Of course, one of these females, we now know, Scott met and married while attending Cal Poly. The other, he may have hardly known. But now, both of these women appear to be permanently gone.

When Kristin Smart's mother was interviewed, she appeared to be under the belief that the last person seen with her daughter, Paul Flores, was the one responsible for her disappearance. When Flores was interviewed in the beginning of the investigation, detectives found him to be very cooperative and didn't believe he had any involvement. After some time had elapsed, detectives again wanted to interview Paul. This time his parents were involved and had hired an attorney, who advised their son not to speak with police. To me, this would make sense. What I mean is that, the boy, showing a normal, candid, truthful demeanor, didn't appear to be hiding anything when Kristin first disappeared (not to mention that there was no apparent motive), but it wasn't until later that investigators would try to make a second attempt at their only suspect. Now, assuming for a minute that the boy actually *is* innocent, I could understand his not wanting to cooperate a second time with detectives, because to do so, when you know you are innocent, only serves to help police to build a case around an innocent person—in other words, he'd be handing officials the resources to wrongfully convict an innocent bystander—himself.

Paul Flores was a young freshman at the time. He was eighteen years old with skinny arms. According to police, a cadaver dog detected the scent of a dead body in Paul's dorm room (or was it peanut butter?). Also, the information sheet about Kristin's disappearance listed her height as 6'1." It sounds like Kristin was as large as a full-grown man. Well, if this were true, how would a kid such as Paul Flores carry a sizable body like this down the stairs, hallways, and lobby of a student dorm building without being seen? Furthermore, as a first year freshman in the dorms, he probably didn't have a vehicle other than a bicycle, so where would he get access to a boat to sink her, or a shovel to bury her? Her body, by the way, has never been found, so whoever is responsible evidently did a good job with the disposal. An immature person such as Paul Flores doesn't strike me as the type to carry out this high level of a crime successfully.

Kristin's mother made it a point to mention that, at one time, she attempted to confront Paul at a gas station where he was working about a year later. She just wanted to ask him if he knew anything at all about her daughter's disappearance and even tried to tell him she wasn't interested punishing him. She said Paul locked himself behind a door and yelled, "Go away!"

This, apparently, was enough to convince Mrs. Smart of Paul's guilt. She believes this young man was able to get away with murdering her daughter. Standing back and looking at this evidence neutrally, I don't see it the same way. I believe the young man's reaction at the gas station had more to do with his immaturity and lack of social etiquette, than it did out of guilt for any crime he may have committed. Remember, Paul Flores couldn't have been more than 19 years old at the time Kristin's mother approached him at this location. Sometimes males at this age haven't discovered themselves yet, nor did he have enough life experience yet to know how to properly address the situation and issue. However, we do know about another young man that she dated, who attended the same college as Kristin, was a senior, and was a little bigger, stronger, and more experienced with life in general than Flores (not to mention that he had his own truck). This man, Scott Peterson, also by coincidence, was being tried for an almost identical crime only six years later, with a preponderance of overwhelming evidence against him. Police were also interviewing the person who provided information that Scott Peterson dated Kristin Smart.

Sheriff Patrick Hedges issued a statement that announced there was no connection was found between Scott Peterson and the Kristin Smart case. He said, "Investigators are not looking at Scott Peterson in connection with the disappearance of Kristin Smart. After consulting with investigators working on the Laci Peterson case, we have determined there is no basis to shift the focus of investigation in the Smart case."

California alone had a reported 17,000 missing females in 2002. (By the way, a large percentage of these were undoubtedly temporary runaways, most of whom came back home the next day after the missing persons report was filed.) This number appears staggering, and as unfortunate as this reality may be, it is perhaps statistics like these that might give a guy such as Scott Peterson the incentive to add just one more to this list. It's unbelievable to most of us, but to a sociopath who is willing to stomp anyone out strictly to further his own personal interests, this factor might help him justify his actions. Scott may have thought that, because this list is already so large, and the cops obviously had their hands full already, what's just one more going to hurt?

Five months before the Laci Peterson case began, another young, pregnant female went missing, and her remains ultimately surfaced in the San Francisco Bay, as well. In May of 2002, Evelyn Hernandez, who lived in San Francisco's Mission District and was eight months pregnant, turned up missing, along with her 5-year-old son, Alex. In July of 2002, just two months after she was reported missing, her headless, limbless torso was found floating in the bay, directly underneath the Golden Gate Bridge. She was a single mother, working to support her son, Alex, while also studying to be a nurse. She had worked at both Walgreen's and Costco, according to her cousin, Berta Hernandez. She was considered very responsible by those who were close to her. They said that her main focus had always been raising her son, Alex, even after beginning a new relationship with a boyfriend, who seemed to have a reasonably stable career. His name was Herman Aguillerra; he was an airline mechanic and part-time chauffeur. It wasn't long before Evelyn became pregnant by Herman.

Investigators believe Hernandez disappeared on or about the night of May 1, 2002, after having spoken to her sister for the last time by telephone. Friends and family contacted Evelyn's boyfriend, when they hadn't heard from her. He then reported to police his girlfriend's disappearance, but not until a full month after Evelyn had gone missing. Two months later her body turned up in the bay, but her son still remains missing to this day.

Her friends and family say that they organized a memorial service and invited the media, but, they said…nobody showed up. The media just weren't interested. Her friends said publicly that they believe the reason the news agencies showed no interest was because Evelyn wasn't white, that she was from El Salvador. When the Hernandez torso was collected from the bay, investigators were fairly certain that this was she, because a tag on the inner, elastic waistband of the clothes read: Motherhood Maternity. In the Laci Peterson case, the identities of the bodies found were confirmed by DNA testing within 4 days. In the Hernandez case, the family had to wait for over a month before the results were in. Hernandez had two sisters who live in the United States—one who lives in Virginia and another who lives in Richmond, California, and who happens to be a deaf-mute. Reina Solis, Evelyn's sister from Richmond, said through an interpreter that she was devastated when a policeman notified her that her sister's remains had been found in the bay, again without a head or limbs. She is holding out hope that her sister's son, Alex, is still alive, and she has kept many of his things at her home, including his crib, toys, and storybooks, in the prospect of his unlikely return.

Again, the burglary across the street from the Petersons' home was not the only case that got increased attention as a result of Laci's disappearance. Now the Evelyn Hernandez case was starting to get more of a push, when it had previously been neglected. Why? She too was pregnant and found in San Francisco Bay, while the prime suspect, who was her boyfriend, reportedly impregnated her while he was married to someone else. Without sufficient proof, the investigators stopped pursuing the case. But now, with the many similarities between her and Laci, the Evelyn Hernandez case has gained some new attention. The lead investigator on that case, for example, was compelled to come forward on national television and explain why, in her opinion, the case had gone cold.

Lead Detective Holly Pera said that there could be a five-year-old boy still alive out there, and that it is incumbent that everything possible should be done to find him. She said that the media are an enormous aid to investigators searching for missing persons, and that she personally had spoken to reporters, who promised police that a sizable article on the case would come out in the newspaper. However, police were notified with an apology that the story would be bumped to the back page because of more pressing stories. On the other hand, over 3,000 articles had already been printed about the Laci Peterson case within the first few months. The Hernandez case had received so little attention, that no one had even bothered to list Alex in the national database for missing and exploited children. His mother's murder investigation has only recently begun to receive some attention, solely because it had become a curious sub-factor in the Peterson case. The Peterson defense team was denied access to the Hernandez investigation files, which they had hoped might corroborate a theory that either case could be the work of a serial killer out to steal unborn babies.

After Evelyn had become pregnant by Mr. Aguillera, she had spoken to her friends about her aspirations of creating a happy, secure family together with him, Alex, and their new baby. Another of her friends talked about how Evelyn had wanted to improve herself, so as to become a better wife for

Herman, demonstrating her desire to build a future with him. The only problem with Evelyn's grand dream was that Aguillera was already married. According to the investigators, Evelyn didn't find out that her boyfriend already had a wife until after she had become pregnant by him. One can only imagine what kind of emotional ups and downs that this woman must have experienced upon hearing this information—emotions that, no doubt, included animosity towards Herman for deceiving her in this way. According to the victim's sister, Aguillera wanted nothing to do with the baby, and that he told her to get rid of it. But for Evelyn, it was too late; she had already made her decision to keep it. Then Evelyn, in her concern for how she might have to raise this child on her own, told Herman that she would go directly to the DA's office, to make sure that she would garnish child support payments from him. This, she knew, would be effective because, as a union airline mechanic, Herman was a W-2 employee. He couldn't quit his hard-earned job to avoid the wage garnishments because he had his *own* family to support. Aguillera's wife doesn't want her husband to cooperate with authorities anymore in this investigation for some reason. I wonder what Herman's wife thought of her husband getting another woman pregnant, or what she thought of the possibility that her husband's paychecks might be reduced for child support payments, as well as the possibility of him making regular visitations to his…other woman and baby. Detective Pera said that Aguillera's wife chose to provide him with an alibi, that he was home with her on the night of Evelyn's disappearance. So the detective said that Aguillera is not a formal suspect, and now they don't have a suspect.

My question is this, if Holly Pera is being called the "lead detective" in this case, why is it that she knows very little about homicide investigation? A wife can never be considered an alibi because she is the mate. Her testimony has zero credibility because of her extreme bias. Any spouse will corroborate an alibi, whether it's true or not, to protect and retain her husband. This legal principle is Homicide 101. How could a "lead detective" not know this?

Herman uses the gas station that the limousine company he works for is contracted with. Evelyn's wallet was found within one block of this location a few days after she went missing. The wallet still had money in it, which indicates that the motive was not robbery. Is this just a coincidence, too? It might be, but after being questioned the first time by detectives, Aguillera hired a defense lawyer and is refusing to discuss the case any further. Here is a possible theory: Herman Aguillera picked up Evelyn Hernandez and her 5-year-old son in his company's limousine for a supposed fun night out. As an experienced chauffeur, Herman knew where all the secluded make-out spots are, especially since the main clientele for limousine service are young couples on prom dates, etc. These romantic spots include hidden areas that overlook the waters of the bay and the view of the Golden Gate Bridge, underneath which Evelyn's body was found floating. Perhaps it made sense to Evelyn that her boyfriend was able to use a limo from his work on a weeknight, since the company wouldn't be as busy as on a Friday or Saturday night. Likewise, Aguillera also realized that it would be less likely that anyone who might inadvertently end up as another witness might be at one these isolated lovers' locales on a weeknight. Limousines are equipped with the most sophisticated power door lock systems available, giving the driver total control over the safety of the frequently drunk and partying young people. After locking his girlfriend and her young son in the rear compartment, he then pulled on his extra large, black leather gloves, and entered the rear compartment, where they were both sitting unsuspectingly. Photos of Herman show him to be a huge man. With one blow, he knocked the 5-year-old unconscious. As his mother screamed, Aguillera put his huge hands around her neck and summarily strangled her to death, so that there was no blood or ballistic evidence whatsoever. He then quietly removed the bodies, one at a time, and threw them into the nearby water, just underneath the Golden Gate Bridge. He felt relieved; the nearest person to the scene was perhaps as far as a quarter mile away, and this woman no longer posed a threat to his livelihood. Now, if the national media were to converge on Evelyn's lover, as they did with Scott Peterson, more than likely the evidence would have eventually caved in on him, leading to his inevitable arrest. As we know, this part of the case never happened. The man got away with it, "Scott-free."

More recently because of the "Peterson connection" the Hernandez case has received, San Francisco homicide detectives have now listed the Evelyn Hernandez case "Top Priority," with the possibility of it being classified as a triple homicide of Evelyn, Alex, and the unborn baby. The only problem with this new ambitious announcement is its poor timing. With over a year already having slipped by, the likelihood of collecting any meaningful evidence to further *that* investigation is all but futile. I'm pretty sure those limos are shampooed weekly.

Evelyn Hernandez's family said that their feelings were crushed, when they saw how diligently law enforcement agencies honed in on a suspect in the Laci Peterson case and "got the guy." They said, "It just isn't fair."

A UC Berkeley professor conducted a study to determine the actual factors that contribute to the level of publicity a missing female case receives. The results of the probe concluded that the level of <u>attractiveness</u>, <u>age</u>, <u>race</u>, and <u>economic status</u> determined the amount of publicity an investigation of this type garnishes.

There was another missing female case right here in Modesto that, according to the victim's mother, was not given that much attention at all; she said that it had been ignored between the Yosemite Slayings and the Chandra Levy case, which took place before and after her daughter's investigation. The female missing was Dena McCluskey, a 36-year-old, known to have had a risky lifestyle of heavy drinking, associating with people who had criminal backgrounds, and filing and recanting domestic violence charges against her boyfriend, Mark Keough, with whom she'd been carrying on a volatile relationship. Three days after she had disappeared police found Dena's car parked on Oakdale Road, a few blocks from her boyfriend's house. They found some of her jewelry, after searching Keough's home and car, but have never been able to collect enough evidence to make an arrest. This man has neither been formally considered a suspect, nor has he been ruled out by police, as was Laci's husband, Scott, prior to those bodies surfacing.

"What is it about these other people that makes them so much more *valuable* than my child?" Dena's mother asked of the other cases that have captured America's attention.

Authorities, however, disagreed with the mother's assessment. Modesto Police sergeant Al Carter responded, "Unfortunately, I don't control what the news media concentrates on. But the fact is that, in this case, we have no *body*, no crime scene, no cooperation from Keough. All of those things put kinks in the investigation."

As the UC Berkeley study indicated, *age* was the second most publicity-drawing factor for missing female cases, and, as we see here, Dena McCluskey was already 36 years old and was also divorced. She, perhaps, was a little old for the mother to still be calling a child.

Together with Chandra Levy's mother, Dena McCluskey's mother formed "Wings of Protection," a support group for family members of missing persons. The organization has 25 members who regularly meet at the spacious home of Dena's mother, in a gated suburb of Modesto. There, the victim's families receive grief counseling, practical advice, and emotional support. "Wings of Protection" also maintains a web site and holds vigils in an effort to enlighten participants on missing persons issues across the nation.

Why did the massive search efforts for Laci not uncover the bodies of other missing persons? For example, many of these victims' parents have complained that no such extensive searching took place for their daughters. But they *did*, in effect! If Laci's disappearance was within a few years of any of these cases, then surely, if any of *those* skeletal remains had been found during the *Laci* searches, then these cases would have made headlines, too. After *all* the searches and investigation so far, not one single human corpse was uncovered during all the searching for Laci; there was not even the mention of an animal carcass being found.

The most highly publicized, recent case of a missing, pregnant woman, other than that of Laci, was that of Theresa Andrews of Kent, Ohio. Theresa, 23, was abducted, then shot to death by Michelle Bica, 39, on September 27, 2000.

Michelle had been looking for pregnant women at Wal-Mart's baby department—there she found Theresa Andrews. After kidnapping her victim at gunpoint, Bica shot her in the back and then performed a crude C-section, carving the infant out of Theresa's uterus. Michelle had lied to her husband and neighbors for months, telling them she was pregnant.

For about the next five days after this unbelievable crime, Michelle pretended that this baby was her own. Somehow the investigation led to her. When police arrived, Michelle Bica committed suicide in a locked bedroom. The toddler is apparently doing fine after all the tumultuous events leading to his birth. When this child reaches adulthood, one can only imagine what he is going to think when informed of the circumstances surrounding his birth—from his gruesome crime scene delivery, to his murderous surrogate mother's thwarted arrest and bloody suicide. Quite often the husband wants his children to be his own flesh and blood, is not willing to adopt, and will only keep a woman as his wife if she can produce them. Perhaps this woman, in her desperation to keep her husband, as well as in her own dreams of finally having a child, made this disastrous decision because she never expected that investigators would believe a person such as her could have committed such an atrocity.

There was a 1995 study conducted by the FBI on the abductions of pregnant women and their infants. Specifically, it dealt with female perpetrators. The study read, "Most of these women are living a lie—before, during and after the abduction. Many have faked a pregnancy, which eventually forces them into a corner. They feel they have no choice but to produce a child by any means necessary. Indeed, infant abductions are the desperate acts of desperate women. As one infant abductor put it, 'I began getting really desperate, trying to figure out what I was gonna do—how I was gonna find someone to give me their baby—now!'"

From one perspective, this sounds similar to the psychological pressures Scott Peterson may have been experiencing. For example, he was living a lie with Amber Frey and her surrounding network of friends and family. He was living this lie—before, during, and after he made the fatal decision to get rid of Laci. Now that he had entrapped himself in a self-inflicted web of lies, he perhaps felt he had no other choice but to…"do it."

In a case such as that of O.J. Simpson, it wasn't hard for one to see that "race" would eventually become an issue. However, it would seem almost impossible that this same factor would actually surface in the Scott Peterson case, as well. Not so, according to one particular individual whom I had interviewed. He was a young, Asian man, who had a degree in cultural anthropology, and has asked to remain anonymous. He was very adamant in his conviction that race was a primary factor in the motive behind Scott Peterson murdering his wife, Laci. This is what he said:

(Disclaimer: The following information may be considered controversial. Certainly no disrespect is intended towards any person, place, or thing. I only print it in the hope that this young man's view may possibly help the investigation in some way. Thank you for your understanding.)

> "During the time Laci had become pregnant, Scott was prompted to think one more time about a subject that had troubled him a little bit in the past, but it was some-

thing he hadn't particularly dwelled on, until now. He knew Laci was, ethnically, only half Caucasian. Her mother, Sharon Rocha, is white, or entirely of European decent. Her stepfather, Ron Grantski, is also Caucasian. These were the people to whom Laci, at first, introduced to Scott, as her parents. In fact, it wasn't until much later that Scott eventually found out that Ron Grantski wasn't Laci's real father—that, in fact, Laci had a real biological father whom Scott just hadn't met yet, and about whom Laci, for some reason, hadn't even told Scott until much later, after of course, Laci's relationship with Scott had been well consummated. Laci's real father is a more recent immigrant from Latin America. This, of course, would make Laci, biologically, half Hispanic. Which would mean that Scott's own son, Connor, when born, would have been twenty-five-percent Hispanic. Perhaps Scott had planned to teach his child that he, too, when grown up, should seek a spouse within his own race. Then Scott, perhaps, realized that he would be unable to teach his son this, for obvious reasons. Connor would be, in fact, part Hispanic, and thus Scott would be a hypocrite for saying so. This might have been unacceptable to Scott. Latin American people do have part Spanish European in their blood. However, most are comprised of Aztec, Mayan, Incan or other Native American heritage, which is technically considered an Asian stock.

"Scott felt a sort of resentment towards Laci for not telling him sooner. He realized, after it was too late, that he could have devoted all that time while at college, towards perhaps, a relationship with another Caucasian person, as he is himself. Likewise, all his brothers and sisters had married *white* as did his parents, of course, and likewise his grandparents, and so on. He, possibly, began to ponder the fact that he would be the only sibling in his family who would be taking a branch of the family tree into a different cultural and ethnic direction, away from which his forefathers had originally intended. Again, he perhaps thought, why should *he* be the only brother in his family who couldn't get a *white* girl? Scott felt that he was definitely 'good enough' to get a white girl. Of course, if asked, his brothers and sisters would not necessarily admit that they had planned it that way. I'm sure they would simply say that that was just how the ball bounced in their circumstances, and perhaps, that is actually true, because, in the "baby boom" generation there obviously were a great deal more people to choose from, compared to Scott's generation, which was far more sparse.

"This racial disparity also might've given Scott more incentive to dispose of Laci's body, if he felt that since Latinas are more commonly reported missing, her case might be given less attention. Unfortunately for him, he apparently forgot that Laci was also half *white*.

"Laci had sharp common sense and social skills. She knew that, when dating young men from prominent white families, admitting you're part Latin American simply doesn't sound that good and might've disqualified her from these young men's consideration as a potential mate with whom to have children. Sometimes, around fraternity and sorority circles, when asked about her nationality she would perhaps respond with the other combination of nationalities that made up her mother such as Italian, Spanish, Greek and Irish. Since these are mostly from southern European nations (except Irish), this would explain her darker skin complexion, and since her parents are, in fact, comprised of a combination of these nationalities, she was actually telling the truth, just not the *entire* truth.

"Later in the pregnancy, Scott had more ample opportunity to see if it wasn't too late in life for him to actually meet and go out with a *white* woman. Of course, we now know the rest of that story. Scott met Amber Frey."

Well, I suppose this man's theory has some plausibility and merit to it. I can't say that I necessarily agree with all of it, but he's certainly entitled to his opinion. He told me that he thought that this was the reason why Dennis Rocha had refrained from doing much talking publicly in the beginning. Instead, the family let Ron Grantski do most of the talking, to make sure a constant flow of public attention was focused on Laci. In both the Polly Klaas and Elizabeth Smart cases, there was a tremendous amount of initial attention; both of these girls were white. He did mention, however, that there was a factor that didn't make sense to him. He said that he thought it was odd that Scott would give "race" more precedence over the fact that Amber already had a child. He thought that this fact would only put Amber on an equal playing field with Laci, but, perhaps in Scott's mind, he seemed to feel that *race* was even more important.

Ironically, I had spoken to one of the guards at Stanislaus County Jail, who told me something that I found kind of interesting. He said that the jail population, just as at most prisons, was divided into three basic, racial segmentations: white, black, and Hispanic. He said that, when Scott was first incarcerated, it was not the black or white populations that were concerned with him, but it was the Hispanics who were rumored to be plotting against him. According to this guard, rumor had it that the motive for targeting Peterson had to do with him dropping a Hispanic man's daughter into the bay. Supposedly, because of the high profile nature of the case, many of them wanted the individual honor of being the one who killed Scott Peterson for the Hispanic "cause." The county guards had to set up a special system to protect Peterson from other inmates, including having him choose his own food tray randomly, so there'd be no risk of tampering, or possibly poisoning him.

Just two weeks after I conducted this interview with the young, cultural anthropologist, a startling, new break in the case was announced. It was broadcasted nationwide that a witness from the jail system came forward with supposed information about a murder-for-hire plot to kill Laci, to be carried out by a couple of members of a large, Central Valley gang, known as the Nazi Low Riders.

According to this individual, Cory Lee Carroll, late in November 2002, he was approached by Scott Peterson in a dark and seedy lounge in Fresno, California, Amber's hometown. The bar was mostly a biker hangout. After playing some pool, watching strip dancers, and drinking, Scott discovered in casual conversation that Carroll had spent some time in prison. Peterson then asked the 34-year-old man if he knew of anyone who might be able to help him carry out a car insurance fraud—basically, to steal his wife's car for him. Carroll said that he didn't do that kind of job, but for $300, he would hook Scott up with someone who did. Scott agreed, and a meeting was planned. Carroll introduced Peterson to two gang members known only as "Dirty" and "Skeeter." Then the four of them went ahead and met in a seedy motel room in an older, run-down part of town. Carroll said that the little, secret meeting took a sharp turn when Peterson changed the subject from car theft to kidnapping his wife. At this point, the eventual informer said that he'd heard enough and got up to leave. He didn't say "murder" or "kill," he just said "kidnap." He said it wasn't until a month or so later when he recognized Scott Peterson on television, as the same person with whom he'd recently had this serious involvement. Melvin King, a retired Fresno police lieutenant, put the individual through a full polygraph examination, evidently with clear and passing results.

Could these possibly be the men whom a witness reportedly saw yelling at a pregnant woman, Christmas Eve morning in East La Loma Park, to "shut her f——n' dog up" and get into a brown van?

Many of the cable stations around this time were airing coverage of this breaking new development. Among the commentators doing segments on it was Geraldo Rivera. (Whose show, by the way, I like.) The special guest who was invited in to comment on the subject was none other than—Mark Fuhrman.

It appeared that Geraldo didn't forewarn Mark as to the nature of all the questions he might be asking. When he asked Fuhrman his opinion of the Nazi Low Rider situation, Mark, at first, had this startled, and almost flustered, look on his face. It was almost as if he was thinking, "My God. After everything I've been through, you actually asked me that question?" Or, almost as if he wanted to say, "How in the hell would I know?"

Mark, however, gave what I thought was an outstanding answer to the question. He basically said that just as with any gangs, whether it's Crypts, Bloods, neo-nazis, low riders, or whatever, you could separate them and question them individually, and possibly bluff them into thinking that their comrades gave up some information, which may lead them to further reveal even more additional facts.

About a day after hearing this break in the news, I received a surprise call. It was the young, cultural anthropologist whom I had just interviewed. He confirmed, "You see, it's all starting to come together now, isn't it?"

I responded, "Yes, this certainly does give at least more substance to that point of view." I told him that I still had some doubts, but that this perspective could possibly play into the overall motive. (Basically, he was implying that, because these men were neo-nazis, this was no coincidence. In other words, Scott obviously had to approach this type of guys, if he had any kind of a racial motive to kill his wife. In that way, the perpetrators wouldn't *just* be doing it for money, but for *principle* as well.)

Cory Carroll said that, after the two gang members finished their meeting a half hour later with Peterson and were leaving, they told him that they were going to take care of something for Scott. Carroll told King, who was administering the polygraph, that he did not immediately learn of the woman's disappearance, because he went back to prison on a parole violation soon after the meeting with the gang members. Perhaps he had heard of Laci by this time, but didn't realize it was the same woman.

There were some questions that arose later about why Carroll hadn't come forward sooner. He apparently made an excuse about being locked down at a facility, without much access to television. Someone later disputed this claim saying that there was no lock down at the jail in question and that he would have had access to television. I believe that it is more realistic that Carroll probably didn't realize at first who these people were about whom he would hear bits and pieces regarding the Laci Peterson case. Remember, Scott was hiding his face from the media to prevent Amber, along with her friends and family, from recognizing him. Perhaps what coverage of the case Carroll *did* see, did not include many close-up shots of Scott, nor was Carroll specifically looking to recognize anyone at the time.

Again, we're also talking about a convict here, someone who wouldn't be as interested in the news as, say, a more educated person would be. Additionally, even when Carroll did make the connection, he was an inmate in the California prison system who, I'm sure, didn't want to incur his own death sentence among other inmates for violating the most crucial, jailyard code of ethics—being a snitch. Also, I'm sure Carroll was concerned at first with being implicated into a heinous kidnapping conspiracy, when all he was serving time for, was nothing more than a minor parole violation. Under these conditions, it makes sense why Carroll didn't come forward until months after the investigation had begun. Carroll also said that the reason why he even chose to come forward at all was because he feared that, if detectives turned up Dirty and Skeeter on their own, this could lead them back to him as the liaison who set up the whole connection between them and their client, Peterson, in the first place—thus implicating himself in what would seem to be a worse way.

After seeing another report on the Peterson case, Carroll, at that time, tried to relay his story to prison officials, and then to a parole officer, but nothing seemed to come of it except, he said, a threat warning him to "keep his mouth shut" from a couple of inmates who had heard of his attempt to betray these gang members. He was released again in early July, but was arrested again shortly in August, this time for driving with a suspended license. Then he shared his story with a cellmate, who convinced him to tell the inmate's attorney, Frank Muna, who practices in Fresno. Muna took the information seriously enough to hire a polygraph examiner, Melvin King.

King, who has been administering polygraph tests for 28 years, said, "My initial thought was, 'Yeah, yeah, this guy's wacko,' because inmates are known to offer information in the hope of getting lenient sentences, but Carroll never asked for special treatment." King then said that Carroll at first rejected the idea of a polygraph because he didn't want to implicate himself in a kidnapping, not because he was about to lie. "I was impressed with his ability to speak clearly, to articulate," King pointed out. "Carroll said, 'I don't want to be charged with a heinous crime, when all I did was arrange a car theft.' After I met and talked with him, my final position is, I believe Mr. Carroll believes it's true. Whether it is, I don't know, but he believes it is." King said that, during the polygraph test, he asked Carroll ten questions, only four of which were relevant to the Peterson case. He stated, "All I can say is, I didn't see any significant signs of deception. I have no stake in this. I'm just saying this guy is somewhat credible."

At the time of this revelation, Cory Lee Carroll was only being held on a parole violation, but records show that Carroll has been in prison several times for possession of stolen property, grand theft, and forgery. He said that Dirty and Skeeter often lived in a beige van with orange and brown stripes and has a place in the back, near the bumper, to hold a generator. Several neighbors reported seeing a tan or brown van, on the morning of December 24, in Peterson's La Loma neighborhood. One of the neighbors, Diane Jackson, told officials that she saw a tan van parked in front of 516 Covena Avenue, with three men standing in front of it, at 11:40 a.m. This address is directly across the street from the Peterson home. Dirty and Skeeter are described as 5' 10" and 5' 8" in height, respectively, and both are white. Carroll is also white. Since Carroll's information surfaced, detectives have not contacted Ms. Jackson to see if she could identify either of them as being the men by the van. Jackson told police in her report that one of the van's doors was ajar, and that a rear door was open.

Other interesting, supposed witnesses were Homer Maldonado and his wife, Helen, who said they left their Phoenix Avenue home at about 9:30 a.m. on December 24th, dropped off a Christmas present, and then went to the USA gas station on Miller Avenue, which is close to a half mile south of the Peterson home. At an adjacent pump, they said they saw a yellowish-tan van with dull paint. The van reeked of cigarette smoke, they said. "They weren't getting gas. They were just there," Homer remembered. According to his account, a man came out of the gas station's mini-mart and a gritty male voice from within the van asked him if he "got the cigs." The Maldonados said that, after leaving the gas station, they saw Laci walking her dog about a block away from the gas station, in front of 211 Covena Avenue. Carroll's attorney, Frank Muna, when asked whether he thought there might be a connection between the sightings of these men in a tan van and the story of Dirty and Skeeter, said, "Quite possibly. The general descriptions match."

Frank Muna later revealed more information about the murder-for-hire plot. He said that, according to Carroll, Scott Peterson offered Dirty and Skeeter $3,000 each to "kidnap" his wife, and $8,000 each to "get rid of her." Former Lt. King denied hearing any of this information during his administration of the polygraph exam. According to Muna, he said that's because King didn't ask that very many questions during the test, nor did he ask if an amount of money was offered. Additionally, Muna said that he didn't reveal the information right away because he wanted the prosecutors to have an opportunity to conduct their own investigation. It would mean a lot more to them, if they heard it for the first time directly from the horse's mouth. He remarked, "We were caught off guard because the story broke before we thought, but we knew up front."

Muna also had suggested the idea that Scott Peterson may have failed to pay most of the money because he fell under such intense public scrutiny and suspicion, that he knew his every move was being watched and didn't want to lead the investigators to his hit men, Dirty and Skeeter. Therefore, the two, disgruntled contract killers, upset that they hadn't been paid, decided to take revenge on their defaulting client. They chose to frame Peterson for the murders by planting the bodies in the bay, knowing that this, of course, was the location of his alibi.

Neither the defense nor the prosecution will bring up Dirty and Skeeter at the trial, because it would only serve to damage both sides. Prosecutors won't introduce them because it contradicts their theory that Scott acted alone. The defense won't bring in a murder-for-hire scenario, because this theory equally implicates Scott for first-degree murder, despite completely disproving the "body-dumping fishing trip" theory. Mark Geragos has said that he believes that the two men seen in the park with a brown van were the ones who abducted and killed Laci. Geragos would be free to pursue this theory because he wouldn't have to worry about the prosecution arguing that these two men were Dirty and Skeeter, hired to carry out Scott's evil scheme. If I were the prosecutor in this case, I might introduce the concept in a different way: simply to serve as further proof that Scott was shopping for various options to do away with Laci. For example, the prosecutors could contend that, after checking into the murder-for-hire method, Scott ultimately settled on doing it himself, to save money, and therefore chose to buy a boat, instead. Again, the point is that Carroll, seemingly with nothing to gain except clearing his name, happened to overhear Scott say "kidnap," when arranging a car theft—furthering the evidence regarding Scott's state of mind, his drive, his seriousness in wanting to make a clean break from his marriage, with no strings attached, and that he had murder on his mind.

Another way to put it would be this: the prosecution could contend that Scott, after learning of the Nazi Low Riders' high prices, decided that the more economical method to get rid of Laci would be to buy a boat and do it himself, which sure beats paying out a total of $22,000. (Especially since it appears that Scott's main incentive to kill Laci was financial; to avoid alimony and child support payments, as well as not having to *split* the proceeds of selling the house with her.)

Carroll said that the kidnap-conspiracy meeting at the motel took place on or about November 29, 2002, at approximately 12:30 p.m. Lee Peterson, Scott's father, said that his son could not have met with gangsters at that time, because he and Laci were driving back from San Diego after Thanksgiving. However, Melvin King said that, while administering the polygraph, he didn't press Carroll on the date, and that the meeting could have been later. King said that he was concentrating on whether Carroll spoke the truth, and not about the meeting.

In response to the inquiry of getting paid for the story, Muna responded, "We accepted no money, we asked for no money. We were offered money but didn't take it." He also said that his client had little to gain by coming forward, because he was just finishing a sentence on a minor parole violation and would be released shortly anyway. Even the staff at the motel where the meeting allegedly took place was interviewed. After being shown a photo of Cory Carroll, they said that yes, they recognized him as someone who had stayed there before, but didn't remember seeing Scott Peterson before. Muna went on to say that investigators were able to track down Dirty—a 46-year-old out of Fresno with a long criminal history. At the time of Laci's disappearance, Dirty was out of prison and didn't have an alibi. However, Skeeter has yet to be found. Cory Lee Carroll is out of custody now and will not talk about the case anymore unless subpoenaed as a witness. Muna concluded, "My client feels he's done everything he can. It's over and done with as far as we're concerned. His conscience is clear."

The Nazi Low Riders, based on other reports of their activity, are what is known as a "certified" prison gang. In other words, they are real. According to this information, they are a prison and street gang supposedly immersed in white supremacy, violence, and drugs. A source close to the investigation said that Amber Frey, out of fear of this gang, secured 24-hour protection. She lives in a gated community and is protected by private guards. Since Amber would play the most pivotal witness role of all in the prosecution's case against Laci's husband, she was being monitored 24/7, according to this source. He said that Laci is deader than hell and it is a very real possibility these individuals could target Amber in an attempt to thwart the state's case. "How safe is Amber, if other people involved are still out there floating around? This is no game," he said.

Regarding the fact that Amber was already a mother, I thought about that one a lot, myself. For the longest time, I was simply stumped. I couldn't understand what could've gotten into the mind of a young man who doesn't have any kids yet, but definitely wants to have them and just throws away a seemingly perfect, clean-slate woman, for one who has *that* kind of mileage already on her. The anthropologist even made a joke about this situation. He said he thought the fact that Scott traded in Laci's "green" Land Rover for a "white" Dodge, was symbolic of him turning in a "Latina" Laci for a "white" Amber. But considering that Amber already had a baby, I thought about it for quite some time, and then, suddenly, "bam," it hit me!

I thought, "My God, I think I finally figured it out." Remember, Scott and Laci both came from families full of "step" siblings. Scott's family was almost like the Brady Bunch; before his parents got married, they each already had three kids from other marriages. The same was true with Laci's family; she and Brent also had a stepsister, Amy. So, perhaps Scott saw Amber as a strong woman (someone who dabbles in body building) who could still have children with him, and he simply felt "ok" with the fact that Amber only had a daughter, and fairly recently at that. Also that Amber had the normal healthy "two" ovaries, not just *one* ovary, as did Laci. Also, unlike Laci, who was the same age as Amber, Amber owned her own house. Personally, I see home ownership as only money. I would've taken the woman with no children, so that we could have our own kids, rather than a woman with someone else's child, who just happens to own her own home. That's just me, though, and I already own my own house. But for a lot of guys, that house might make it worthwhile to forego the fact that the woman has a kid already. Scott, of course, owned his own home, too, but there was only one problem—Laci was still on the deed.

Over thirty years ago here in Northern California, baby girl Vogt's killing led to the current state law Scott Peterson is being charged with violating—murdering his unborn son, Conner, one month from birth. The earlier homicide occurred on a rural road in Amador County, when Robert Harrison Keeler randomly encountered his ex-wife there while she was taking a walk. Both Robert and his ex-wife Teresa Keeler were from Stockton, which is just north of Modesto; the year was 1969. When Keeler saw his ex-wife's enlarged belly and discovered she was 8 months pregnant by another man, he went into a jealous rage. Teresa apparently admitted it was true, then the enraged ex-husband told her, "You sure are pregnant. I'm going to stomp it out of you." And he proceeded to pin the pregnant woman up against a car to secure his aim, then with full force he gave a hard up-thrust with his knee directly into her swelled abdomen. The baby girl was delivered stillborn at a nearby Stockton hospital.

Since the mother survived the attack, and her ex-husband only aborted the child inside her on the spot and against her will, as he had threatened he would, the state could not prosecute him for homicide, but only assault and battery as an alternative consolation. The state law that was in effect at the time of this violent incident had been written in 1850 and did not include an unborn child as a human being, therefore the California State Supreme Court was bound to uphold this legislation. In a response of intense fury, that same year California legislators updated the state law to cover violent crime resulting in the death of a fetus as "murder." The newly written legislation, that state congressional leaders passed without hesitation, now renders Scott, who currently sits awaiting trial, eligible for the death penalty.

Part of the philosophy that went into the original legislation of 1850, that was being systematically upheld in 1969 by the state supreme court, was from a quatrain by Lord Coke, a 17th century English legal scholar. It read, "If a woman be quick with childe (and) if a man beat her, whereby the childe dyeth in her body, and she is delivered of a dead childe, this is a great misprision (misdemeanor), and no murder, but if the childe be born alive and dyeth of the potion, battery or other cause, this is murder."

Associate Justice Stanley Mosk cited this quote as historical precedence that early California lawmakers did not intend to protect a fetus, which contributed to the Supreme Court upholding. This, in turn, led the state legislature to promptly change the law. This is good, because any man who deliberately kicks his knee hard into the abdomen of an 8-month pregnant female in an attempt to kill her child, is not guilty of any great misdemeanor. I see this activity only as a *felony* in the first degree. Such behavior, in my opinion, is far worse than robbing a liquor store at gunpoint, assuming that there are no casualties from the robbery. The violent crime of intentionally killing a woman's baby, by inflicting great injury to her body and that of her child, involves the murder of another human being, as well as causing great bodily injury to the mother, resulting in intense physical pain and suffering along with long-term psychological trauma. A murder statute for a crime this serious is appropriate.

On Wednesday, May 7, 2003, in Washington, D.C., the Rocha family authorized the use of the names of Laci and Conner for federal legislation that would make the killing of an unborn child a federal violation when resulting from a violent crime. In a letter made public on Capitol Hill, the family stated: "As the family of Laci Peterson and her unborn son, Conner, this bill is very close to our hearts. We have not only lost our future with our daughter and sister, but with our grandson and nephew, as well."

The bill had been previously titled the "Unborn Victims of Violence Act." Now, with the high-profile family's alliance, the bill was given a significant public relations boost. Many of those elected officials naturally would be influenced by this development, because it gives a renewed interest to the matter across greater segments of voting constituents within their districts. The legislation would permit the federal government to charge violators with the homicide of a fetus, if it dies while in the commission of a federal crime. Twenty-six states, including California, allow murder charges in violent deaths of fetuses. The laws in fourteen other states protect an unborn child at any stage of growth. California and eleven other states cover only those fetuses that have reached a certain level of development. For example, a fetus in California is protected by state law if it passes the "embryonic stage," which is generally considered to be seven or eight weeks. However, the federal legislation goes further than California's law because it covers a fetus at *any* stage of development.

Just a few years before Laci's family's involvement, in 2001, the bill had passed through the House of Representatives by a seemingly comfortable margin, a 252–172 vote, but it failed to win Senate approval. This same bill specifically excluded abortion, but regardless, strong pro-choice senators voted "no" on the Unborn Victims of Violence Act, because they dismissed it as nothing more than a backdoor strategy for pro-life lobbyists to use in an effort to undermine abortion rights.

Here is a statement made by Kate Michelman, President of NARAL Pro Choice America: "It is a sad statement that anti-choice leaders are willing to use a family's tragedy to continue their campaign to steadily take away a woman's right to choose. The only thing new about this bill is the length to which anti-choice lawmakers and advocates are willing to go to exploit a family's pain in order to move their own political agenda."

As we can see, this bill had received a certain amount of opposition from pro-choice lobbyists who said that passing it as law would only serve as further ammunition for the pro-life leaders to use in their greater quest to outlaw abortion. The only flaw in this argument is that the bill has absolutely nothing to do with abortion. It only has to do with violent crime. I mean, yes, I can understand how these pro-choice activists might fear that a federal law against "killing a fetus" could eventually take on a blanket interpretation by some pro-life activists that might also include the "killing a fetus" with instruments used by a surgeon, even if it was the woman's choice. But perhaps a better way to put it, regarding its affiliation to abortion, would be: The new law would actually be giving increased strength to the pro-choice movement, because it protects a woman's right to choose to have her baby. In other words, if a woman is happily pregnant because she wants to be, then a perpetrator should *not* be allowed to take that "choice" away from her, by aborting her child for her without her consent. This way a woman could retain both the right to choose having an abortion and the right to choose having a child.

Some normally outspoken pro-choice groups took a back seat and stayed relatively low-key since the high-profile family's involvement arose. Groups such as the National Organization for Women, who have traditionally opposed such legislation, seemed to have been temporarily rendered gun shy due to what they refer to as "respect for the family." For example, here is a statement that Kim Gandy, executive vice president of NOW, had previously made after the 2001 House vote: "This bill is being sold as an effort to deter violence against women, but it ignores pregnant women. (If you ask me, I'd say it *emphasizes* pregnant women.) It is nothing more than a poorly disguised attempt to elevate fetal rights. This is a challenge to a woman's fundamental right to abortion."

The family members of Laci wrote in a letter to Washington: "When we heard about this bill, we immediately thought of placing a request to have it named Laci and Conner's Law in their honor."

Regarding President Bush's support of the measure, White House Spokesman Ari Fleischer announced: "The President does believe that, when an unborn child is injured or killed during the commission of a crime of violence, the law should recognize what most people immediately realize, and that is that such a crime has two victims."

The week of May 20, 2003, Sharon Rocha and Kim Petersen, Executive Director of the Sund/Carrington Foundation, were flown out to Washington, D.C., to meet President George W. Bush. The trip was primarily focused on them meeting and working with the various senators and congressmen who were engineering the bill. The evening of Wednesday, May 21, 2003, Sharon and Kim attended a fundraising dinner with President Bush. After speaking to his wife on the phone, Ron Grantski told the media, "I talked to Sharon on the telephone, and she's very excited about being there. She's been meeting with different senators and representatives about the new law." Mr. Grantski then went on to thank all of us who had attended Laci's Memorial Service, as well as those who provided the facility and crowd control for the event.

After returning from her meeting with the President, Sharon Rocha hired some attorneys to help her retrieve certain items that belonged to her daughter. Among these personal items were a wedding dress and a baby crib. According to the statement by attorneys Albert G. Clark and Adam J. Stewart, Scott Peterson's parents and his attorney have prevented his wife's family from entering the couple's Covena Avenue home and retrieving personal items. The statement also included a list of 22 items that family members wanted back, including Laci's diplomas, yearbooks, and private journals. They even wanted her watering can that had the words "Laci's Garden" printed on it. Regarding the attorneys' statement, Sharon Rocha responded to the media with, "The statement that you have is the absolute truth. I'm not going to comment beyond that."

There had been some behind-the-scenes legal haggling between Mark Geragos and the Rochas, just prior to this information being announced. Among the concerns to which Geragos responded was the notion that gathering up any belongings or personal items whatsoever from the supposed crime scene would simply be "unthinkable," because, he claimed, the defense team had not completed *its* investigation yet. Geragos, who said that he'd been working with the police investigators and DA's office to log in evidence, predicted that the process would be completed in ten days and would have an "amicable solution" for the two families at that time. He said that his team and the prosecutors on the case had reached an agreement to release the Laci and Conner's remains to their family with an "accelerated process." A judge had ordered that the bodies were to remain held in the Contra Costa County Coroner's office until further notice. Geragos stated publicly, "It's an awful situation, and we're going to work our way through it with as much dignity as we can. There are two families here that have lost a grandson."

Scott's mother, Jackie Peterson, confirmed that her and her husband had been in the house recently, but said that nothing had been disturbed. She said that when they were in Modesto, which had been quite frequent, with all their son's court hearings that they attended, "We keep it clean. It was sitting there for four months, getting overrun, and people were taking things from the grounds. Missing are two glass hurricane lanterns, loose bricks from a pile near the patio, and a patio chess set that had marble frog figurines for the playing pieces."

Jackie went on to say that she had left frequent phone messages for Sharon, but had never received a return call. She commented that, if Sharon simply would have given her a call, then she could have made it easier and given her a new key, because they had changed all the locks and the alarm code in the house. Instead of Sharon herself calling Jackie, it was Sharon's lawyer who contacted her with the request. Jackie said, "Since they initiated going through a lawyer, we were advised to go through a lawyer, too. We hadn't done that before with them. We had always talked."

It almost seems as if Jackie Peterson might have been trying to manipulate some of the Rochas' behavior through the implementation of a crude punishment and reward system. Sharon Rocha was clearly doing the right thing by not contacting Jackie Peterson directly. For if she had, Sharon would only be subjecting herself to more sob stories from the murderer's mother, who, naturally, would be trying to tug at the victim's mother's sympathies. Jackie already had admitted publicly that she was deeply insulted for not being invited to the Laci Memorial Service, and here she seemed to be implying that, if the Rochas simply had remained in friendly contact with them, then there would be no the need to go through attorneys and a court hearing in order to access the home and personal belongings.

In that original request by the Rochas for a court order allowing access to the property, Sharon had written that she had been watering the potted plants around the lawn and backyard, and that she had made an arrangement to pick them up. Upon arriving, she discovered the plants had been moved to the front yard, and that some of them were dead.

Sick of Jackie's attitude, among other things, the Rochas stormed into 523 Covena Avenue, breaking the front door padlock, and then loading up seven different vehicles with Laci's belongings on the morning of Friday, May 30, 2003. This was prior to a scheduled walk-thru that was to be videotaped by Mark Geragos' crew that Tuesday. After cutting the padlock, the family used a key to open a deadbolt, which set off an alarm that summoned police to the slain woman's home. The Modesto Police had long before relinquished control of the home to the Rochas, but as mentioned, it was Mark Geragos who was refusing to surrender control, out of a stated concern that the family could taint the crime scene.

They loaded a rocking chair for the expected baby, a mattress and bed frame, clothing, a large box containing a stroller, a wedding dress, jewelry, and many other personal items. Laci's brother, Brent Rocha, was one of several people moving furnishings from the house into four pick-up trucks, two sport utility vehicles, and a minivan. Police arrived, as the family was removing the items, and ruled it "a civil dispute" between the Rochas and the Petersons. Attorneys representing Laci's family said that the family had permission to go in and remove some articles, while acknowledging that they had jumped the gun on a previous agreement arranged with Mark Geragos to enter the home at a later date. According to Adam Stewart, one of the Rocha attorneys, the Peterson and Rocha families had been in dispute over these listed items, and the terms under which they could enter and retrieve them, for quite some time. He said that Sharon had grown frustrated over the slow pace of discussions, "We weren't getting anything done. She went the appropriate route. She tried to deal with it family-to-family and lawyer-to-lawyer and finally took matters into her own hands. It was against my advice as a lawyer, but as a parent, I would say, 'Go for it.' Everything on that list was removed, which we're happy about." These items also included Laci's diplomas and journals, a crib, photographs, and numerous baby items. Also, according to Stewart, Geragos had previously given the Rochas Laci's Christmas presents, two Tiffany lamps, and a set of salt and pepper shakers.

Meanwhile, Scott's parents and lawyers were expressing outrage over the unauthorized break-in. Jackie, Scott's mother, said, "Those going into the Covena Avenue home that Friday had absolutely no permission to be in that house." Scott's father, Lee, agreed. He said that the Rochas had burglarized it, and thus should be held accountable. He was ignored.

Capt. Greg Savelli said in a statement. The police department "does not anticipate taking any further action."

The Stanislaus County District Attorneys office corroborated that sentiment. Chief Deputy DA John Goold said, "Any claim over ownership is a civil dispute between the Petersons and the Rochas."

Scott's other attorney, Kirk McAllister, had custody of some of the requested items at his office by the Monday before the break-in. He apparently had been waiting for the Rochas to come over and pick them up. He said, "I still have things for the

Rochas sitting in my front conference room. I don't know why they need to break in."

Another Rocha attorney, Albert Clark, noted, "It would be *ridiculous* to suggest the Rochas were breaking into the home. I apologize for it coming down to this. This is not the way we operate. This is for Laci, Conner and Laci's family. It is not for the media or Mr. Scott Peterson's defense in any way, shape or form. It's depressing that it's come down to this."

Jackie Peterson said that she was planning to let Sharon into the house, as long as Sharon was accompanied by representatives from Scott's legal defense team. Jackie remarked, "I have a lot of empathy for Sharon. (Pause) But she does not have a right to go in our house and take what she wants." The house, legally, does belong to the Petersons because, when Laci died, Scott, as the husband, inherited her half. Under the state Probate Code, Scott would lose any right to the house, if he is convicted of playing a role in Laci's death. But in the meantime, a person in this country is innocent until proven guilty, thus giving Scott's parents current custody and ownership rights to the house until the criminal proceedings have concluded. Jackie, trying to look like she was expressing dismay, said "Yesterday we see a coroner's report about a baby, and today we're talking about salt and pepper shakers."

Lee Peterson, on *Larry King Live*, said, "Instead of grieving, Sharon apparently planned this break-in."

Not long after this broadcast, the Petersons had made their way up from San Diego for more of their son's court hearings. Upon entering the Modesto Red Lion Inn where they had been staying for free courtesy of the management, the Petersons were in for a bit of a surprise. Brad Saltzman, the general manager, politely told them that they could probably find a better rate at another hotel. Saltzman had seen the Larry King segment in which Lee Peterson had accused Sharon Rocha of being a burglar. Even though the hotel was continuing to provide interview rooms for TV networks, the management didn't feel that it was necessary to continue providing a free (or even a discounted room) to the parents of the accused murderer. The sentiment about the Petersons had clearly evolved within the last month since Scott had been charged with his wife Laci's murder.

Brad Saltzman's decision was one of many that reflected the conscience of the community here in Modesto. Since then the young Saltzman has moved on to more rewarding ventures in his career. Brad had become somewhat famous in all the frenzy over the case, since he had provided the volunteer search and command center, as well as many other central functions. Many major hotel chains made management offers to Saltzman, but he politely turned them down for another plan that he had in mind. As a result of all his involvement in the Peterson case, investors were eager to sponsor a large, entrepreneurial project of Saltzman's, that capitalized on one of the fastest growing trends on the U.S. market today, the low-carb diet. These popular programs include the Atkins, Zone, South Beach, and Slim Fast diets. Many of you, of course, are already familiar with this phenomenon, which has swept across America. For those who aren't, it's hard to find a restaurant today, that doesn't have menu items specifically for this diet. Personally, I don't know too much about it, except that I know of at least one friend who is actively on this type of diet, and occasionally, I see different books on the subject at the grocery stores.

Evidently, Brad Saltzman is one of their success stories; he claimed that he lost twenty pounds, thanks to this new discipline. With Mr. Saltzman's talent and insight as a business manager, he has since launched "Pure Foods," a chain of specialty food outlets that sells only foods specifically meant for low-carb diets. So far, he has locations in Beverly Hills, Modesto, and Santa Monica, and by the way things are going, it won't be long before the demand for this popular regimen requires Brad to open many more locations in other parts of the state and country, as well. His first location opened its doors in early December 2003, at 1820 Wilshire Blvd., Santa Monica. All the proceeds from the grand opening, which was held on Wednesday, December 17, 2003, were donated to the Laci Peterson Fund. Pure Foods is a one-stop shopping source, offering over 1,000 low-carb, sugar-free, and low-fat products. The store also includes books, vitamins and other items, stocking products for the Atkins, Zone, South Beach, and Slim Fast diets. After browsing his web site, I could clearly see that Brad Saltzman has established a multi-million-dollar operation, with all kinds of nationwide vending and franchising opportunities available.

After this chapter was written, Saltzman was opening new stores at a rate of about one per month.

During the time that the fiasco at the Peterson house was going on, the criminal lawyers in the Peterson case were arguing in court about the legality of the wiretapped phone calls. Investigators intercepted 69 calls between Scott Peterson and his attorney Kirk McAllister, by mistake, among hundreds of other calls Scott had been making during the first several months after his wife's disappearance. The wiretapping portion of the investigation is legal, except for the attorney-client privilege; none of these calls may be monitored by law enforcement officials during their investigation. The constitutionality of this privilege lies within the basic ethics that, likewise, the defense is not allowed to wiretap conversations between detectives working on a case, and the prosecutors to whom they are submitting their findings.

Among the emotional outpourings in tribute to Laci, several songs have been written for her. Some of these album tracks include "Remembering Laci" by John Strand, "Straight to Heaven" by Tony Handy, and "Laci's Song" by Jim Maris. There have been countless *unpublished* works created in Laci's honor, as well, including poems, paintings, and various other renditions of art.

Among all the tabloid reports on the Peterson case, one lady told me she saw an article titled "I Caught Laci's Head," which was supposedly about a homeless fisherman in Richmond, who happened to "catch" Laci's head, while he was trolling for rock cod in the San Francisco Bay.

Here are some "name" coincidences that occurred during the investigation. During all the Scott Peterson hearings taking place at the courthouse, there had been a prominent, missing persons flyer posted on most of the nearby utility poles. It read: "Missing—Laci Ferguson, Modesto," etc., etc. "Laci" *Ferguson*? These flyers remained up for months, so one could only assume that this person had been missing for a long time, or maybe still *is* missing. Does this missing woman from Modesto really have the name *Laci*? I'm sure it was a legitimate coincidence, but it makes one ponder for a moment about the possibility that the name Laci might have been this person's *middle* name instead. The middle name could have been shifted to the first name spot in an attempt to get more search, media and investigative resources allocated to *that* case.

On one of the nightly talk shows, I believe it was *On the Record* with Greta Van Susteren, a short time after the legendary

Dr. Henry Lee had been hired by the defense team, a special guest appeared on the program. His name was "Henry Lee," and he was a journalist covering the case for the *San Francisco Examiner*. Right away, I just assumed, of course, that the almost identical name similarity was only a coincidence. It was such an obvious coincidence that surely *someone* on the expert panel of guests would have made reference to it, you know, maybe as a joke or something, during the course of the program. No one ever did. I thought, well, hasn't "Dr." Henry Lee been on this show before? I checked my back records, and sure enough, he had been on several times before. Oh well, maybe they all just forgot, or perhaps no one even thought of the coincidence at all...Or *was* it a coincidence?...I'm just teasing, Greta. I love your show. And I've read some of Henry Lee's articles, too; he's a good reporter.

The name "Scott" is somewhat common as an American first name for males, and the name "Peterson" is an even more common last name. Several name coincidences occurred during the multi-national frenzy over the Peterson case. For example, the producers of *Terminator 3: Rise of the Machines* had to change a main character's name from "Scott Peterson" to "Scott Mason." The screenplay for this movie had already been written prior to Laci's disappearance, but ironically, the Scott Peterson character had a fiancée, who had also been kidnapped.

Perhaps the most interesting name coincidence of all was the mistaken identity of a Modesto resident named J. Scott Peterson. The 56-year-old is partially bald and wears glasses. He goes by his middle name, Scott, and says that most people who know him don't know that Scott is not his first name. He came to Modesto with his wife and four children 19 years ago.

Before the accused murderer, Scott Peterson, went to jail, J. Scott said that people did not hesitate to call him, thinking they were calling the notorious one. Both the murder suspect and J. Scott were listed right next to each other in the phonebook. J. Scott said, "Most of the people were calling to ask, 'How did it feel to kill your wife?' One guy said he was keeping me in his prayers." The calls since Christmas became more and more intense, as Laci's disappearance began gripping America's heart strings. He continued, "It was flabbergasting to me that I would get so many calls. I couldn't understand what possessed them to call. I would say, 'Why would he (Scott L. Peterson) want to talk to *you*?' It's amazing to me that people would call, but if that's the worst thing that happens to me, I'll be in pretty good shape." He changed his phone number three times, and said people still managed to get through and call.

Enough was enough, sick of all the misdirected harassment, J. Scott Peterson and his wife moved to Utah three months after Laci's disappearance. They said that this wasn't the only reason for the move, but it certainly had contributed to it. I could just picture this guy being invited to appear on the *David Letterman Show*. I could just see Dave introducing his special guest. "Ladies and Gentlemen, tonight we have J. Scott Peterson, a resident of Modesto, whose name had been mistaken for the notorious Scott Peterson." Then the man makes his way across stage to take a seat in front of the host's desk. After a few questions, the talk-show commentator could introduce yet another guest by the name of Scott Peterson (again, by picking up any phonebook, this wouldn't be too hard to find). Then he could have both men stand and face each other to shake hands for a photograph. Together, before a televised audience of millions, the two Scott Petersons could swap stories about who had the funniest or most interesting mishap that resulted from being a Scott Peterson.

Charles Manson lives in a city right next to Modesto. Not the one in prison, but just some guy with the exact same name. When he was interviewed during all the hoopla, he said that he got so tired of the identity characterization, that he moved out of California for a few years. But then he said he came back because wherever he went, he got harassed just the same. Now here he is right next to Modesto, still having difficulty to this day with his name. When I heard this, I couldn't understand why this man still, after thirty years since the Charles Manson case, has not yet changed his name? Charles Manson is one of the most widely publicized mass murderers in all modern history. His case, O.J.'s, and the Lindbergh Trial are considered to be the first, second, and third biggest trials of the century.

As a final note about identity coincidences, the *Modesto Bee* reported on May 24, 2003, that the investigation briefly examined a Laci look-alike who was living in the La Loma neighborhood at the time of the disappearance. Additionally, Mark Geragos even made a comment about this woman: he said even though she resembled Laci, the time of her pregnancy "debunks" the whole prosecution theory of a mistaken identity on Christmas Eve morning. She was pregnant, but had had her baby in October. Also the woman, of all things, happened to be a prosecutor, and she claimed that she didn't walk her dog that day. The most unbelievable portion of this similarity is the dog. According to the *Bee's* report, the Laci look-alike's dog is a golden retriever and its name, believe it or not, is McKenzie.

7

DNA—The Forensic Evidence

Stanislaus Superior Court Judge Al Girolami ordered the Contra Costa County Coroner's Office to allow Scott Peterson's defense team to examine the bodies of Laci Peterson and her son, Conner, with their own expert witnesses. The victims' remains, since surfacing along the Richmond shoreline in April, were in different stages of decomposition. After the coroner performed immediate autopsies on both cadavers, the results revealed no obvious cause of death.

The examination was an agreed upon order, signed by all parties involved in the case—Deputy DA David Harris, defense attorney Kirk McAllister, and the judge. The order had limitations, including that no more than eight individuals from the defense team could be present: four people from the DA's office, two coroner officials, and a physician to be picked by the coroner's office. The examination was to be limited to visual inspection, including photos, videotapes, X-rays, and another autopsy restricted to taking a "reasonable" amount of tissue and fluid samples for testing. Also the exam was to be limited to a single day between, 9 a.m. and 5 p.m., and had to be done at the Contra Costa County Coroner's lab in Martinez, unless the prosecution, defense, and coroner all agreed otherwise. Peterson's defense team was required to pay for its own exam, was required to furnish its own equipment, and was not to be charged for the use of the coroner's office.

The defense examination and autopsy took place on Monday, August 11, 2003. The purpose of the second inspection, of course, was so that the defense team could look for evidence that might help clear its client, Scott Peterson, of double murder charges. Of the eight members present from the defense team were criminalist Dr. Henry Lee and forensic pathologist Dr. Cyril Wecht. Dr. Lee is the Chief Emeritus for Scientific Services, Chair Professor at University of New Haven Forensic Science Program, Research Professor in Molecular Cell Biology at the University of Connecticut, and the former Commissioner of Public Safety for the State of Connecticut. He served as that state's Chief Criminalist from 1979 to 2000 and was the driving force behind establishing a modern forensic lab in Connecticut. He has received numerous awards for his work and has helped police around the world with over 6,000 investigations. Dr. Cyril Wecht, who is a renowned forensic pathologist, is the coroner for Allegheny County, Pennsylvania. Both doctors were expert witnesses in the O.J. Simpson trial.

The defense team brought in their own medical instruments in cases on wheels. They had brown paper bags for collection, and other items, as well. Doctors Lee and Wecht were inside the Martinez Coroner's office for about 2 hours before returning to the Peterson home, ninety miles away, in Modesto, the listed crime scene.

When Mark Geragos was interviewed after the inspection, he kept his remarks brief. Regarding the two doctors, he mentioned, "Both are thought of in their fields as the foremost experts. Given the consequences in this case, and given, I think initially at least, some of the investigative things that were done, I think it was important to get the best people in the field." (I wonder if he also chose them because he wanted to win a high-profile case?)

Before going into detail about their findings here in this chapter, as well as more findings we'll look at in the Preliminary Hearing chapter, I'll give a basic review on DNA, its principles, purpose and uses, then I'll go into a more elaborate review, in terms of its use as criminal evidence.

To start off with, I wanted to mention something regarding being summoned to jury duty. If you're ever called and would actually like to serve on a jury, I strongly recommend that you know what DNA stands for. DNA stands for deoxyribonucleic acid. If you are ever called to serve on a jury to which forensic evidence will be presented, most likely a prosecutor will ask you about this. The purpose for him asking this question, of course, would be to get as many well-educated people on the jury as possible, especially if it is a circumstantial case, in which the DNA evidence will be used largely to carry the burden of proof. It's an interesting statistic, but evidently about 6 out of 10 well-educated people still get stumped on this very basic question.

Within the nuclei of the cell are the chromosomes that carry the genes. There are literally thousands of genes carried by a chromosome, which determines the physical attributes of a person. Chromosomes occur in pairs, and likewise, so do the genes they carry. An individual inherits one gene from each parent, in order to fill each set of pairs that determine each genetic characteristic. Every cell contains DNA (except *red* blood cells), and it is considered the blueprint of life. The DNA in the nucleus of any single cell contains all the genetic information necessary to grow an entire human body, from top to bottom. DNA in an individual's blood is the same as the DNA in his or her saliva, skin tissue, hair, and bone. Also, DNA never changes throughout a person's life—it always remains the same, from birth to death.

The whole DNA molecule is twisted tightly in small conglomerations that make up the chromosomes. Every healthy individual has 46 chromosomes, 1 pair of sex chromosomes (X and Y for males, and two X chromosomes for females), and 22 pairs of autosomes (any chromosome that's not a sex chromosome). A human receives an X chromosome, plus 22 autosomes, from his or her mother, and either an X or a Y chromosome, plus 22 autosomes, from his or her father.

In the human body, there are an estimated ten trillion cells. If fully stretched out, the human DNA strand has been approximated to be about six feet long. The complete set of genetic instructions for a person is known as the human genome. It is made up of about 6 billion base pairs, and approximately 0.1 percent of those (roughly about 6 million) may be different between any two humans. Each individual's DNA has identifiable differences, with the exception of identical twins. The goal of forensic DNA analysis is to find and compare what two genetic specimens have in common, their similarities, and differences. The different DNA combinations or genes randomly mark the chromosomes at certain locations, called "loci." Except for sex chromosomes in men, human chromosomes come only in pairs. Since this is the case, there will always be a duplicate of any given DNA combination or gene, at a specific locus in healthy individuals. All in all, there are tens of thousands of genes implemented along the vast human genome, although the precise number still has not definitively been determined.

The term "allele" refers to genetic variations at certain loci. Each person has two alleles at any particular locus, which may be identical or completely different, one inherited from each parent. If the DNA sequences that make up the locus are different, than it is called heterozygous. If the code is identical, then the locus is called homozygous.

In a criminal trial, physical evidence may be limited to pieces of fabric, or strands of hair, that the prosecution must somehow link conclusively to the defendant. DNA evidence is the closest method developed by science, that can conclusively tie a person to a crime scene beyond a reasonable doubt, or more important, to rule out suspects, in order to prevent the wrong person from being convicted.

Two things are needed to prove a match between a DNA sample left at a crime scene with that of a suspect. These include a DNA profile using molecular biology procedures, and applying the principles of population genetics to prove the match mathematically.

The key to DNA evidence lies in comparing the DNA left at a crime scene with a suspect's DNA in those regions of the chromosome that differ. These areas of the genome that comprise a lot of diversity are called polymorphic regions. These include *sequence* polymorphisms and *length* polymorphisms.

Sequence polymorphisms are usually simple substitutions of one or two bases in the genes themselves, which also serve as templates for protein production. Despite vast human complexity, genes comprise only 5 percent of the human genome. The other 95 percent of the genome does not code for any protein, but serves to regulate gene expression during development, serves to aid or impede cellular mechanisms from reading nearby genes and producing protein, and as the building blocks for chromosomal architecture.

Length polymorphisms are just differences in the physical length of the DNA molecule. Non-coding DNA is loaded with length polymorphisms. DNA evidence uses a special kind of length polymorphism found in non-coding areas, called <u>variable</u> <u>number</u> <u>tandem</u> <u>repeats</u> (<u>VNTRs</u>). These specific variations come from stretches of brief, but identical, repeat sequences of DNA. A specific combination might be repeated anywhere from one to thirty times in a row, thus giving these regions their name. Depending on how many duplicates of a VNTR there are, the size of a DNA segment may be longer or shorter. A unique advantage with DNA evidence is that the number of tandem repeats at each locus on a chromosome differs between persons. There will be a certain number of repeats for any given VNTR in an individual's DNA.

<u>Restriction</u> <u>Fragment</u> <u>Length</u> <u>Polymorphism</u> (<u>RFLP</u>) analysis is the basic protocol used to identify a person's DNA profile. With this, scientific investigators can determine the number of VNTR repeats at a number of distinctive loci to determine the make-up of an individual's DNA type.

There will be a specific amount of repeats in the VNTR region, when one looks at a particular individual's DNA. An investigator, to make a DNA "fingerprint," must count the number of repeats for a specific person for a particular VNTR region. There are two numbers of repeats in each VNTR area for each person, one from each parent, receiving both counts. If this is done for a number of various VNTR areas, an investigator can build a profile for someone that is statistically unique. The resulting DNA profile can then be compared to the one left at the crime scene by the perpetrator, to see if there's a match.

In a nutshell, here's how it works:

1. Isolate the DNA.
2. Split the DNA into shorter fragments containing known VNTR regions.
3. Arrange the DNA fragments by size. (A process called gel electrophoresis)
4. Compare the DNA fragments in various specimens.

DNA was first used as evidence in a courtroom in 1985, but was only used to rule out a defendant. It wasn't until 1988 that DNA evidence was used by prosecutors to win a conviction. Throughout the earliest times of DNA's courtroom appearances, defense lawyers were able to exploit the *complexity* of this new scientific evidence, as a means of raising a reasonable doubt. For instance, with the reams of information, laden with mathematical formulas, passed on to jurors for study as evidence during deliberations, this material could easily be interpreted by defense attorneys as having vast room for error, thus perpetuating the concept of reasonable doubt. However, since those early days, leaps and bounds of progress have been made to streamline and simplify the process, so that DNA evidence can be more easily comprehended by the average juror.

Some of these improvements include the amount of DNA needed for adequate testing, more sources from which to pull DNA samples, expanded DNA databases, more advanced training, and better science education, in general. Now, with a technology called polymerse chain reaction (PCR), much smaller samples of DNA can be amplified; therefore, tiny amounts of a particular DNA sequence can be duplicated exponentially within a matter of hours. New ways have been devised to extract DNA specimens from sources that were once considered either too difficult or too contaminated to deal with. Now several countries, including the U.S., Britain, and Canada, have set up elaborate databases, with hundreds of thousands of unique DNA profiles. The British police have an online database of more than 360,000 profiles that they compare to crime scene samples; more than 500 positive matches come up per week. This helps by reducing much of the mathematical reasonable doubt; however, this also raises civil liberty issues, as authorities ponder the idea of including every citizen in the database for the sake of thoroughness.

Furthermore, to reduce the probability of DNA evidence becoming contaminated, crime labs across the country have developed formal procedures for handling and processing evidence. In the courtroom, prosecutors have become more skilled at presenting scientific evidence. Matching DNA profiles can either link a suspect to a crime, or it can potentially exonerate an innocent person. After DNA evidence had been studied from their cases, at least 10 innocent people have been freed from death row here in the United States. Of the DNA profiles compared by the FBI, about thirty percent of them result in the exclusion of a suspect.

Outside of the courtroom, DNA evidence is found to be useful for paternity testing, so that authorities can determine if two individuals are related.

The Stanislaus County Coroner's Office received the bodies the evening of Thursday, August 21, 2003, after a court document was made public on Monday, August 18, 2003, indicating that the remains of Laci Peterson and her son, Conner, would be released to the family no later than Friday. At that time, a defense specialist still needed to conduct an X-ray exam of the fetus.

Approximately four months after Laci and Conner's bodies had washed ashore from San Francisco Bay, their remains finally had been returned to Stanislaus County. Regarding the transfer, Stanislaus County Sheriff Les Weidman said, "We are holding them as a courtesy to the family." He also said that his office was waiting for Laci's family to make arrangements, and he wouldn't elaborate further.

Earlier that day, District Attorney James Brazelton issued a brief statement. He announced, "No comments will be made regarding any release of the remains of Laci and Conner Peterson from the Contra Costa County Coroner's facility. The district attorney requests that all parties respect the privacy of the Rocha family in this time of mourning." Brazelton also emphasized that other law enforcement agencies should "refrain" from making any further comments publicly on the subject, as well.

In a written statement released the week before, Sharon Rocha and other family members urged the media to be sensitive regarding the matter. The statement read, "Please treat her in death respectfully, so that we as her family will be allowed to lay her and Conner to rest in dignity and peace, when the time comes. We ask that you respect our privacy and understand our pain, as we grieve for our beautiful Laci and baby Conner."

Since most cases similar to this one are *not* as high-profile, and do not normally receive a second defense team autopsy and examination, the episode raised some questions in the forensic community. Santa Clara County Coroner and Chief Medical Examiner Dr. Gregory Schmunk had said, "There's no reason to do X-rays at this stage. It scientifically makes no sense. Bodies routinely are X-rayed before an autopsy is performed, and those results are provided to both sides. After an autopsy is performed, the subject's body is in a different condition, making it impossible to directly compare X-ray results. More accurate methods exist to determine elements such as how old Conner was when he died, and whether he was in his mother's womb at the time. I have no idea why the defense would want to do this. It's difficult to say what is going through their heads. Maybe they're looking for something *specific*."

Perhaps the "specific" thing the defense was looking for during this exam was simply anything that might help add up to reasonable doubt.

On Monday, August 25, 2003, the Rocha family decided that the burial ceremony to be held for Laci and Conner would be closed to the public. The family spokesperson, Kim Petersen said, "They held the public memorial and appreciate the outpouring of support from the community. If they choose to do anything else, it will be done in private."

Friday, August 29, 2003, after a funeral mass at St. Joseph's Catholic Church in Modesto, a long procession of Cadillacs, Lincolns, and Chryslers wound its way behind two, white limousines carrying Laci Peterson's family and the white-gloved pallbearers to the rolling, green slopes of a quiet cemetery in Escalon. This was Burwood Cemetery, just outside of Modesto, where the bodies of Laci Peterson and her son, Conner, were laid to rest. There were about 250 relatives and friends who attended the private burial ceremony. During the 30-

minute service, Stanislaus and San Joaquin County sheriff's deputies stood discreetly in dark suits and sunglasses across from the cemetery.

Mourners released two doves representing Laci and Conner, and 20 more that represented angels. Those who attended marveled in tranquility, as they gazed skyward at the white-feathered flock, which swirled twice before whispering away to the north and slowly fading into the pillowy, white apparitions that adorned the greater blue heavens. A moment of silence fell over the assembled gathering by the gravesite, as some wept, and others held hands. Reverend Joseph Illo officiated at the service. Here are a few excerpts from his sermon:

> Blessed are those who mourn, for they shall be comforted. It goes without saying how much all of us have grieved with you, dear Sharon and the rest of the family and friends. We have wept quietly with you, Sharon, for Laci represents every daughter whose mother has had to bury her. Laci reminds us that great evil can come at any time to the most beautiful of God's children. In Laci's death, we come face to face with our own death; her suffering is our suffering.
>
> If any death was senseless, Laci's was. Why did she and Conner die? What insanity drove the killer to destroy such beauty and such life? A young mother and her son. For this, there is no direct answer. I don't offer one, and neither do the Gospels. But while there is no rationale, no direct answer to death, there is a meaning—a meaning beyond human logic. In God's grace, earthly suffering is an inoculation against eternal suffering.
>
> How close her death is to Christ's is strikingly evident in the very chronology of this tragedy. Lost on Christmas Eve, Laci became a carefully wrapped gift to be opened later; she and Conner portrayed the Mother and Child at

the heart of the Christian mystery. Found on Good Friday, the day of Christ's death, her death is joined to that of her savior. This remarkable timeframe—from Christmas—to—Easter, is certainly God's sign that the deaths of this mother and son were not meaningless, that Laci and Conner are with God.

This was a very significant observation of symbolism that fit perfectly into such a ceremony. I believe that this Reverend had put a tremendous amount of heart and soul into his words. For the entire sermon, one may check the Laci Peterson web site for a full rendition, and the newspapers should carry it as well.

As Laci and Conner were lowered into the ground in a single coffin, Ron Grantski addressed the mourners with hints of anger in his painful utterance, "She was the light of my life. The animal that did this to her is going to pay."

Afterwards, the mourners left the new grave decorated with lilies and sunflowers, as they slowly drifted away in the early afternoon sunshine.

On Tuesday, September 2, 2003, Jackie Peterson found out about the private funeral service and burial that had been held four days earlier. After emerging from one of their son's court hearings, Scott's parents said they were devastated that they were not told in advance about the services to be held for their daughter-in-law and their grandson. Lee and Jackie Peterson were *not* among the 250 or so people invited to the funeral, for which Sharon had made most of the arrangements.

Just days before, Jackie, trying to sound innocuous, had sent Sharon an e-mail that ultimately was publicized on national television, as well as in local media outlets. It read, "We are trying to appeal to your heart. Though by law, you are granted the decision on how to handle the remains of all our loved ones, we ask you to postpone the service until such time as Scott is exonerated and we can all join together as a family to mourn your daughter, Scott's wife, our and your grandson, and Scott's son who has been taken from all of us so cruelly."

In a response, Adam Stewart, a lawyer representing the Rocha family, told the Petersons to stop attempting to contact the Rochas. He said, "The family wishes to be left alone during this difficult time." Then, a few days later, when the Petersons got upset upon discovering that Laci's burial service had transpired without their knowledge, Stewart responded that the Rochas did not want them at the funeral. The attorney explained, "There is no etiquette for the circumstances we're confronted with here. We don't feel it was appropriate for them to be invited or present (at the funeral)." He went on, "Sharon is very distraught and upset. She is very upset that, two days after the funeral, Jackie would release these e-mails to the news media. Was Jackie really concerned about being there, or was she more concerned about eliciting sympathy for her son?"

Calling the situation *hurtful*, Jackie Peterson said, "My thoughts were that Laci would have been so upset about it (ignoring Scott's family)."

In hearing this opinion of Jackie's, like most people, I, naturally, disagreed. I doubt that Laci would have been upset (as Scott's mother put it) that the Petersons were not invited. First, Scott's parents birthed the man who allegedly killed Laci. Second, Scott's parents were defending him. Assuming for a minute that Scott did, in fact, put his hands around Laci's neck to strangle her, one can only imagine the rush of thoughts that must have gone through this young, pregnant woman's mind in that last three or four minutes of consciousness before her death. As Laci looks into the cold murderous eyes of the man she once considered her loving husband, he slowly squeezes his masculine fingers tighter and tighter around her throat, until her last breath of air is no more. The actual knowledge that this man, who is supposed to love her has decided, for some insane reason that is unknown to Laci, that she must die, and must endure, not only the terrible suffering of her last moments before death, but must die with what only could have lingered on her struggling, dying lips, the unanswered question of, "Why?" In other words, as Laci looks down from Heaven upon the participants involved, I'm sure she is proud of her immediate family's sentiment toward her in-laws, who only exhibit desperate impulses of grabbing at any straws to defend their evil son.

Outside the Stanislaus County Superior Court, Lee Peterson commented, "If 250 people can attend, surely there's room for the grandparents of the baby. I would just have wished to have been there and had a chance to see them find their rest together and bring some finality to it."

The plastic sheeting and tape found near the bodies of Laci and Conner when they washed up had raised speculation and theories of how these items may have played into the case, and what it meant to both the prosecution and the defense. Even though the court-imposed gag order was currently in effect during the time this information had been reported, experts continued to give their professional opinions of these findings. Regarding this evidence, there appeared to be an equal number of theories pointing at Scott Peterson's guilt, as there were scenarios suggesting his innocence.

The two main theories that resulted from these findings are as follows: If the clear, plastic sheeting from the bay can be microscopically connected to any that had been collected as evidence during the search warrants executed on Scott's warehouse, then this, of course, points to his guilt. If, on the other hand, it is determined that the tape around Conner's neck was wrapped there after his birth, then the defense could argue that this could be the work of a satanic cult, especially since Scott could not have had contact with Conner, because the baby hadn't been born yet.

A sizable portion of distinct, clear plastic sheeting was recovered, about 50 yards from the location of Laci's body, along with what appeared to be a length of black, plastic electrical tape wrapped around it. Likewise, another length of black plastic, similar to the type used for roofing or gardening, was found, also 50 yards from the body. These items were among 31 chosen by the defense to further examine, all of which were pulled from the bay and then logged in as evidence. Conner's body was recovered with a narrow loop of plastic tape wrapped one time around his neck, then extending out in a circle that resembled a bowknot.

Other experts have speculated that this tape around Conner's neck was simply ocean debris that had become entangled with the body. This would be an argument the prosecution most likely would make, given the inevitability of the item's submission as evidence. The likelihood of the tape around Conner's neck *not* being presented during the trial is highly unlikely, because there is no doubt as to the magnitude of importance that this little piece of forensic evidence could play, given its direct physical involvement with one of the victims.

The plastic sheeting was forensically analyzed; however, at this writing, the results were not yet available. One theory suggests that the plastic, if linked to Conner, could be a defense point worth arguing. That theory would simply insinuate that the boy was born before he was killed, casting doubt on the charges against Scott, who fell under such heavy police surveillance after Laci's disappearance, that he presumably could *not* have had the opportunity to commit *that* particular murder.

Forensic pathologists have suggested publicly that a body wrapped in plastic would be expected to decompose more slowly than one exposed to the elements. Now, assuming that both bodies were *not* wrapped in plastic, there are several other reasons why an adult female will decompose faster than a baby. For instance, adult stomachs contain bacteria, which are considered a large element in decomposition, while the stomachs of fetuses do not store this component. Also, cold water tends to preserve small bodies better, because adults have more fat, which keeps the body warmer, allowing bacteria to incubate and mature more effectively, thus breaking down tissues more rapidly. Likewise, scavengers, such as crabs and fish, would be naturally more inclined to seek large food sources first, rather than small ones.

Other experts have speculated that, once Laci's body had sufficiently decomposed, the fetus was then expelled from the womb in a phenomenon known as "coffin birth." In this scenario, Conner's body would have remained reasonably protected from the oceanic elements for quite some time.

The logo "Target Products Ltd." was printed on the wad of clear sheeting. This was traced back to the Canada-based company that manufactures it. The firm produces cement, stucco, and grout commonly used in mining, building, and agriculture. The name, by the way, has apparently no connection to the American retailer Target stores, but the company does have retail outlets within the United States. Here in California, the distributors are located in Sacramento, Long Beach, and San Diego. An attorney with Scott Peterson's defense team, Matt Dalton, had contacted the company, according to Bob Sanford, the owner of Spec-West Inc., in Sacramento. The lawyer contacted the Sacramento materials supplier in June of 2003, to acquire a sample of the plastic sheeting specifically showing the Target logo.

The type of plastic found was determined to be that of a polyethylene sheeting commonly used to wrap industrial pallets. The director for the Sacramento store said that the material discovered with the bodies is a heavier gauge than that of typical pallet wrap, and is normally used to protect shipments traveling a longer distance, specifically in this case, from Canada. Spec-West, which is a small company, says that products supplied by Target comprise only 5 percent of its total inventory. The company typically sells pallets to contractors. The director said he didn't know whether records would indicate that Scott Peterson had made a purchase or not, but he said he was surprised prosecutors had not contacted the company yet. "Why wouldn't police want something like this?" he pondered.

One of the experts suggested that perhaps the prosecution might know something that the public and the defense do not know. For example, if they had tested similar tarping recovered from Peterson's warehouse, and the test proved a match to the material discovered near the bodies, they need not research it any further, because the results conclude all they need. Another suggestion would simply be that the prosecution may have determined that the plastic is not related to the bodies, and found no need for speculation because, with the voluminous circumstantial evidence of the mere location of these bodies being so close to the location of Scott's Christmas Eve fishing alibi, conjecture about the plastic would only serve to cloud an overwhelming and abiding conviction of guilt that already points to the defendant.

It's entirely possible that if, in fact, the prosecution has determined—that the material found near the bodies and the material found in Scott's warehouse are a molecular-structure match, then the defense may want to undercut the statistical probability of this connection, by showing that the sample they obtained from Spec-West Inc. is also an exact molecular-structure match, thus demonstrating that the plastic found in the bay didn't necessarily come from the roll in Scott's warehouse, and technically showing that *anyone* could have put that plastic out there. However, the only flaw in this argument, if the defense chooses to use it, would be that the *percentage* of people purchasing this particular product at Spec-West Inc., or any of the few other locations that sell it, is so small compared to the overall population, that statistical probability alone links Scott's warehouse plastic to the bay plastic beyond a reasonable doubt.

If the prosecution does have a match between the two plastics, this is simply one more error made by an inexperienced killer. In other words, Scott, having never disposed of a body before, may not have anticipated that the investigation would use microscopes to match these materials. According to one law professor, in crimes of passion or crimes committed by an inexperienced offender, the perpetrator often makes mistakes, and that's how we catch them. The defendant may have chosen to use materials that, without his knowing, could be traced back to him. Scott, perhaps, overestimated his ability to sink the bodies completely in a way that they could never surface again during his lifetime. However, this also may have been his first time ever disposing of bodies, or perhaps he became overconfident and took shortcuts, while disposing of Laci and Conner, because if he was the one who sank Kristin Smart's body, while he was still at Cal Poly, she never again surfaced. (Again, just a possibility.) But this again demonstrates the reality of the "inexperienced killer" principle.

According to toxicology tests taken at the time of the autopsy, Laci was shown to have caffeine in her system at the time she died, while her unborn son, Conner, did not. The subsequent issue this factor had raised was whether or not this finding could mean that Conner was already born alive and separate from his mother at the time of their murders. Investigators find this particular type of testing useful in determining whether a poisoning has occurred or not. The toxicology documents also specified whether or not Laci had the date-rape drug GHB in her remaining tissues, but they indicated that no such traces were found. This had been considered a possibility, since Scott's character was so clean. It made sense that he may have killed Laci and Conner more humanely, by rendering her unconscious before taking their lives. However, toxicology testing performed only on skeletal muscle that has reached this level of decomposition, would only identify caffeine and PEA (a decomposition product).

The date-rape drug GHB is a depressant that can render people unconscious, especially when it is mixed with alcohol. In asking for this test, the investigators wanted to clear this theory as a possibility. Gamma hydroxy butyrate (GHB) can be hard to detect during testing, because it metabolizes so rapidly in the bloodstream. In low doses, GHB depresses a person's inhibitions and produces a high or euphoric feeling, making it a popular drug in the club scene. One pathologist said that, if the drug had appeared in this investigation, it could have been an indication that Laci might have been drugged, in an attempt to subdue her before her murder. He said, "That would be the obvious inference. I don't know why they looked for that, unless they had some indication that he had access to it. I don't think decomposition would enhance the ability to find it, certainly. GHB is pretty difficult to find, even in a case where it's been used."

Forensic analysts concluded that the presence of caffeine in Laci's body, and none in her son's body, was *not* an indication that Conner was outside his mother's womb at the time she was killed. However, it's being speculated that Scott Peterson's defense team could try to use these toxicology reports, to further their satanic cult theories. For instance, if any strange chemicals were found in Laci's system that include some with a ritualistic connection, such as embalming fluids, or an unusual herb only normally found in the making of voodoo dolls, then Geragos undoubtedly could press the issue. It again makes one seriously ponder for a moment…is Mark Geragos actually going to try to use this theory? Or is he just bluffing, so that the prosecution might drop their guard or be a little less prepared to handle whatever *real* defense he may ultimately present as his case-in-chief?

Three forensic experts unanimously agreed that it would be uncommon to find measurable amounts of caffeine in the body of an unborn infant, even if the mother *had* ingested large quantities of it. This, of course, would suggest that the toxicology tests performed on Laci were meaningless. One of the experts said that the odds of caffeine passing into the fetus are minimal to nil, and that trace amounts could get through, but actually trying to find it for a toxicology report is an exercise in futility.

One expert on child deaths frequently reviews toxicology reports on fetuses whose mothers are suspected of drug abuse. She said she has never come across an unborn child with measurable amounts of caffeine in its system, and with the usual amount of caffeine that adults have, it just wouldn't show up in a fetus. It was also mentioned that the placenta is more effective in blocking out caffeine than other chemicals, such as cocaine. Coffee, tea, soda, some medications, and chocolate are common sources of caffeine, which normally stays in the human body for several days after consumption.

One of Laci's friends, who asked to remain anonymous, said that, as a substitute schoolteacher, Laci enjoyed drinking coffee; however, she avoided the beverage once she became pregnant because of the caffeine ingredient. The pathologist who specialized in child death acknowledged that the Peterson's defense team might attempt to say that Laci drank something with caffeine in it after she gave birth. Moreover, he said, "The world could also end tomorrow. They can blow smoke with it, but the fact that it was not in the baby certainly is *not* proof that the baby had to have been born." It was noted that Laci could've had many opportunities to consume something with caffeine in it.

Dr. Cyril Wecht, who, with Dr. Henry Lee, was one of the primary defense-team experts to examine the remains during the second autopsy, went on *Larry King Live* shortly thereafter. Here are some excerpts of what he said regarding that autopsy. "This baby, a small body mass, could *not* have been floating free in that water for these 3 ½ months and have remained intact to the point that it was. The sex was immediately determined, I think, even by a non-physician, when the baby was discovered on a Sunday night. If that baby had been lying out for *all* that time, the external genitalia would have slipped off, it would have decomposed. I believe that this baby was sequestered within the mother's uterus and did not come out as a free-floating object for several weeks, until the mother had already been in the water for a period of time. I do not believe that this baby was forcibly removed from the mother's womb. We will see from Laci's autopsy report if there is a slash through her anterior abdominal wall and through the uterus. I doubt there will be such an injury."

Regarding the satanic-cult theory, Dr. Wecht went on to say, "There are about 50,000 murders in America. Let's say about half are women, and I bet you, of those 20 to 25,000 women who are married, probably 75 to 80 percent of their husbands have engaged in adultery, and I doubt that means they murdered their wives. So, you know, the business of trying Scott Peterson based upon adultery, I think is very, very unethical, improper, and unjust. Regarding that Scott Peterson is a sociopath, I think the evidence leads *away* from Scott Peterson, to suggest that a father is going to do this, not only to his wife, that's one thing, but then to take the baby and cut up the baby and tie it around its neck. So I just want to make it clear, I'm not suggesting that this dumps on Scott Peterson, but I do *not* buy the satanic cult. One more thing on the satanic cult, too. People keep talking about Geragos and the satanic cult. Remember that everyone on the panel understands clearly, but I think maybe for viewers and listeners should be told about is that the defense doesn't have to prove anything. It is the prosecution that has to prove something. The defense doesn't have to prove a single thing."

Here, I believe Dr. Wecht was saying that it's natural for the general public to disregard Geragos's notion of a satanic cult theory as lunacy, but that it's perfectly normal, under the framework of our American criminal justice system, that a defense lawyer may raise several ulterior motives, simply as *possible* theories, to help raise doubt regarding the one that incriminates his client.

Note that Dr. Cyril Wecht is a member of the *defense* team, which Mark Geragos is leading and floating the satanic cult theory from; but again, with Dr. Wecht, a key expert on the Peterson team, not agreeing with the possibility of this scenario again raises the doubt of whether Geragos ultimately will choose this theme for a defense.

Among the data acquired by investigators when they collected the two computers from the Peterson home was evidence of Scott looking up information on the date-rape drug GHB. On another evening, Dr. Henry Lee was also a guest on *Larry King Live*. When he was asked about this finding, Dr. Lee, in his response, first defined again what GHB stands for, and then elaborated: "In human bodies we produce a small amount of GHB in our system, so if you find a trace amount of GHB, not necessary somebody drugged, because our body naturally produces small amounts of GHB. GHB in contrast to public belief, is not going to say disable somebody, only subconscious people will still have some other conscious and GHB has a life within the blood that's pretty fast, usually between two to four hours it's gone. And then they go through urinating, by twelve hours you are already metabolized. So vomiting material that is kind of interesting whether or not trace amounts that could be what the body produced. If a large amount, definitely that is proof some drug has been used."

Regarding the autopsy, Dr. Henry Lee was then asked if "cause of death" could ever be determined. He responded with, "Well, the manner of death includes <u>homicide</u>, <u>suicide</u>, and <u>accidental</u>, but they also have a fourth one called <u>undetermined</u>. That's why this case became *homicide*. And the cause of death is undetermined, so by process of elimination, prosecution tried to say 'Must be strangulation' because they did not find any gun shell, no stabbing wall, no blunt object, and no drugs were found in her system. So, by the process of elimination, they have to come up with something that could be a strangulation. Strangulation, of course, GHB maybe disabled her somewhat then the strangulation to cover why they did not find any blood in the house."

Prior to the autopsy, there were some body parts from a woman found in Davis, California, which is just north of Modesto on Highway 99. These body parts, although ruled out as those of an older woman, were nevertheless the same types of limbs that Laci was missing when *her* body was discovered. Greta Van Susteren had both Dr. Henry Lee and Dr. Michael Baden on her show after this discovery was made. Here are some excerpts.

Remarks by Dr. Michael Baden: "The medical examiner can very quickly, on examining the parts, visually determine whether they're human, non-human, whether they're female, male, age, sex and race. And if the size of the individual doesn't match Laci, if the sizes of the arms or legs don't match, then that could be an exclusion, and that can be done within hours of looking at the remains. Things like DNA analysis, which takes five days or so, can absolutely include or exclude Laci. But there are body parts missing from Laci, unfortunately."

Greta then commented that the body parts found were not only the same ones missing from Laci, but that they too were badly decomposed, and even mummified.

Dr. Baden responded with, "We all have the same body parts. So when bodies are discovered, we all have arms and legs and heads and torsos, and they have to be looked at. The FBI does have a bureau that has a database that matches missing body parts with reported missing people, and I'm sure that's being looked into also, to see if there's any match of people who've been reported as missing."

Then Greta asked Dr. Henry Lee his opinion. Here is his response: "Well, of course, now you find a bag with body parts that Dr. Baden just talked about, I agree with him 100 percent. Of course DNA is something that definitely they have to 'type.' But as you say, it's a mixture, some are mummified, some are bone remains, others are relatively fresh, which is indicative to me it's a collection of a different time period. It's not from one time. More likely, I don't think that that is Laci Peterson's body."

Regarding the possible cause of death, Dr. Lee said, "It's very difficult to tell. Of course, you have to look at any other physical evidence associated with the body, such as her clothing. Do we have any obvious damage or other indicators, because forensic pathologists look at the body, and criminalists will look at other associated avenues."

Then Greta asked Dr. Lee if he would be testifying at all for this case. (This episode was, of course, aired prior to Dr. Lee's public announcement of his joining the Peterson defense team.) Smiling, Dr. Lee half-jokingly responded, "Why you are so sharp, you asked me this question right away. I can't really deny or confirm."

Greta, trying to probe a little deeper, then asked, "Can you deny or confirm whether or not you've been contacted by both the prosecution and defense?"

Dr. Lee lightheartedly replied, "I don't know, uh, I don't speak English. Some people talk to me, I don't know who called me." Chuckles from the other panelists filled the studio.

Greta also asked Dr. Lee what he thought the most important forensic clues are in this case. He responded, "Well, so far they found a hair on a pair of pliers. That hair was microscopically similar to Laci Peterson's. Of course, they found some cement material in his boat, and they collected a lot of material from his house, which we really don't know what's the major piece of evidence linked to him yet. So far, I don't think any earthshaking piece of physical evidence can prove one way or the other."

Greta finally asked Dr. Lee, "Supposing you were hired by one side in this case, what's the protocol, how do you go back and investigate? What are the steps that you'd take?"

Dr. Lee said, "OK, well, it doesn't matter which side hires a forensic scientist. We just look at the scientific truths. We really don't take sides. Does not matter if prosecution retains us, or defense retains us, we give the same answer. The first thing we have to review is all the documentation, try to reconstruct the pieces together, from the scene, to the body. What's the linkage? How can we link the body, clothing, to the house. Of course, any sort of fabric material found in the house, also found on her body, that can be innocently transferred. What we look at has to be some foul play, or some force was involved. Let's say, in the house you found a large pool of blood, even washed, maybe we can find some clue, because today DNA STR methol, you can really look at a decomposed or aged blood stain linked to somebody." He then mentioned that they could determine what kind of hair it was, if it was dead, or growing, if it still had tissue attached, or even blood, which could help to see if there was some force involved.

Regarding secondary transfer: I remember one night, I believe it was on *Larry King Live*, Dr. Henry Lee was a special guest, along with the usual nightly panelists, mostly lawyers, discussing the case. The issue of "secondary transfer" came up as a possible way Laci's hair may have gotten on Scott's boat without her body ever having been on the craft. One of the panelists was former Judge Jeanine Ferris Pirro, now currently the District Attorney of Westchester, New York. Not only does she have an impressive legal career, but she also remains a very attractive and voluptuous lady. It was she who inquired of Dr. Lee about how "secondary transfer" may have resulted in Laci's hair being on the boat without Laci ever having been there. I can't recall the exact words, but I do remember that Dr. Lee (whom buildings have been named after) responded with something like this: "Well, if one of your hairs gets on me, then I go home and use my bathroom, and your hair gets in my bathroom, where it is discovered the next morning and identified as yours, does this mean that you and I got somethin' goin' on?"

If there had been a studio audience for this primetime show, it most certainly would have erupted in laughter at this moment. Judge Jeanine Pirro at first got a little flustered, and said, "No, gosh, I don't think so." Some of the other panelists snickered a little. The point of Dr. Lee's joke was basically that to conclude Scott murdered Laci because her hair was found in his boat would be equally as ludicrous an assumption, or as Dr. Lee put it, a quantum leap. (Also, it sounded like possibly Dr. Henry Lee was up for some game.)

When Dr. Henry Lee was testifying during the O.J. Simpson trial, he managed to get a good reaction from the whole courtroom. From the stand, Dr. Lee had addressed one of the defense lawyers by one of the other team member's names. When the lawyer corrected Dr. Lee by identifying himself, Dr. Lee, who is Asian, said to the mostly-white panel, "Oh, you guys all look the same to me." The entire courtroom erupted into laughter.

Dr. Henry Lee had made a similar joke with similar results while testifying at the William Kennedy Smith rape trial. We'll all have to wait and see what kind of improvisation he may have up his sleeve for the Scott Peterson trial.

Some time after this chapter had already been written, it was announced that Dr. Henry Lee was awarded his own weekly television show, to be airing on Court TV. The name of the show is *Trace Evidence: The Case Files of Dr. Henry Lee*. The man's success seems to be growing at an exponential rate.

8

Scott Peterson vs. O.J.

I thought it might be interesting to discuss the similarities between these two cases since, not only have both been treated by the national media with more fervor than most wars, but also, so many in the legal profession came forward, after the O.J. verdict was out, with extremely insightful ideas that were released just simply...too late, after the fact. I mean, after an Olympic championship chess match, the loser can't say, "Wait, I think I'd rather make this move, this move, and this move instead." Sorry, big guy, the game is over. In other words, let's take the hindsight we've learned from one case and actually *apply* it to the new case just getting started. Besides both being trials of the century, there were many similarities between the Peterson case and O.J.'s. Here is a list I've made of those similarities:

1. Both took place in beautiful California, and both cases involved *beautiful* participants.

2. Both cases involved a double homicide punishable by death.

3. Both these defendants admitted to bleeding in their trucks on the days their wives were murdered, O.J. in his Ford Bronco and Peterson in his Ford F-150.
4. O.J. Simpson said during his interrogation that he plays golf and bleeds all the time. Scott Peterson said in public interviews that *he* plays golf, works with farm equipment, and bleeds all the time. (I occasionally play golf too, and to this day I don't understand how anybody can cut themselves while playing this game.)
5. Both Nicole Brown and Laci Rocha were nominated to be Homecoming Princesses at their high schools.
6. Both defendants were in possession of close to $10,000.00 in cash and a disguise at the time of their arrests. (There was also some debate as to whether or not Scott was in possession of a handgun at this time; we do, however, know that O.J. was.)
7. Mark Geragos has hired many of the same expert witnesses that Robert Shapiro hired in O.J.'s trial, such as Dr. Henry Lee from Connecticut, as well as Jo Ellan Dimitrius as a jury consultant.
8. Another similarity between the two cases is how Mark Geragos appeared to be settling on the "rush to judgement" defense, which, as we all know, Johnnie Cochran successfully employed for O.J.
9. Just as the defense did with Mark Fuhrman in O.J.'s trial, the defense in the Peterson case planned to demonize detective Al Brochini, who found some of the key evidence against Scott.

10. Both cases involved a deadly love triangle. In Modesto, it was Laci, Scott, and Amber. In Brentwood, it was O.J., Nicole, and Ron.

O.J. Simpson finally came out of hiding for the first time since *his* trial and gave an in-depth interview to *Playboy* magazine in October 2003, regarding his viewpoints on the upcoming Scott Peterson trial. Here are some excerpts from that interview.

P.B.: Are there parallels between your case and the Scott Peterson case?

O.J.: I heard that Scott Peterson had $10,000 on him when he was arrested. Well, they said I had $10,000 when I was arrested, but I had $3 or something. (He doesn't bother to mention that Al Cowlings had $10,000 on *him* at the time of their arrest, which O.J. undoubtedly handed him before they got caught.) You never hear about it when it proves untrue. The first report on CNN about the Peterson case said that he had changed his look and was 30 miles from the Mexican border. It gave the impression that they caught him fleeing the country. They didn't say that's where he lives. They didn't say he may have changed his looks, so he could go out without everybody recognizing him—so he could go

	out on the golf course. They created the impression that he was fleeing, so he's guilty. I'm not saying that he isn't, but I don't pretend to know.
P.B.:	Are you resentful that your acquittal wasn't enough to exonerate you in the minds of most Americans?
O.J.:	If the trial hadn't been on TV, most people would feel differently. I was tried by the media before I was tried in court. Look at Scott Peterson. Ask anyone in America about him. They'll say the guy is guilty. But we haven't heard one shred of evidence.
P.B.:	(Regarding O.J.'s daughter calling 911 on him.) How many teenagers call 911 just because they were reprimanded?
O.J.:	Evidently it happens quite often. When the police came, they knew immediately what it was, and yet it became a media event because someone sold the story. I don't know if Scott Peterson or Robert Blake is guilty. I have my opinion, but I would never say it publicly. Until these guys are proven guilty, they are innocent.
P.B.:	(Regarding golf.) How often do you play?
O.J.:	Pretty much every day.

P.B.: What do you get from golf?

O.J.: Scott Peterson was out playing golf, and people were saying, "What kind of guy is this? These may be his wife's remains, and he's going to play golf. Well, when I got back from Chicago after Nicole was murdered, I wanted to get on a golf course. I wanted to get away from all the shit—all the hurt, all the pain. It's the only place I can go to get away from everything. I didn't go, but I had that feeling. I know that far more executives would be in therapy, if it weren't for golf. A few of his friends helped Vitas Gerulaitis get off drugs, and then his addiction became golf. I used to play with him every day.

P.B.: Is golf an addiction for you?

O.J.: It is. Next to sex, it is the single most addictive thing I've ever been into.

P.B.: Did you have an altercation on a Florida golf course with a man who called you a killer?

O.J.: That's one of the few times I did lose my temper. Fortunately, he was a lot bigger than me, so it wasn't like I was picking on somebody. First he was like, "Hey, Juice." Then, "There are snipers out there. I hope they don't shoot." Then he said something like "You're a f——g asshole." I dropped my bag and went over. I knew I couldn't hit the guy, but I got right up on him. I realized he was a big nothing because he let me get right up on him. If anything happened, I was going to get a couple of quick shots in. If he withstood that, I was going to get my ass kicked. I was so mad I was yelling, spraying saliva all over him, making sure I was extra juicy. (O.J. then said that nothing ultimately came of it.)

P.B.: You were charged and acquitted in a road rage incident. It was reported that you cut off some guy, got in his face, screamed at him and yanked off his glasses. What happened?

O.J.: I was driving my kids home. We were all fine, and all of a sudden this guy's on my tail. I stopped, got out and looked to see if something was wrong with my car. He got out and said, "You cut me off!" I said, "Man, you chased me down." He was in my face and I said, "Man, look—f—k you." Then they tried to prosecute me. They said that I took the guy's glasses off his face? Allegedly, that's my crime. For that, they asked for the maximum sentence of 17 years. It was the most amazing thing I ever heard. If the kids hadn't been in the car, I would have made a deal. I would have taken anger management. I wouldn't have run the risk of going to jail. But because I've preached to them, "You've got to stand up; you can't let people run over you," I had to go to court and fight this. (O.J. was acquitted at this trial also. It was tried in Miami, and his murder case was tried in L.A. O.J. said that any major city has mostly African-Americans on the juries.)

I thought it was interesting that it took a case like Scott Peterson's to finally draw O.J. out of hiding after ten years.

Part III

9

The Preliminary Hearing

It was the evening of Wednesday, October 29, 2003. Even though I lived nearby, I thought I'd try to get a good, early spot in front of the courthouse. Here I was in my big, white van, camping down the street from the tent-city media circus forming in front of the Stanislaus County Court House. It was just a coincidence that I had a vehicle like this, since I was temporarily using it for my work, but, interestingly enough, it bore a striking resemblance to many of the news-station vehicles. The next morning at 9:30 a.m. was the first day of the Scott Peterson preliminary hearing, for which we had all been waiting for so long. It was still quite warm out. During the week it had reached the 90's, unusual for October. We were, of course, in the Central Valley. This event coincided with the fires that were raging out of control in Southern California. Despite many reporters detaching themselves from the Laci story to pursue that one, it was hard to even get near the courthouse in Modesto.

The next morning, I parked alongside many large vans that had their network stations' logos painted on them and had large antennas and satellite dishes sprouting out their roofs. I made my way into the media-only access area, where a badge was required for entry, and began setting up not too far from Ted Rowland's crew from KTVU.

This particular type of hearing, for those who may not be as familiar with our legal system, is the most important hearing prior to any felony trial. This is where it's determined whether there is enough evidence to hold the case over for a trial. A judge, during the preliminary hearing, determines whether the charges are serious enough to constitute a felony, and thus decides whether the case should go on to superior court. During the proceeding prosecutors need only to present enough evidence to raise a reasonable suspicion indicating the defendant is "probably" responsible for the crime. The district attorney, who is *elected* by constituents within that county district, indicts a defendant, and the judge, who is *appointed* by the governor of the state, confirms or denies that indictment through the preliminary hearing process. Very rarely are indictments denied at this stage, mainly because of the low threshold of incriminating evidence needed to continue the process for consideration by a jury in actual trial.

The other proceeding, which also serves the same purpose as the preliminary hearing, is the grand jury. When a grand jury is convened it is composed of citizens, usually of some prominent status, who can also confirm an indictment for trial. The difference between the two is that the grand jury is "private," while the preliminary hearing is "public." This means that defense lawyers may cross-examine prosecution witnesses during the preliminary hearing but *not* during the grand jury proceeding. There are pros and cons to both processes. For example, prosecutors in the O.J. Simpson trial chose to take the case to the grand jury, mainly because they felt they had more than enough evidence for a conviction and didn't want to wait for the lead investigators on the case to complete a few more interviews that prosecutors thought were taking much too long. That indictment, however, was overturned by a judge, because some of the evidence had already leaked out to the media, such as the 911 tapes of Nicole Simpson screaming, and it was felt this might have influenced the grand jurors. The DA again filed the criminal complaint to be heard by preliminary hearing, and then from there, it went on to trial.

On the first day of Scott Peterson's preliminary hearing, Laci's parents, relatives, and friends occupied three entire rows of the filled courtroom, and Scott's family consumed almost two more. Lee and Jackie Peterson wore blue and yellow lapel pins, to signify the ribbons worn during the search for Laci.

This first day of the hearing focused mainly on one small piece of evidence, the single, brown hair found in the pliers at the bottom of Scott's boat. An FBI biochemist, Constance Fisher, who was called to the stand as an expert witness by prosecutors, testified that the hair most likely belonged to Laci Peterson, as determined through the process of mitochondrial DNA testing. However, this particular type of DNA testing is not wholeheartedly accepted by the legal community nationwide. It's a little newer than traditional DNA testing, and is not considered as reliable. Thus, it gave Mark Geragos fuel for a heavy cross-examination. He spent the entire afternoon trying to cast doubt on the reliability of this evidence and attempted to argue against its admissibility in court. Geragos naturally tried to contend that the investigators mishandled the single strand. Basically, the testing determined that the hair could have belonged to Laci, her brother (her sister Amy had a different mother), or her mother, but definitely ruled out the possibility of it being one of Scott's hairs. Fisher explained the difference between nuclear DNA and mitochondrial DNA. Mitochondrial DNA is passed down from the mother, and all maternal family members share the same, but unlike nuclear DNA, which is found in the nucleus of a cell and positively identifies tissues, mitochondrial DNA is found elsewhere in a cell and is simply less reliable for identification purposes. Under heavy questioning Fisher admitted that if the samples had been taken years apart, then it is possible the tests might have shown different results.

This testimony naturally supported the prosecution's contention that Scott, after killing his wife, put her in the back of his boat, then drove to the Berkeley Marina, and, of course, dumped her body into the bay during his *supposed* Christmas Eve fishing trip.

Stanislaus County District Attorney James Brazelton had previously said that the evidence presented during this hearing would "open some eyes." However, because of the long, boring hours of meticulous details involved in presenting this scientific evidence, many in the packed courtroom, that seats 70, were having difficulty keeping their eyes from *closing*. The only thing remotely exciting to the observers this first day was Mark Geragos's attempt to "ban" Amber Frey's attorney, Gloria Allred, from the courtroom. Allred responded by telling the judge that excluding her would only interfere with her ability to represent her client and would be "unprecedented and unwise." Judge Girolami allowed her to stay; however, he admonished her not to discuss the testimony of any other witnesses with Amber, who appeared to be the star witness against Peterson. He said, "You can give her advice, but you cannot include what witnesses have said." All witnesses are kept out of the courtroom before giving testimony, except the parents of Laci and Scott, as well as Laci's sister, Amy.

Mark Geragos claimed that, after Modesto Police checked out the hair from the evidence locker, it suddenly became two strands. Prosecutors naturally contended that the hair simply split while inside the evidence envelope. I couldn't understand why Geragos couldn't see the ridiculousness of his claim. If investigators knew that *they* had listed the finding as a *single* hair, then to plant a second hair would only force police to make excuses for how the one hair became two. Let us say, hypothetically, that the investigators deliberately planted the second hair as Geragos contends. What plausible benefit could the prosecution possibility derive from this action, since the evidence was already listed by *detectives* as *one* hair, and *not* two? Since when did the police or the prosecution ever claim that it had *always* been two hairs? Such a contention by Geragos, if realistically weighed and balanced in the mind of a juror, would only subtract from the credibility of the high-profile defense lawyer, who was obviously very biased in his opinion.

Fisher, however, simply testified that "there was no evidence of any contamination in this case."

Because mitochondrial DNA testing is considered to be a *novel* technique, state law requires a special proceeding to be held, known as a "Kelly Fry" hearing, to determine the validity of such evidence. Judge Girolami agreed to hold such a hearing, citing that, up until now, California courts have not accepted the admissibility of such analysis as forensic evidence. Fisher testified for the prosecution that the process is generally accepted by the scientific community. She remarked, "Children are learning this in high school. They're doing this in biology labs across the country."

According to prosecution documents, twelve state courts and one federal court *have* ruled that mitochondrial DNA evidence *is* admissible. Senior Deputy DA Dave Harris said, "The court will see that there is nothing new and novel in this particular type of technique."

FBI technicians compared the hair found in Scott's boat to a DNA sample on a test swab from Sharon Rocha, designated as "SR2." Their comparison resulted in a match. The hair was also compared to a blood sample from Scott, which excluded him. Authorities had retrieved the Peterson blood sample after obtaining a warrant for Scott's "person." These results satisfied the prosecution, but I thought it would make even more sense for FBI DNA experts to compare Scott's *hair* rather than just his *blood*, to the hair found in his boat.

Based on a comparison of the DNA from the hair specimen to an FBI database, Fisher testified that one in every 112 Caucasians would be expected to have the same DNA sequence, as would one in every 159 Hispanics. Under cross-examination by the defense, Fisher acknowledged that this was the first case in which she had testified specifically about the admissibility of mitochondrial DNA as evidence, and that she never had testified in a California state court before. She did, however, confirm that she's testified in fourteen other DNA-related cases.

Constance Fisher testified for approximately four hours. Whether or not the hair actually belonged to Laci, the FBI forensic investigator's information during testimony was time-consuming to discern. The hair could not be tested for the highly accurate nuclear DNA because there was no follicle attached. Instead, she had to test the substance outside the nucleus, the mitochondrial DNA, which is less precise for identification but is always inherited from the mother.

At the end of the day, family members from both sides exited the courtroom separately, so as not to cross paths. Scott Peterson's mother, Jackie, left the courthouse while holding on to Mark Geragos's arm.

Day 2 of the prelim continued with the same subject matter of DNA, again specifically in the context of Laci's hair found in the fishing pliers on Scott's boat. FBI investigator Constance Fisher, just as the day before, was the only witness who testified the second day. Geragos continued with a lengthy cross-examination, thus spreading the testimony out and consuming the entire day in court. One of the angles he tried to use, in an attempt to discredit the prosecution witness, was that the FBI used faulty equipment during the analysis, which tainted the results.

Then Geragos attempted to show that the FBI hadn't followed proper guidelines, by asking Fisher why the FBI hadn't extracted DNA from one of Laci's bone samples and then compared it to the hair. The expert witness responded that it wouldn't have been necessary, since they already had a saliva sample from Laci's mother, which has proven to be easier to extract DNA from than a bone sample. Geragos read that FBI guidelines "should" include a comparison with a second tissue sample. Fisher responded, "'Should' has wiggle room in it. There is a difference between 'should' and 'must.'"

Geragos also took a pot shot at the computer program used to collect the data. Fisher said the program was written by a lab employee who no longer worked at that facility, and that it did have a built-in program error, but technicians checked the results manually. Geragos, in a flare of wanna-be Perry Mason, asked "Was he fired for incompetence?"

The FBI supervisor responded that the programmer left to go study to become a lawyer. With the question having backfired on the defense lawyer, the packed courtroom roared with laughter at him, including Scott Peterson, who was wearing a light gray suit and a red tie. Scott chuckled, then briefly shook his head from side to side, as he smiled, trying to pretend that he was just one of the guys.

Geragos had told Judge Girolami the day before that there was a "raging debate" still currently ongoing in courtrooms nationwide regarding the admissibility of mitochondrial DNA evidence. The judge acknowledged, "There's some dispute of its use in the forensic setting."

Geragos, again, on the second day asserted that the reliability of mitochondrial DNA is a "raging debate" in the scientific community. FBI biochemist Constance Fisher responded, "If it's a debate, I wouldn't call it a big one."

The hair evidence, as we know, is considered critical in that the prosecution may use it to argue that Scott transported Laci's body in his boat to the Berkeley Marina on the day she disappeared.

By the third day of the preliminary hearing, some of the letters Scott had been writing to various acquaintances were beginning to make some headlines. Laci's college friend Heather Richardson, who currently resides in Ventura County, stated publicly, "He makes references to memories of Laci. It's a little irritating to us. We were their best friends, and Scott doesn't have unique thoughts for us. He writes generally the same stuff to everybody. He avoids writing in detail about the double-murder case against him. He never says, 'I didn't do this,' but it's inconceivable in his mind that he had anything to do with it. It's kind of cryptic, as far as I'm concerned. It's not exactly what you'd expect from someone facing what he is. It's like he is not realizing the reality of the situation he's in." Heather went on to say that, in one of Scott's letters to her and her husband Mike, he said, "In an upcoming forum, you will be able to see the evidence my team has put together." She mentioned that she thought he was referring to the preliminary hearing.

Heather also mentioned that the Simi Valley fires that week burned right to their property line. She said, "Good or bad, it's nice to be preoccupied down here, so the hearing is not always everything I think about. At this point, we're just waiting to hear all the evidence."

Ted Rowlands of KTVU was able to provide some excerpts from these letters, written by Scott within the first month or so of his incarceration. Here are some of those excerpts:

> "I was told they were gone on the car ride to Modesto by detectives...I didn't believe...wouldn't believe them. I only knew it was true on the next morning when I saw the paper."
>
> "I woke up early today to a crashing cell door, I figured it must be after midnight and therefore Laci's birthday...I lay in this bunk dreaming about her, being able to hold her and Conner. As the morning went on, all I could do was lay here in tears."
>
> —Scott Peterson

I noticed Scott didn't refer to Laci and Conner by name in the first letter. Some people thought this might have meant that he had already distanced himself so far from his wife and son, that he could've been having difficulty living the lie needed to sound emotional.

Relatives from both sides of the Laci Peterson tragedy took the witness stand on the third day of the prelim. When Laci's mother, Sharon Rocha, approached the stand, a hush fell over the courtroom. She appeared to be cool, calm, and collected, and when not answering questions, Sharon simply looked straight ahead. She said, "Laci and I were very close. We talked probably at least every day or every couple of days."

Sharon testified that Laci called her at 8 p.m. the night before her disappearance. She said she was talking to a friend on the other line when Laci called, so the conversation lasted only a couple of minutes, since the other person was still on hold. She said her pregnant 27-year-old daughter was tired and that, before they hung up, they confirmed plans for Laci and Scott to attend Christmas Eve dinner at Sharon's. It was the last time Sharon Rocha would ever talk to her popular daughter.

Sharon then testified that Scott Peterson called her the next night to say that her daughter was missing. She said, "I was getting really scared by then, when he said 'missing.' When he said 'missing,' that's what concerned me. It wasn't that she wasn't there, or he couldn't find her, but that she was *missing*."

Sharon told the jammed courtroom that she thought "the world" of Scott *before* December 24, 2002.

While cross-examining Sharon, Mark Geragos asked her if her daughter had ever confided in her about any serious marital problems before. Sharon responded that, no, Laci hadn't.

Laci's half-sister Amy testified that the couple had visited the hair salon where she worked at 5:45 p.m., December 23, 2002. Amy cut Scott's hair that night, and testified that he mentioned he'd do her a favor the by picking up a gift basket for their grandfather the next day at Vella Farms, near the Del

Rio Country Club, where Scott told her he was planning to go golfing in the morning.

Lee Peterson, Scott's father, testified that he reached his son by cell phone between approximately noon and 2 p.m., Christmas Eve day. He said they only spoke for a few minutes about plans for Christmas. He conceded that Scott didn't tell him he went fishing in the bay that day. He also admitted Scott never told him he bought a boat, but then added that his son had previously made large purchases before and also hadn't told him about those. He said these purchases included a motorcycle, a catamaran, and the Ford F-150 he used to tow the boat with. I'd like to know where the motorcycle and catamaran are today.

Lee Peterson concluded his testimony by saying, "I proudly say Scott's my son."

All three relatives testified Scott never told any of them about a boat, nor did he tell any of them about a Christmas Eve fishing trip. And according to Sharon and Amy, Laci knew nothing about the boat, or at least never mentioned that she did. Also, both Amy and Sharon testified that neither of them knew at the time about Scott's affair with Fresno masseuse Amber Frey.

Amy mentioned that one early indication that something might have been wrong on Christmas Eve was that Scott never picked up the gift basket he agreed to retrieve. She testified that a Vella Farms employee called her towards the store's closing time on December 24th, because the gift had not been picked up yet. Amy then tried to reach Scott on his cell phone, and then tried the house phone, but there was no answer either way. She then drove to the store to collect the gift herself.

Prosecutor Rick Distaso kept Laci's sister on the witness stand for a seemingly lengthy period. He asked very specific questions about the exact garments her sister was wearing the night she cut Scott's hair. Amy Rocha responded that Laci wore a black blouse with cream flowers and beige pants. Scott told investigators that Laci was wearing black pants and a white blouse before going out to walk the dog. Potential defense eyewitnesses told investigators they saw Laci wearing black pants and a white top the morning she disappeared. Laci's body washed up in beige maternity pants.

Less than two hours later, Amy said Scott called Sharon and told her Laci was missing. Scott met Sharon at Dry Creek Park, where the search began, where Laci had supposedly walked their dog. Detective Jon Evers, who was first on the scene, testified, "Scott was upset. Sharon was upset. Foul play was suspected almost immediately. I remember Laci's mom, Sharon, crying. She was very, very, very upset. When Scott walked up, he appeared to be very upset."

The Peterson's maid, Margarita Nava, also took the stand that morning. She testified that she saw Laci when she arrived on December 23, 2002. She said Laci looked fine, but appeared tired. Nava said she opened the Petersons' window blinds that morning.

Geragos may have already caught this tidbit of testimony while reviewing the transcripts from the preliminary hearing. During the actual trial in front of the jury, Geragos could argue the fact that the maid had to open the blinds, which disproves the notion that Laci did it herself every morning. Likewise, the prosecution could counter this argument by saying the maid had only been there a grand total of 4 times. Who opened the blinds the other 361 days of the year? Obviously, Laci did.

Nava testified that she cleaned the couple's Modesto house the day before Laci went missing. The chemicals she said she used were water and a pine oil-based cleaner on the kitchen tile floor, but she only used bleach in the bathrooms. Investigators found evidence pointing to the use of two separate chemicals used to clean the kitchen, suggesting that the house had been cleaned yet again the very next day, when Scott's wife was nowhere to be found. One forensic criminalist said that, if the maid said she used cleaner X, and investigators discovered evidence of cleaner Y, it means someone else cleaned with Y sometime after Nava mopped the floor on December 23.

Earlier in the investigation, police said they had detected a strong odor of bleach in the Peterson home the night Laci went missing. Prosecutors, however, did not question Officer Jon Evers, who was first on the scene that night, about a smell of bleach. Instead, Evers's testimony focused mainly on Scott Peterson's story, which began with him leaving in the morning to go fishing in San Francisco Bay at about 9:30 a.m., while Laci prepared to take the dog for a walk in East La Loma Park. Evers did say, however, that they found two mops and a bucket that were still wet, just outside the door. Evers later testified that he did *not* smell bleach in the home that first night.

Evers was a patrolman at the time of the disappearance, and he stated that, when he arrived at the Peterson house, Scott relayed the story that, when he arrived home from fishing, Laci was not there. Evers then testified that Peterson told him that he ate some slices of pizza, took a shower, and then called some relatives and friends. He also mentioned that Scott, when questioned by another officer, "couldn't say" what type of fish he was trying to catch. The officer even testified that he heard Ron

Grantski ask Scott why he had left so late to go fishing. Scott, evidently, had no answer.

On Day 4 of the preliminary hearing, the defense called its forensic expert witness. William Shields, a professor of environmental and forest biology at New York State University, was called to the stand. He testified that the FBI was using flawed testing methods when determining the genetic makeup of the hair from the pliers, which had resulted in a link to Laci. William Shields fired away at the use of mitochondrial DNA, saying that *it* and the protocol behind the testing were unreliable. He said that FBI DNA tests could lead to false exclusions and inclusions of possible matches, which according to him, would mean that the hair could have originated from someone other than Laci. He contended that the statistic would be closer to inclusion of one in nine Caucasians, as opposed to 1 in every 159, per FBI analyst Constance Fisher.

Prosecutors were no cream puffs at opening up cracks in the defense witness's testimony. First, they questioned his professional experience with mitochondrial DNA forensics. Shields admitted, under cross-examination by Deputy DA Dave Harris, that he was *not* a forensic scientist, had little training in forensics, and even less experience in a forensic laboratory. He further acknowledged that he was neither a PhD, nor did he hold a doctorate in any type of DNA field. At times the questioning became heated, as Shields struggled to get out answers to Deputy DA Harris's penetrating queries. Repeatedly Shields avoided answering whether mitochondrial DNA testing was "generally accepted" in the scientific community, by citing that it was up to a judge to decide.

As a maximum-security inmate at Stanislaus County Jail, Scott had already begun receiving a considerable amount of mail. This had additionally been referred to as his *fan* mail. Naturally, as notorious an individual as he had become, he was attracting a lot of attention, and women were writing to him. There are always a small percentage of women, in a society as large as ours, who are drawn to a man in prison, such as Scott. There was some discussion on a segment of *Larry King Live* about this very issue. Guest Jeanine Pirro happened to mention that many women, for various reasons, are attracted to the "bad boys," including some who just want to nurture them. Also, Ms. Pirro emphasized that many women want to be associated with a celebrity. Scott is now currently both, so it becomes no surprise that his number of groupies may be growing.

Nancy Grace asked the panel, "What is behind the phenomenon of people on trial for murder getting stacks and stacks of love letters, marriage proposals, you name it?"

Dr. Robi Ludwig responded with, "Well, these are suicidal women. I say that half in jest. But really, these are women who are very desperate, who are not able to have normal relationships, so they feel that, if they can have a relationship with a man in jail, and I think Jeanine is right, there is a celebrity factor here. If he's infamous, he's the bad boy, they can convert them, they can get the attention. It's this false intimacy they can't get in a normal way."

For the next few days of courtroom testimony, attorneys continued to hammer away at the single human hair found wrapped in the pliers under the seat of Scott's secret boat that nobody knew about until the day Laci disappeared. This was the human hair that "could" be Laci's, but definitely did *not* come from Scott's scalp.

Regarding the pliers, Modesto defense lawyer Ernie Spokes commented, "Maybe Scott grabbed them from the kitchen drawer. Laci had access to the drawer all the time."

Personally, I use needle nose pliers whenever I go fishing, to remove the hooks from the lips of the fishes' mouths, so I can usually throw the creatures back in alive and watch them swim away. One time I caught the same bluegill so many times out of this one Modesto fishing hole, that a friend who was with me said, "That fish's lips are shot-to-shit."

A sturgeon fisherman named Robert Kisner said publicly, "I have five or six pairs of pliers in my boat and more in the tool box. But my woman's hair ain't on any of 'em."

Over the next few days, Jon Evers, as well as several other officers, continued testifying regarding possible sources of the hair, as well as their findings on what appeared to be a possible crime scene clean up. This testimony included an account of a throw rug bunched up at the foot of the door leading out to the garage, which seemed to imply that Scott may have dragged a body out this way.

After a few more days of coma-inducing mitochondrial DNA testimony, the prelim took a more lively turn. Detective Al Brochini took the stand and testified that he found a loaded .22 caliber semiautomatic handgun in the glove compartment of Scott's truck, which of course was the vehicle he had taken to the Berkeley Marina. At this moment Sharon Rocha, with what appeared to be a look of shock and disgust on her face, got up to exit the courtroom.

Based on the detective's testimony, Scott had said that he last fired a gun about a month before his wife's disappearance. Scott consented to have his hands tested for gun blast residue, but he also asked the detective whether exhaust from an outboard boat motor might trigger a false positive. The results of such a test were not available.

While under cross-examination by Kirk McAllister, Brochini said that, when Scott wasn't looking, he took the gun and put it in his pocket. Together the two men drove to Peterson's warehouse, and then to the police station. As minimal a score for the defense as this may be, it does strike one as being a little odd that Brochini would handle the confiscation of the gun in this manner. It would seem to make more sense that Scott naturally would understand that he was under a certain amount of suspicion by being the spouse, so I wouldn't think that Scott would interpret the officer's need to confiscate the gun as evidence, or because it was illegal to carry one in a vehicle, as anything more than normal procedure. Brochini, on the other hand, may have thought that if he *let* Scott see that he was taking the weapon as evidence, that this might have caused the prime suspect to freeze up and become less cooperative during the investigation, which at that point was only a missing persons case.

Brochini testified that Amber Frey said that Scott had told her on December 9th that he had "lost" his wife, and he also testified that Scott went ahead and bought a 14-foot boat the very next day. Brochini also testified about the wiretapped calls between Scott and Amber. He testified about Amber calling in on the tip line on December 30, 2002, and that she agreed to cooperate in the investigation, by allowing detectives to record any and all telephone conversations between her and her fraudulent lover. Brochini testified that, the very next night (New Year's Eve), during the candlelight vigil, while Scott was in the crowd of Laci supporters at La Loma Park, he called Amber on his cell phone and said that he was out of the country, that it was his first holiday without his wife, and that he would be able to be with Frey more exclusively by about January 25.

Brochini testified that Scott was driving a maroon Mercedes on the day he was arrested. He had used his mother's name to purchase the vehicle with 36 one hundred dollar bills as payment, which implies that Peterson wanted to avoid any kind of paper trail. Brochini also said Peterson had altered his appearance. Based on Brochini's statements, the car seller asked Peterson about his female first name of Jacqueline. Scott evidently replied that his parents had given him the name, and that he usually goes by "Jac." Brochini said the seller told him Scott said it was "A Boy Named Sue" kind of thing. (There's a Johnnie Cash song called "A Boy Name Sue.") He then said Peterson provided the seller with a fake number that Scott claimed to be a Florida driver's license number.

Brochini testified that Scott Peterson said that he had washed the clothes he was wearing upon returning from his trip, because they were wet from fishing. Although the hamper was overflowing with his soiled clothing, Scott chose, for some reason, to wash only the three items he had worn *that* day, the detective said. He also testified that Scott told him the fishing trip was a last-minute decision because, "it was too cold to go golfing." (If it was too cold to go golfing, I would imagine it would be even *colder* on the San Francisco Bay in the middle of winter. If you asked me, I would say the complete opposite would be more normal, to golf on a cooler day, and to fish on a warmer day.)

Brochini testified that Scott told him his wife was mopping the floor that morning. The housekeeper testified she had mopped the floor the day before.

Several months after the bodies were found, Amber Frey got pregnant again. This wasn't reported until about the time of the middle of the preliminary hearing. The leak somehow got out, and the media just exploded into another feeding frenzy. All the panelists on television were drilling all these questions right at Gloria Allred, who at first said nothing but had this big ear-to-ear smile on her face. I don't think this smile meant anything more than the fact that she couldn't believe such a huge deal was being made over something like this. She probably didn't know who the had leaked this gossip, but she seemed to be enjoying all the attention, as it hit. Yes, she did confirm the rumor to be true.

Like everyone else, I had my own opinions as to how this development may have affected the trial. Before I discuss the effects this factor might have in a legal arena, I want to discuss some of the personal reasons Amber may have had for this rather sudden surprise. For example, my initial, gut reaction was quite different from anything I heard on TV, or from anyone else for that matter. The first thing I felt was that Amber, to some extent, was deliberately rubbing a certain amount of spite in Scott's face. Again, we can't forget that, no matter how much worldwide attention this case was getting, at one time Amber had put her whole heart and soul into believing this man was the one for her. As shocking as the murder of his wife must have been to her, this (believe it or not) may have been only secondary in importance to the shattering of the great expectations she had built up for a future with this young man. I could almost sense from the recorded phone conversations she had with Scott that Amber deliberately and rebelliously steered away from the detectives' guidelines, to pursue her own personal investigation, as well. In fact, I almost got the sense that she was not fearful of

Scott harming her in any physical way, and that she felt she had more control of him than that. But what I did find strongly rising in her sentiments from these conversations was the fact that Scott had lied to her about something as serious as being married, and that reporting the affair to the police was her way of punishing him for lying to her. The pregnancy, which, undoubtedly, Amber knew would eventually get back to Scott, seemed to say for her, "Ha! This could've been you! But you lied to me, so there!" Also probably, "I got pregnant with someone better than you anyway. So I'm going to enjoy the rest of my life, as my children grow up. But you're gonna have to sit there and eat shit until you die in that jail cell. That's what you get for trying to deceive me, you loser."

I'm sure most modern liberal-minded women would probably not admit this much. In fact, the ones giving commentary on the shows said more or less exactly what I expected them to say regarding this development: "Oh, she's just, you know, getting on with her life and certainly isn't going to let her involvement in this case stop her from pursuing her own personal dreams, even if she does it right now before the trial even begins, whether she has to testify or not. She doesn't care. Her life is more important to her."

Yes, even I, too, agree with this assessment. I think this also is part of the whole development.

I remember one of the days when I was over at the courthouse along with the hordes of other reporters. At the time, I had put this little incident on the back burner, because my primary focus during the hearings was to cover the case itself as it unfolded. The most exciting parts of these episodes usually occurred when family members, lawyers, and detectives associated with the case either entered or exited the building. It occasionally got a little boring between these sequences, so sometimes we journalists just hung out and socialized with one another or went to get some food, or whatever. On one of these days, I happened to be talking to one of the hot dog vendors just outside the courthouse. I figured that day that, rather than make the walk downtown, I'd simply get a Polish dog instead. The vendor seemed rather eager to talk to me for some reason, although I had seen other reporters nearby in whom he didn't show the same interest. I guess he might've thought I was kind of important or something. Since it was only small talk, I didn't bother to ask his name. He was a shorter guy, maybe in his late 40s, with a plump, round face and wire-rimmed glasses. He seemed to be somewhat opinionated about the Peterson case and also the role the media were taking in it. For example, he asked half lightheartedly, if I knew that Scott Peterson was innocent until proven guilty. And at first I started to answer his question seriously. I said, "Well, yes, of course..." then I stopped and kind of laughed. "What are you asking *me* this for?" I asked him.

He replied, "Well, it seems you reporters have already convicted this guy, before he can get a fair trial."

It seemed as if this person might've been messing with me a little, so I thought that maybe I'd just mess with him in return a little. He seemed to want to express an opinion in a bold manner to me for some reason, even though I knew he probably didn't know a whole lot about what he was referring to. So I said, "Yeah, well, I admit, I was the guy who wrote the article that got the police to arrest Peterson."

I looked at his face to see his reaction. He just stood there, staring back at me with this blank look. So, I said, "You know, the article that described how he killed her, put her in his boat, and dropped her in the bay when he went fishing..." He continued to just stare back, not knowing what to say.

After pausing a second, I said, "I'm just kidding." Then, I told him that I was remaining fairly neutral about it at this stage of the proceedings. However I could certainly understand why he might have felt that way, seeing this convergence of media here every day. But I went ahead and explained to him that the majority of the information being reported was directly from law enforcement agencies, family members, or lawyers, usually in the form of specially allocated press conferences. In other words, I told him, the majority of the media were merely reporting the actual facts of the case as they unfolded and really not much more than that. I went on to mention that a lot of media people had expressed rather dismal opinions of Scott Peterson due to the preponderance of evidence against him. Some of this evidence included the bodies washing up in the area where Peterson's alibi was. I asked the hot dog guy if he didn't believe that this factor didn't at least cast a reasonable amount of suspicion on the prime suspect. His response was, "Me?" He pointed to himself, then looked around. Then he said, "Maybe the guy is guilty. I don't know."

I asked him, "Well, don't you like the fact that we (the media) are here? I mean doesn't it bring a lot more business to you?"

He exclaimed, "What? Are you kidding? You were one of the only guys nice enough to even buy a hot dog. Most of them all have expense accounts and go to the fanciest restaurants here in downtown. All *these* guys do is get in my way."

We talked briefly but amiably for a few more minutes, before I went on to make the rounds. Before we knew it, Jackie and Lee Peterson were making their way out of the courthouse. Mark Geragos had partially disguised himself with big black rimmed sunglasses and, along with another lawyer, made his way to the left of the building. This had caused the crowd to diverge, steering some of the reporters away from the main thrust that was now converging on Scott's parents, who walked in the opposite direction, to the right of the building, toward the general vicinity of the hot dog vendor I had just been talking to.

About thirty or so journalists were clamoring around the older Petersons with microphones, notepads, and cameras, forming a large cluster, and making them hardly visible. Suddenly, one of them, perhaps Lee, turned at a bit of a sharp angle, forcing the mob and some of their equipment to move directly toward the square, aluminum, hot dog stand. The hot dog guy tried to yell, "Hey, stop!" But it was too late. The mob, not able to control who was pushing whom, apparently bumped the stand with just enough force to tip it over on its side, leaving buns spilled everywhere, napkins flying in the wind, and a few plastic ketchup and mustard bottles sprawled out onto the asphalt. The hot dog guy went ballistic. He yelled over at the crowd of journalists, "I hope you guys have enough money to pay for my doctor bills," while raising his middle finger at them.

One of the male reporters sternly yelled back to him, "Hey, settle down over there."

A couple of the female reporters and I bent over to help him pick up some of the jumble out of the gutter. Then we lifted the unit back into place. The hot dog guy was all excited and jumping around. "Damn" he blurted, "I knew it! I knew that was gonna happen. This is my livelihood! Did you hear what that guy said?"

Trying to hold back my own chuckles, I reassured him that it appeared to be just one of those accidental things that happen, and that it wasn't really anyone's fault.

Back inside the courthouse there was some ongoing FBI testimony about a surveillance camera stationed across the street from the Peterson home on a utility pole during the days and weeks after the disappearance. The camera was installed mainly to monitor Scott Peterson's movements. If Evelyn Hernandez's family heard about this, they must have been furious to learn that law enforcement agencies actually have these resources at their disposal, but they never bothered to use any of it for *their* daughter, perhaps because these resources are only used on cases in which their departments are under the gun. The Hernandezes must have been struck with a combination of emotions, including anger and depression. It must have further broken their hearts to realize that police really *do* have the resources with which to catch murderers, but again, Evelyn and her family were apparently not worth lifting a finger for. One unique finding caught on film by this camera was the perpetrator in the act of the burglary that occurred while Scott was in L.A. the weekend of January 18, 2003. This was the burglary that was only reported as an unknown person associated with the case, who had taken Laci's wedding dress, and that no charges were going to be filed by the DA's office regarding the incident.

More recently, this person's identity was revealed publicly as Kimberly Ann McGregor, a neighbor who had been active in the searches for Laci. When I heard this, I tried to climb into this person's mind and figure out what she may have been thinking that may have driven her to commit this crime. Living in the area, plus being known for helping in the searches, she may have thought she could access the home, unnoticed. Her original motive, I believe, was probably just to gather some very noteworthy souvenirs from her involvement in a "trial of the new century." I believe that when her eyes locked onto that one-and-only Laci Peterson *wedding* dress, this woman experienced delusions of grandeur. She probably had dollar signs in her eyes, which may have blinded her better judgement. She could probably only imagine what such an item would bring on the black market, as if she had raided King Tut's tomb. She, having been approached by reporters before in the case, probably couldn't stop thinking how fast and how fat a check—possibly a hundred thousand dollars—might be written to her by a national tabloid.

During the next few days of testimony, it surfaced that Scott Peterson had rented a private mailbox on December 23, 2002, the day before his wife went missing. Amber, disheartened that she couldn't spend the holidays with her new boyfriend, called Scott to suggest that they should exchange gifts. Scott apparently told her to send the present to his private mailbox.

In further testimony by Al Brochini, he said that, when he went with Scott Peterson to the warehouse, Scott informed him that there was no electricity. Brochini testified that he believed Peterson at the time and proceeded to look around with his flashlight. He said it didn't occur to him while there to try to find a light switch anyway, despite what Scott told him. His testimony suggested Peterson might've had a motive for saying there was no electricity, so as to hinder the inspection for evidence that Scott knew might *be* there, because he naturally would be afraid he may have overlooked something earlier during his amateur, crime-scene clean up. This notion was corroborated by the fact that records indicate Scott transmitted a fax from his warehouse the previous morning, which suggests that he only could have done so with an ample light source.

McAllister asked the detective, "At no point while you're at the warehouse is he trying to kick you out or prevent you from doing anything you want to do there, right?"

"Other than see," Brochini answered.

Other factors came out during continued examination of witnesses, including the fact that Scott's whereabouts were tracked beginning immediately after the disappearance of his wife. Scott evidently revisited the shores of the San Francisco Bay three times in the days just following Laci's disappearance. This, by the way, was prior to the media making these bay searches public. Police watched Scott Peterson rent a different car on three separate occasions and tailed him as he drove directly to the San Francisco Bay on January 5, 6 and 9. He apparently got out and briefly gazed out over the water before driving away.

Al Brochini testified, "On Peterson's first trip, he stood at the boat launch and gazed out at the water for five minutes. Peterson didn't make any other stops on the roughly 170-mile round trip. On the second trip, he made no stops on the outbound leg, stared out into the bay about two minutes after arriving at the Berkeley Marina, and immediately began doing counter-surveillance tactics when he left. On the third trip, Peterson drove to the marina in a rented truck, briefly got out and then drove to a reservoir near Santa Nella. He stayed that night at a hotel in Bakersfield."

Brochini also said that, on Peterson's second trip to the marina, he tried to lose the shadowing officers when he left by stopping his car on the side of the highway, making u-turns in the middle of city blocks, and driving through parking lots.

One possibility that occurred to me was that Scott may have been re-evaluating the vastness of the bay in terms of the search effort's potential of actually recovering Laci's body there. He may have wanted to see again with his own eyes what investigators and divers may be looking at and make a judgement in his own conceited mind, perhaps to reassure himself that they could never find her there.

During this testimony of Peterson's suspicious return visits to the bay, the defense tried to claim the bay searches had already been announced in the papers, suggesting that Scott only behaved as any normal husband would, observing the progress in his wife's search. The prosecution claimed this took place prior to the public announcements.

Sharon Rocha felt compelled to exit the courtroom again when the focus of the hearing shifted to the recovery and condition of the remains of her daughter and grandson. Contra Costa County Forensic Pathologist Brian Peterson (no relation to Scott) testified regarding the conditions of the bodies. He said Laci Peterson's body was missing the head, neck, forearms, hands, feet, and part of the lower left leg. There were no indications of bullet, saw, or chew marks that he said he could identify on Laci's body. He said Laci's remains were severely decomposed, and that almost all internal organs were gone, leaving a skeletal torso. The only internal organ that remained intact was the uterus, he added, which showed no indication of having been cut.

Brian Peterson testified that Conner's body showed considerably less decomposition than that of his mother, which he said could be attributed to the baby being protected inside the body of the mother. Geragos pointed to a bag with duct tape stuck to it found near Conner's body, and to 1 ½ loops of tape around Conner's neck that was knotted and ran along his chest and under his arm. He then suggested the difference in decomposition between the two bodies may have been caused by Conner being wrapped in the bag and secured by the duct tape. Brian Peterson acknowledged this notion as a possibility, but he downplayed it as being *not* very likely, nor one he would even suggest.

The prosecution decided not to call Amber Frey to the witness stand during the preliminary hearing. They, of course, gave no specific reason for this. However, one can assume that this decision served several purposes. It would prevent the state's star witness from an unnecessarily grueling cross-examination by the defense. This then would prevent the defense from trying to lock Amber in to statements she'd be unable to change at trial. There was plenty of evidence already presented against Scott Peterson that should've been more than sufficient to hold him over for trial, given the lower threshold of suspicion required during the preliminary hearing for the murder charges to be formally confirmed.

Among other tidbits at the hearing, Mark Geragos had asked Al Brochini under cross-examination whether he had handled Laci's hairbrush, while examining the pliers found in Scott's boat. Brochini said he did not. (Gee, I wonder what Geragos might have been implying here?)

Criminalist Rodney Oswalt, of the state Department of Justice, testified that there were *two* hair fragments, when the evidence arrived at the lab in Ripon. One fragment, he said, was 4 3/8 inches and the other 1 5/8 inches in length. Interestingly, the evidence was logged in originally as being one strand, *six* inches in length. He said it was entirely possible that the strand, having been clamped in the needle-nose pliers, may have broken later.

Brochini also acknowledged having covertly called in a tip to a Laci hot line being operated by Scott's family. He said his purpose was to conduct a type of sting operation, which was intended to see if the Petersons would actually report the tip back to police, even if it seemed to condemn Scott. No further information was provided regarding the result of this sting. I certainly was hoping to find out the result. I thought it would be uniquely interesting to see how the family members reacted to the investigator's bait without them knowing about the police involvement.

Detective Phil Owen testified that he interviewed several people regarding their observations on the morning Laci disappeared. He said John and Kharma Souza told him that they saw a suspicious-looking man in a puffy jacket and blue jeans, who "popped out of the bushes," as they went by on a trail in East La Loma Park that morning. Detective Owen then said that at about 10:45 that morning at that same infamous location, Diana Campos, an employee at a nearby hospital, saw a pregnant woman walking a golden retriever with two men along a path in the park. Owen testified that Campos described the woman as six to seven months pregnant with straight, shoulder-length hair, and she described the men as extremely dirty. The detective said the witness heard one of the men use profanity when telling the pregnant woman to shut her dog up.

Investigators found evidence that Scott had made three cement anchors in his warehouse. One of the anchors was in the boat; the other two are missing.

Judge Girolami ruled that he would allow the disputed mitochondrial DNA evidence to be considered in the decision of this hearing, as well as for evidence in the actual trial.

Defense lawyer Jeffrey Fieger had said publicly, a few months before the trial, that Peterson's biggest problem or mistake was that he talked and talked to the media, right up until he was arrested. I disagree. Here's why. What Fieger said is basically true about incriminating oneself and Scott locking himself into a story he could never change, but this defense lawyer must have forgotten that, during the first few weeks of the investigation, Scott was coming under titanic pressure from high-profile media, law enforcement, and family to say something, or at least to answer some questions. He refused. He refused to talk to police, he refused a polygraph, and he refused to talk to the media. He even refused to talk to his father-in-law, Dennis Rocha, who was growing more and more suspicious and resentful by the day. This "avoidance" factor alone cast more public suspicion on Peterson than anything else the case had mustered so far.

Believe me, Scott knew his rights, and he tried his hardest not to talk to anyone. Again, what Fieger did not seem to consider was the fact that Scott had to say something publicly or face total character crucifixion. He didn't have a choice. There were simply no two ways about it. To clarify this point even more, just imagine how Peterson would look, if he continued to hide in a corner with his head buried in the sand, especially with Laci's family publicly pleading with him to cooperate. Imagine what all of us would think of him then, everyone on planet Earth wondering what deep, dark secret Scott was hiding. As much as the young man *had* the constitutional right to remain silent, his right to immunity from self-incrimination, and the right to a fair trial, he'd have to be guilty as hell not to speak out, when any family member of a victim of an abduction would speak out, as did Marc Klaas, John Walsh, the Smarts, etc.

Ultimately, just as the defense lawyer said he would, Scott *did* incriminate himself through public statements. To explain away why cops found blood in his truck, Peterson admitted to bleeding in his truck and in the house on the day Laci disappeared. He said that he had cut his knuckle on his toolbox. He also stated that since he works around farm equipment, he cuts himself all the time—that when men cut themselves, men bleed. If Scott was really as smart as he thinks he is, yes, he did the right thing by speaking out, but he never should have admitted to all this bleeding, especially to bleeding on the same day that Laci disappeared. The only plausible explanation for the blood to a right-minded juror would be that, since Scott doesn't kill his wife every day, the use of the murder weapon, along with the ensuing struggle, resulted in a haphazard laceration, which caused Scott to bleed in both his house and his truck, thus Scott needed to scramble for some lame excuse to explain the blood, which inevitably would be discovered.

That was the end of the ballgame right there, as far as I was concerned. Case closed. I occasionally work around heavy equipment with my truck, too, and the times I've cut myself enough to actually bleed have only been about once every 2 years. In fact, the last time it happened to me was about 18 months ago. I put my hand over the cut, walked into a building, got a bandage for it, and never bled in my truck at all, let alone my house! Scott worked in the *sales* end of the industry. He probably never even got on a tractor before in his life.

Even if Scott took out Laci from behind or smothered her in her sleep, in which case, there was hardly a struggle, Scott's panic-stricken, nervous state could easily have caused him to haphazardly cut himself or Laci during the preparation of her body for disposal in the bay. He perhaps had to twist chicken wire around her and Connor's bodies with pliers, as well as secure the cement anchor weights he had just made in his shop. If Scott used these sharp tools, objects, and materials, all while trying to race against the clock, with a million panicking thoughts rushing through his head, the slightest disrupting noise could have caused a slip of his hand, thus causing an accidental minor injury.

Geragos may be smarter than we think. Let me explain. A lot of us were looking at the guy as if he were a total idiot. For example, when he announced publicly that the police were using "voodoo" methods of investigation, it was *he*, Geragos, who was floating a "satanic cult" defense theory. People were saying that Geragos was just a flagrant hypocrite because of the voodoo statements, and also because of the announcement he made in which he stated that he believed Scott was proved guilty because of where the bodies were found, which he quickly recanted, once he was hired on as the defense. So, as I said, the greater moral majority of people, if they don't already, should understand this about Geragos. Unfortunately, the reality is that the majority of the population thinks he must be "the bomb" (the absolute champion of champion lawyers), simply because he's on TV a lot. But what that vast majority of the populace *doesn't* realize is the fact that he's only on TV because he became famous from one case, Winona Ryder's, which, by the way, he *lost* because he's only a very average attorney. I believe, for example, a lawyer such as Gerry Spence would have won an acquittal, if *he* had had this actress as *his* client. I should also mention that Geragos was on another high-profile case that was not as well publicized, the Susan McDougal case (part of the "Whitewater" scandal), which according to Jeffrey Fieger, Geragos *also* lost. After that Geragos' fame continued to escalate when he was hired by Congressman Gary Condit, who, by the way, never even became a suspect in the Chandra Levy case, so Geragos never had to actually *do* anything there, except become more famous, making his resume that much more attractive to cable TV commentators for guest spots. But I'll mention once again, that he may be only very average by "talent," but he's very "special" by experience, and that, in turn, gives him that extra edge over the millions of other "average" lawyers out there.

Here is how Geragos might be smarter than many of us actually think. I certainly don't believe that Geragos is the bomb, but I *do* believe that his past experience may have taught him the power of a pre-emptive strike, which perhaps he may be plotting and scheming at this very moment. What he could be planning is a card player's bluff. Everybody knows you simply don't show your hand of cards to the opponent whose defeat means the world to you. In fact, a smart player, if he's convincing enough, might be able to actually sell you the idea of a phony hand. In other words, Geragos has known all along that he's not really going to use a "satanic cult" defense, but he wants to convince the general public, and especially the prosecution, that he *will*. The obvious benefit of such a distraction is that it could fool the opponent into dropping his guard a little bit.

I was a little concerned when I learned that prosecutor Rick Distaso is only 36 years old. I would have expected DA Brazelton to have chosen more mature prosecutors. Perhaps attorneys in their fifties would be more appropriate for a trial of this magnitude because, if nothing else the jury might be more comfortable being told what to do by someone who at least *appears* more established. That way, they would be neither too young nor too old; they would be just about right, in my opinion. Anyway, let's not underestimate Distaso; you never know, maybe he's a prodigy. But of course, let the prosecution beware that Geragos could very easily be coming in with a more "clear choice" defense that stands head and shoulders above any of the others. To get a better idea of what that *actual* defense might *be*, take a look at Chapter 10—Potential Closing Arguments, and I think you'll get an idea of the possible juggernaut force of Panzer divisions he could be rolling and smashing into France with. Perhaps Geragos wants all of us to underestimate the depth of his scientific, legal, technological, and economic resources, which would be much easier to do, if we all thought he were actually going to use the satanic cult defense.

Most of us are probably aware that, if the defense were to use the satanic cult theory, then the jury would not deliberate for even five minutes. The unanimous verdict would be "guilty." So, the question is, why would Geragos, of all people, not know this? Jeffrey Fieger observed that he thought the defendant might have an adequate claim for an appeal if Mark Geragos were actually incompetent enough to use the satanic theory. Fieger was implying that the only verdict that could ever result from choosing such a defense would be "guilty." I suppose I could've made this a lot simpler by saying, "I believe Mark Geragos is floating the satanic cult defense only as a bluff."

Speaking of prosecutor Rick Distaso, when we finally got to see a little sample of his style, which wasn't until closer to the change of venue hearing, when the gag order wasn't active (not lifted, just not active), he gave me some concern regarding his potential effectiveness. See Chapter 10 for more details on this.

After the twelve-day preliminary hearing concluded, Judge Girolami declared Scott Peterson would be held to answer to charges of double, premeditated murder, confirming the necessity of a felony criminal trial in superior court. The judge's ruling followed a short day in court, in which testimony of Scott's arrest revealed that he was in possession of $15,000 cash in small bills and had extensive camping gear with him, which included a camp stove, a water purifier, and a fishing pole, as well as other survival gear he had in his vehicle.

10

Into the Realm of Nightmare

After the preliminary hearing ruling that Scott Peterson would be required to stand trial on double-murder charges there was another brief arraignment in which Peterson was required to give another plea, which, of course, was "not guilty." Proceedings then began almost immediately for consideration of changing the venue for the trial away from Modesto, due to the massive publicity.

The Chief Deputy DA for Stanislaus County said, "It's expensive. It's expensive to take all the witnesses, and all the law enforcement people, and all the evidence to where we would be located. If we believe it's proper to be here, we'll oppose the motion. We'd like to have the case here, if it can be tried here."

Judge Girolami had indicated earlier in a July hearing that moving the trial would not be a "desirable option" and would result in "considerable hardship" for the witnesses and "added expense" to the public. If Girolami decided to grant a change of venue, then the court would be faced with two possible options: moving the trial to another county or bussing the jurors *in* from another county. According to some veteran criminal attorneys here in Modesto, Girolami is known for being a very cost-conscious judge.

Naturally, it was the defense that filed the motion citing that the overwhelming publicity in the case may have tainted the Stanislaus County jury pool. After seeing the tent-city media circus out front of the Modesto courthouse every day, I couldn't see a judge *not* granting this motion. If ever there were such a need for this kind of motion, with *these* circumstances, surely this case had to be one of them.

After the first change of venue hearing, despite the gag order, Mark Geragos went before the cameras and threw a couple of cheap shots at the prosecution's case. The first one had to do with the height level of the microphones he was speaking into; he said they must've been set up for the Modesto Police Department because they were "kind of low." In the second cheap shot, he said everyone felt Peterson was entitled to a fair trial, except the prosecution, of course.

I'm sure most people saw those remarks exactly for what they were, cheap shots, but some people who haven't pre-determined Scott's guilt or innocence yet, might be influenced by these subtle innuendos. For example, some might see Geragos' cleverness as kind of a "cool" trait and therefore, they might, deep down inside, be secretly rooting for his victory. This instance is only one of many small building blocks needed to successfully build a case against the opponent. For example, in the O.J. trial, Johnnie Cochran used this tool of making a few cheap shots to put some holes in the prosecution's case, ultimately with a successful result. He went on *Larry King Live* when the trial was just beginning and said that the only reason Chris Darden was picked for the case was because he is *black*.

Then, smooth Johnnie went on to say that the prosecution needed to appoint a black man to serve as an apologist for a racist, and that Chris Darden was nothing but a stooge for the white man. (Ironically, if you look at the old photos or news clips of Gil Garcetti, the District Attorney at the time, he does look like the whitest man in America.) To say the least, Chris Darden wasn't very happy with this. Because he was working for the DA, Darden was under strict orders not to speak to the media. He couldn't say squat. But Cochran, on the other hand, only worked for O.J., allowing him to get up there every night and just freely speak his mind.

My first reaction to hearing Johnnie Cochran's announcement about Darden only being hired because he's black was, "Oh, and as if Johnnie wasn't?" Cochran sure wasn't hired by O.J. because he's *white*, I'll tell you that right now.

Don't get me wrong, I actually admire Johnnie Cochran a lot. He is, without a doubt, a very skilled swordsman with his tongue. He is one of the best of the best at what he does. I consider him to be a very talented man and a very talented lawyer. However, some people have compared him to the likes of a fast-talking riverboat gambler, or a smooth-talking, blue suede shoe salesman on a fat commission. He definitely has the gift of gab. Some musicians can seduce people with their fingers on the fret board of a guitar. Well, Johnnie Cochran clearly has the ability to seduce people with his tongue. He can just dance with his tongue, almost like magic. He's the type of attraction you'd have seen in a circus sideshow a hundred years ago. They could sell tickets to see showings of him as if he were some kind of elephant man or something. As the spectators anxiously await, the curtain finally is drawn, and there he is—The World's Greatest Bullshit Artist. And he could just entertain the crowd by taking them on an exciting roller coaster ride of rhetoric with his tongue, and people would simply be mesmerized. I'm just kidding, Johnnie. Seriously, you're great.

In a request to move the trial, the defense cited a "lynch mob" atmosphere and "poisonous" news coverage. In a 21-page motion backed by 8,000 more documents, Mark Geragos wrote, "Only a change of venue can ensure that Mr. Peterson obtains the fair and impartial trial to which he is constitutionally entitled. The widespread, pervasive and negative nature of the media reports surrounding this case have made it impossible to seat a fair and unbiased jury in Stanislaus County."

Included in the defense motion were a range of factors, comprised of some 8,000 news articles covering the case, two surveys conducted by sociologists showing the impossibility of seating an impartial jury in Stanislaus County, as well as what Geragos referred to as "political overtones" in the case. According to the defense attorney, these "political overtones" included California Attorney General Bill Lockyer referring to the odds of convicting Peterson as a "slam dunk," as well as citing Laci's mother, Sharon Rocha, lobbying in Washington, D.C., for federal legislation against fetal murder. The filing also cited a number of unique incidents likewise pointing to the necessity of a venue change. These included:

- On May 9, a person allegedly slashed one of Peterson's attorney's car tires, while it was parked out front of the jailhouse, while he was visiting his client.

- That same month, local residents accosted a Peterson lawyer, while he was trying to eat in a restaurant, for defending the murderer.

- More recently, there was a vehicle parked outside of Scott Peterson's warehouse, advertising a hateful message about him painted on the windshield.

- Geragos noted that Modesto Mayor Carmen Sabatino said he didn't believe Scott Peterson could get a fair trial in Stanislaus County.

- An angry mob of more than 200 people was awaiting Peterson's arrival at the Modesto jailhouse, the night he was arrested, shouting and holding signs with slanderous messages of hate and contempt for the accused killer.

During the change of venue hearings and prior to the judgment being rendered, there was much debate by the media about the size of Modesto being a factor. One panelist, speaking from a defense standpoint, said that Modesto was just a tiny, rural town. This was a gross understatement or mischaracterization, depending on how you look at it, of the city's proportions. To put it more accurately, it is one of the larger central California metropolises along U.S. Highway 99. It has a population of about 200,000, which is comparable to Fremont or Berkeley, California. Similarly to Modesto, these cities aren't considered large, as are San Francisco or Sacramento, but are medium-sized cities of about the same population, except Modesto is more spread out. In fact, George Lucas, the famous Hollywood producer, grew up here and went to the same high school as Laci. He filmed his first movie *American Graffiti* on the now-famous McHenry Boulevard, which, I can attest, runs for what seems like miles and miles, lined with businesses and commercial properties. This spokesperson was clearly trying to create the impression that Laci was a local hero in a fledgling community, and that nobody residing here could possibly be unbiased towards her.

The defense's request to have the trial moved was widely expected. Several months prior, Geragos had announced that he intended to seek a venue change, and publicly confirmed his intent at the close of the preliminary hearing. According to the defense request, Geragos said grand-scale media coverage of this case had been undeniably biased against Mr. Peterson. He also mentioned that potential jurors from Merced, San Joaquin, Sacramento, Tuolumne, Fresno, and Contra Costa counties "are in the same media market" and have likewise been saturated with news on the high-profile double-murder case. In the event a jury *were* to be brought in from a neighboring county, the defense would be required to approve such a ruling. Geragos had already made it clear he had no intention of accepting this compromise, and would hold out only for an actual move of the *entire* proceedings.

During one of the change of venue hearings, Jackie Peterson (Scott's mother) approached not one, but two homicide detectives separately in the courtroom hall and snapped at them that they should be ashamed of themselves for what they've done. Boy, all I've got to say about that is that, if I had been a detective working hard on this case, and a woman with tubes hanging out of her face came up to me and said such a thing, I'd turn to her and say, "Oh, do you mean I should be ashamed of myself for bringing a cold-blooded killer to justice?" Pointing a finger at her, I'd continue, "Look lady, we're simply not going to let the prime suspect in a double-homicide go free, just because he happens to be *your* son!"

Not to sound insensitive about Mrs. Peterson's condition, but those homicide detectives working on a difficult case such as this, are obviously not stupid. They would know that anything that the *mother* of the suspect says is so biased, that it has zero credibility. I'm sure they just scoffed at her and blew that one off.

Sharon Rocha (Laci's mother) filed a $5-million wrongful death lawsuit against her son-in-law, accused murderer Scott Peterson, in December 2003, one month before the criminal trial was scheduled to begin. If I were in her shoes, I wouldn't do that...yet. Here's why: He wouldn't be able to pay anything if he were to receive the death penalty, now would he? Or, life without parole, for that matter. But on the other hand, if Scott is acquitted and goes free, he then will be bankrupted of any future assets he can earn, until the amount of the settlement is paid off. So in the unlikely event that he does go free, this would give the grieving mother of the victim an alternative (consolation) form of justice. But again, she can file that *after* the criminal trial is over—only if she has to. But by filing it now, enough potential jurors will have been saturated with this knowledge that this could, to some degree, affect the psychology of any potential juror. For example, a juror might believe that Sharon would really like for Scott Peterson to pay her 5 million dollars, and that the only way for that to happen would be to acquit him, so he could go free and do his pay-per-view interviews, or whatever way he chooses to capitalize on his notoriety. Again, in that way, Mrs. Rocha could get paid, which, unfortunately, might have the appearance of being what she really wants, since she filed her suit even before the criminal trial ever began.

More likely, she was only seeking justice, and monetary gain was not her actual intention, but clearly, not just by the way I described it, but by general psychology, a lot of people might also get the other subliminal impression, which would have a serious detrimental affect on the outcome of Mrs. Rocha's side of the case. Or perhaps she simply might feel intimidated by the Peterson family's dream team and is feeling pessimistic about the possible outcome, especially since it had been proven in recent history that, even with all the evidence going against a defendant, money and fame sometimes still wins out, as with the O.J. case. Or, still perhaps, she may be feeling just as strong as ever about the evidence against her son-in-law, and confident of his eventual conviction in a criminal court, but she might be simply filing this civil action strictly as a routine motion in this serious of a capital crime, doing everything she possibly can in this situation, as any mother of a murder victim would do.

Plus, another factor may be getting to Mrs. Rocha: on the evening talk shows, many supposedly reputable panel members keep insisting over and over again that there is simply not enough evidence in the prosecution's case to convict Scott. Bullshit. The reason these panel members continue to push that idea, despite the preponderance of evidence that continues to stack against Peterson, is for one reason and one reason only: They think there is still a glimmer of hope that *they*, "the panelist" defense attorneys, might get hired on by the Peterson family to the new dream team of the latest trial of the century, especially since they just saw Mark Geragos get hired by the Peterson family right off of the evening television circuit.

These panels of so-called experts are mostly made up of defense lawyers. Why? Because prosecutors work for the state and are under orders not to discuss current cases with the media. Most defense lawyers, on the other hand, work for themselves in their own private practices, so no one is going to tell them not to go on TV and make names for themselves, which brings more business to their practices, thus more bottom-line dollars for *them*. Since the state is more experienced at appointing attorneys to cases, they obviously are going to be more rigid in their policies and clearly already has chosen their prosecutors in this case. In other words, you won't see too many prosecutors going on TV for their big chance at getting in on the trial of the century. If you did, I'm sure the "slam-dunk" theory would be riveted out into the American public every bit as forcefully as the "reasonable doubt" theory currently is.

Sometimes a defense lawyer can get hired on a big case by appealing to the emotions of the accused defendant's family and by planting false seeds of hope, that *this* particular defense attorney might be the hero who could come through for them, or that the family might think *this* individual could be more influential over the jury. So, it's not hard to see that prosecutors would not be able to get hired on a case by using the same standards. Another reason why defense lawyers speak out more than prosecutors do is that they can't get sued for saying that a man might be innocent. But it's known that people *have* been sued for trying to say someone is guilty, even though their right to "have an opinion" is guaranteed by the First Amendment. Gary Condit, for example, is suing the tabloid *National Enquirer* for $209 million for having *assumed* him to be responsible for Chandra Levy's murder, throughout their coverage of that case. (By the way, since Condit was still an elected official at the time of the allegations, this made him "fair game" to the media, which our constitution guarantees. In other words, in a free country, you're allowed to call your leader a "bum," if you so wish. This is why the Bushes have invited Jay Leno to the White

House for dinner in the past. It's their attempt at preventive maintenance, from being made sport of.)

Experienced defense lawyers including these panelists, know that families of accused killers are a great deal more gullible and desperate than are district attorney's offices. They know this to be true because, how often is a well-off family put in a situation where they need to think fast and hire "the right" defense (dream) team, or their son might be sitting on death row soon, if they don't? But DA offices, on the other hand, try murder cases on a regular basis. Therefore, they have more experience and skill at appointing trial lawyers than the average parents of an accused murderer do. In addition, district attorney's offices usually stay within their own county's pool of qualified staff for these appointments and rarely, even in high-profile cases, do they go outside those parameters for "special" prosecutors. For this reason, these defense lawyers on TV feel that, hey, you never know. It's possible to get a call or message from the Petersons, saying that they really liked his commentary broadcasted on the case in defense of their son and want to reward the individual with a spot on their dream team, which may or may not even be necessary.

Regarding the case, one of my employees mentioned to me, that he thought there was enough evidence against Scott, and that it looked pretty certain that he was guilty, but then he said, "After watching the commentary on it last night, I guess I was wrong. Apparently there's not nearly enough evidence to convict Scott, according to this legal panel." So I explained briefly, but in enough detail, to him why there seemed to be this favorable bias towards Scott in the media. He was floored. He thought this was something I should really point out. But I played it down, because the shows do occasionally have guests speaking from a prosecutorial standpoint, and these programs, I think, do a decent job of keeping most of the reporting fair and balanced, but as was mentioned earlier, there are some factors, mainly in the legal industry, which can sway public opinion.

I'll even say that, if I were one of these defense lawyers who serves as a nightly panelist, I'd give my honest opinion, but I'm sure I would feel compelled to stay within the boundaries of my profession, as well. This, I suppose, is one of the advantages to being a journalist—we can stay more neutral in our opinions, since we are not as affected by the case, as are people in the legal profession. In fact, I would not even be bringing up any of this at all, if it were not for the possibility that, if an average person such as my employee, after viewing nightly coverage of "Laci," actually thought there was no longer much hope for the prosecution's case after all, then it would begin to make more sense why Sharon Rocha may have started to feel that her son-in-law now has a greater chance of getting off than she previously had believed, and thus she felt the need to be pre-emptive and filed this lawsuit as early as she could. Since a certain line of thought may be subliminally affecting the victims' rights, without them necessarily being fully aware of it, I decided it might be worth discussing.

As it turns out, a family only has *one* year from the time of a murder to file a wrongful death lawsuit. This is why Fred Goldman had to file his civil suit against O.J. prior to the conclusion of the criminal trial. This, perhaps, clarifies the Rochas' decision to file so early. They simply may not have had a choice. It might've been *now* or *never*.

More recently, however, this civil legislation has been updated. Now the statute of limitations for filing a wrongful death lawsuit has been extended to two years, although other reasons still exist for the filing early. Modesto attorney Adam Stewart, who represents Sharon Rocha, stated "The family wants to be sure that Scott suffers the greatest of civil and criminal penalties to the greatest extent that our legal system allows. Mrs. Rocha wants to make sure justice is done, whether it's in a civil court or a criminal court."

I perceived this statement to be somewhat of a milestone in the case. What I mean is that, up until this point, we hadn't heard any actual direct reference or accusation by Laci's family regarding Scott's guilt. With all the defensive public statements coming from Scott's parents, this legal statement from Laci's family is clearly what the public had been waiting to hear from them in regards to their belief about their son-in-law.

In the court documents she filed, Sharon Rocha alleged that "Scott Peterson planned and prepared to assault, batter, and murder Laci Denise Peterson," then killed her and their child in the couple's Modesto home.

Here is an excerpt from the lawsuit: "The imposition of substantial punitive and exemplary damages will in this case be both justified and necessary in order to send out a message from this court to all persons in the United States and throughout the world that such vicious and outrageous savagery inflicted by one human being upon another shall be met with the severest of civil penalties."

The lawsuit seeks in excess of $5 million in damages, as well as reimbursement for funeral expenses, burial costs, legal fees, and other compensation. Perhaps Sharon may have figured that, even if Scott does land on death row, whatever is left of his estate should be liquidated, to compensate for these expenses. I also sincerely like how Sharon deliberately did not invite Scott's family to the funeral, but is going ahead and floating them the bill for it. Right on, Sharon! Just as President George W. Bush tipped his hat to you, Mrs. Rocha, so do I as well.

The lawsuit was filed actually as two separate actions. Sharon Rocha filed the first one as an "individual" bringing wrongful death action against the accused. The second, she filed as an "administrator" of Laci Peterson's estate, and it is entered as a "survival action."

Mark Geragos's brother Matt is handling the civil defense for Scott Peterson. In their Los Angeles-based law firm of Geragos and Geragos, it is Matt Geragos who heads the civil litigation department. As we know, in the criminal trial, a defendant must be found guilty beyond a reasonable doubt, with a *unanimous* verdict from the jurors, in order to convict. However, in a civil litigation trial, a jury needs only to find a defendant liable by a *preponderance* of the evidence. In other words, in a civil matter that only deals with monetary compensation, only nine out of 12 jurors are needed to find a defendant responsible for the murders of which he is accused.

Usually in a civil case, with a lower threshold required for judgement, if a defendant is found guilty in a criminal trial, that generally paves the way for a favorable judgement for the plaintiff in a civil proceeding, as well. The largest compensations generally awarded in civil suits come from "punitive" damages, which require proof of "clear and convincing" evidence. This standard is easier to meet than the criminal one. However, it is more difficult to reach than the civil standard alone.

Citing dwindling funds from the Peterson camp to cover legal costs, Mark Geragos has demanded that prosecutors return the $15,000 in cash that was seized when Scott was arrested, as well as his Ford F-150 truck. The truck was fairly new, so altogether with the cash, Geragos is looking at scraping up another $30,000 this way from his client.

The civil case, of course, is not likely to get underway until the criminal trial has concluded. In the event of not only a criminal conviction, but perhaps a capital sentence, as well, Peterson would be allowed to leave his maximum-security, death row cell, to attend a civil deposition. Unlike the criminal trial, in which Scott retains the constitutional right to plead the Fifth and remain silent, here he would be required to testify and answer all the plaintiff's attorneys' questions. Assuming a long shot and Scott is acquitted, the plaintiffs may seek to subpoena him, and if he refuses to appear, the court can enter judgement against him by default. However, if Scott answers the subpoena by showing up, but he refuses to answer questions by remaining silent on the stand, he could be held in contempt, which is criminal, and he could be sent to jail.

Before moving on to the final results of the change of venue hearing, and what these results could mean, here is a hodge-podge of interesting, miscellaneous facts and figures relating to the case.

Scott had a certain amount of odds in his favor, on which he gambled heavily when he made the decision to abort Laci and Connor. Since he was a career salesman, I hate to say it, but we are dealing with a skilled, bullshit artist—someone who knows how to paint pictures in people's minds, and knows how to tell people what they want to hear. From a skill of lying standpoint, being a salesman is an advantage after a murder, when he can sound smooth, convincing, and reassuring. But from a credibility standpoint, there are many people who simply know from experience not to trust what a salesman tells them, especially when he has a significant motive to lie.

I've even known young women who have said that one of their most important criteria, when determining the eligibility of a bachelor, is to make absolutely certain that the young man's career has nothing to do with sales. These girls obviously are sick of being lied to about major things that affect their relationships.

All in all, from the time Scott Peterson met Amber Frey, around November 19, 2002, up until their last call on February 19, 2003, he called her 125 times, and she dialed him 119 times. As enormous as these numbers may sound, keep in mind that cell phone records indicate every time a user even dials a particular number. Therefore, it can safely be assumed that each party might only have reached the other directly in about one out of every 4 attempts, and for the majority of those unsuccessful attempts, neither of them left messages. We then can assume more realistically that closer to a quarter of these calls resulted in an actual conversation between Scott and Amber.

I remember watching a television news excerpt, in which a reporter asked Scott's father Lee Peterson if he didn't agree that his son had acted "oddly" at the beginning of the investigation. Mr. Peterson's response was, "What is oddly?...Is there a playbook for how someone must behave under these circumstances?"

The reporter apparently said nothing more. Well, I feel Mr. Peterson *did* have a good point here. There is no such playbook for a spouse suspected of murder to adhere to. However, I think I may be able to better answer Lee's questions to the reporter. First, what she meant by "oddly" was the fact that your son Scott was the *only* member of Laci's family who didn't cooperate with police. Second, the police were not the only ones Scott was avoiding. He, unlike all the other family members, refused to make comments to the press. At this point, his behavior would at least invoke a reasonable amount of suspicion to a homicide investigator, who, without any obvious suspects, must at least give this factor some consideration. For instance, it goes without saying that family members who are genuinely concerned that their loved ones may never return aggressively seek publicity to help solve their cases. Scott "oddly" had no interest in doing this.

After the prelim, and during the series of hearings regarding change of venue, it was announced that the Petersons had taken out a $100,000 loan against Scott and Laci's house on Covena Avenue. The reason they gave for this was that it was collateral they were holding against their son for money they lent him for legal fees of that amount. After thinking about this, what struck me as odd was that, with the Petersons' *own* high-level of involvement and participation in their son's case, why would they be even the least bit concerned about him eventually paying them back for legal costs, when the money issue would surely be overshadowed by the reality of death row looming over their son's head? The conclusion I came to was this: Sharon Rocha had just filed a wrongful death suit against Lee and Jackie Peterson's son. Naturally, the Petersons don't want any of Sharon's family's attacks against *their* family to be successful. By taking out a second mortgage, the Petersons are effectively taking most of the equity out of the home, so as to leave it "valueless" in the event of a wrongful death judgement against their son, which Sharon may then collect by seizing the assets, including the largest of these, which is the house. This way the Petersons have made a chess move that forces the bank that holds the mortgage into the number one spot to collect liens on the property, putting the judgement of Rocha's lawsuit as secondary for collection purposes. The bank cannot retrieve the money from Scott's parents, who are the recipients of the original loan amount, because they would, of course, claim that this money belonged to Scott, not them, and thus was consumed by his expensive, defense costs.

In an attempt to block the ruling of the preliminary hearing, Geragos filed a motion seeking to dismiss the double-murder charges. This type of motion is commonly filed after most preliminary hearings in which charges are confirmed for trial, particularly in death penalty cases. The actual motion was twelve pages long. Here are a few excerpts from that motion:

"The police, from the very beginning, decided that their job was to put Scott Peterson on death row (perhaps just because he inconvenienced them by executing his Fifth Amendment privilege *also* from the very beginning). They deliberately ignored any exculpatory evidence, and from day one worked only toward the goal of putting Scott in the gas chamber. (By the way, for many years California has used the gas chamber for executions, but more recently has administered only lethal injections.) There was no evidence at all at the preliminary hearing suggesting Laci's cause of death or Conner's cause of death. It also stretches credulity that an alleged 'murderer on a run for the border' stopped on the way to Mexico to play nine or 18 holes while heading north. Only the geographically challenged would miss the fact that Scott was headed north, which, then and now, is the direction of the *Canadian* border."

Geragos called the prosecution's case "extraordinarily feeble." He wrote that they had only established Scott Peterson as an unfaithful husband, who happened to go fishing on the "same day his wife tragically disappeared."

The basis of the defense motion asserted that there would be no reasonable cause to order Scott to stand trial because the prosecution failed to show at the preliminary hearing that the deaths actually involved a crime. Neither, he said, did they present any physical or circumstantial evidence to indicate Peterson had murdered his wife and unborn son.

This motion was scheduled and heard by Judge Marie Silveira. Her ruling was to uphold the previous ruling: Scott Peterson would stand trial.

One observation I made early on regarding Mark Geragos was that he looked an awful lot like "Meathead" from the *All in the Family,* TV show with Archie Bunker.

During this same hearing, we heard a little sample of Rick Distaso's arguments in courtroom action. This was right before the case was transferred. Apparently the gag order was either lifted or ignored, because many of us saw on TV excerpts of both Geragos and Distaso giving arguments during this defense-filed hearing, in which they tried to throw out the previous judge's ruling from the preliminary exam. Perhaps the reason for no continued gag order during *this* hearing was because it required the courtroom of another judge, since she would be required to make a ruling on another judge's ruling. A new courtroom with a different magistrate would perhaps mean *no gag order.* But anyway, during this hearing we were able to get a first taste of what Rick Distaso's style was like. The clip that I saw showed him responding to a claim Geragos was making about the overmedia-exposed alibi of Scott, which Geragos defended by saying that Scott was not decorating the Christmas tree before going fishing later that day, but rather, that he had gone that *morning.*

Distaso pointed his finger at the judge and then sharply responded with, "People don't just wrap duct tape around themselves and then jump into the bay." Cute. One commentator said it was the first time we heard a little fire from the prosecution, who'd been somewhat subdoed until now. My response to hearing this prosecution argument was a little more like, "Uh oh." What I mean is that this sounded like Distaso fired a shot that went completely in left field from his target. For example, when did Geragos ever contend that they thought Laci committed suicide? I think it was pretty obvious what Geragos was asserting and, of course, that was simply that strangers kidnapped Laci and put the bodies in the bay, to frame Scott. I cringed a little when I heard Distaso's response because he snapped at the judge, as if she should've just known this or something. I think any experienced prosecutor would know that you don't just tell a judge what to do. If it weren't for the majority perspective on this high-profile case and the serious nature of the offense, then Distaso potentially could've been doomed here.

There had been some concerns about whether Distaso and the prosecution would call Cory Carroll, the liaison between Scott and the two Nazi Low Rider hit men with the seedy, tan van, to the witness stand. I have confidence in Distaso as a good prosecutor, but here's what I would do, if I were in his shoes. I'd at least put Cory Carroll on the potential witness list, as an ace in the hole, just in case Geragos plans to call a witness named Diane Campos. I'd have Carroll subpoenaed and ready to go at a moment's notice. Here's why: Right now Mark Geragos's most pivotal witness is Diane Campos, who was the hospital employee who took her morning break in nearby La Loma Park. She is the one who claimed she saw a pregnant female, about Laci's age and matching her description, with a golden retriever that apparently was barking aggressively, and two men that she described as "extremely" dirty that were telling Laci to shut her f———-g dog up.

Geragos seems to almost brag about this witness of his. Every time I've seen him make reference to her, he appears to have such a smug look on face, almost a bit of foolish pride. Assuming this jury has legitimately only received a very *general* media exposure to the case, and perhaps doesn't know about very specific witnesses, such as Cory Carroll, (but maybe they already know about the obvious ones, such as Amber Frey), then Distaso could be straight out of luck, if Geragos calls Ms. Campos to the stand. The testimony of this witness *alone* could be interpreted by the jury as a cause for "reasonable doubt."

Remember, Cory Carroll never said whether he knew that these individuals actually ever went ahead and committed the crime. All he said was that he set up a meeting for Scott Peterson to meet these guys about a car theft, sat in on part of the meeting, and inadvertently heard Peterson inquire about the possibility of kidnapping his wife. For all we know, Scott may have been just shopping around for ways to get rid of Laci, but may have ultimately decided the Nazis were a little too expensive, and perhaps thought a more economical approach to the situation would be to get a small boat and do it himself.

But, either way, whether the jurors believe that Dirty and Skeeter did it, or that Scott did it with his boat, Distaso would still cover his ass. This way, Diane Campos's testimony, along with Carroll's, would only corroborate both theories. For Distaso's information, just in case there is any doubt in his mind about Carroll as a witness, if I were on the jury, and I heard *all* these witnesses, there is simply *no way* I would find Scott anything *but* guilty. With this kind of testimony, it is obvious that either Scott *did* it, or he hired *these* guys to do it. For the jury to believe just a couple of *random* guys did it for no apparent reason, when all this *obvious* motive is blistering from Scott's character, would be absolute lunacy.

Naturally, Distaso might fear that Geragos will tell the jury during closing arguments that the prosecution expects them to believe two entirely different scenarios regarding what happened, and because the burden of proof lies on the accusers, Geragos perhaps might tell the jury that even Distaso doesn't know what happened—hey, was it a murder-for-hire plot? Or did Scott do it? He doesn't even know.

The only flaw in this argument, if Geragos chooses to use it, would be that, when two plausible scenarios exist, one pointing to the defendant's guilt, and the other to his innocence, by law, the jury must choose the one that points to his innocence. However, from the potential testimonies of these particular witnesses, both scenarios would point to Scott's guilt. The jury would have no choice other than to convict Scott Peterson. Distaso could rest assured; either way, he would win. On the other hand, if Distaso fails to call Carroll as a witness, and Geragos goes ahead and calls Campos, the prosecution may be screwed. Now we suddenly have two plausible scenarios, one of Scott's guilt, the other, of his innocence.

If Distaso is worried about Carroll's credibility, he should remember that this witness had absolutely nothing to gain by telling this story. He was only temporarily in custody on very minor charges. There could not have been a motive to make a deal with prosecutors because he never needed a deal. He's not that serious of an offender, by proof of his criminal record.

The legalities of the following situation could turn either way, but I hope those in the legal community, especially in this case, can use it to their advantage. Let me explain: Perhaps Distaso could tell the judge and Geragos up front that he plans to call Carroll only as an "if then" witness, meaning that, the prosecution will call Carroll as a witness, *only* if Geragos calls Campos as a witness. Otherwise, Distaso could explain he has no intention of calling Carroll.

Geragos has yet another witness, who could corroborate the Campos testimony. This particular witness is a police reservist, who happened to see two men shouting at a pregnant female to get into a crusty, tan van. Quite frankly, I don't really think Distaso *has* a choice. With these kinds of circumstances, what else can he do? He had better call Carroll as a witness. The people of the state of California are absolutely entitled to a competent presentation of the prosecution's case. Under *these* conditions, I believe, leaving Carroll out as a witness could be a disastrous mistake, a blunder that will go down in legal history. Otherwise, Geragos may even think to say that these kidnappers of Laci *did* have a motive. She knew her neighbors across the street were leaving for a few days, and perhaps, when she went out to walk her dog that morning, she thought it was odd that these dirty men were carrying the neighbors belongings, including a large safe, from their house into an old rusty van. These burglars had to take care of their only witness.

Judge Girolami reached a decision in the defense's request for change of venue. He allowed the trial to be moved.

A few days after this announcement, several students, who had participated in the surveys used as criteria in the judge's ruling, came forward. This was the 10-county Scott Peterson bias survey compiled by 65 students and overseen by criminal justice professor Stephen Schoenthaler at Cal State Stanislaus. The original results of these questionnaires suggested that more jurors without bias could be located in the Bay Area and Southern California, compared to those available in Stanislaus County. The professor said he had these students poll 1,175 prospective jurors randomly by telephone in late November and early December. He said anywhere from 114 to 122 persons responded in each of California's eight largest counties, as well as San Joaquin and Stanislaus counties. Geragos submitted the survey as an official case exhibit, and the judge referred to it when explaining his ruling to move the trial.

The students admitted to falsifying these survey results. Six students, all seniors, said they made up every answer on all the surveys they submitted because they found it difficult to gather legitimate data. They said they fabricated the results because they were short on time and money.

The class syllabus handed out at the beginning of the fall semester stipulated that 20% of that course's grade would be based on the survey project. Here is the project description from that course outline:

"Each student will be assigned to survey public opinion, attitudes and knowledge on the telephone from 20 people in various parts of California, to test hypotheses that will be done in class. The survey typically takes five or six hours to complete and an hour of practice."

The students said that the surveys required numerous, lengthy, long-distance calls, and that they were given no money for reimbursement. Another senior said she struggled to complete half of the required surveys, then she gave up and faked the rest. Another said she refused to cheat, but didn't have the resources to do the survey, so she didn't—accepting that her grade would be lowered from an "A" to a "C." Also, in violation of survey ethics, three of these eight students said they used answers provided by friends and relatives.

The college students came forward to speak to the media. However, they didn't want to be identified. One sophomore participant said, "We falsified the info. The stuff we submitted wasn't true."

After being informed of the student confessions, Schoenthaler said, "I'm stunned and find it hard to believe. It seems impossible that I could have missed something like that." The professor had given his classes the assignment only two days before Thanksgiving weekend.

A 22-year-old student said, "It's just an asinine thing to make a student do a week before finals. There is no way Schoenthaler can say this is legitimate, because he wasn't there when we supposedly made it up."

A 21 year old reflected, "You just make it up. It's bogus."

A 35-year-old student said, "This is a death penalty case. This guy's life is on the line. I'm absolutely outraged."

Schoenthaler said that while the survey was being conducted, he required students to include the phone numbers they supposedly called when recording data, but that he had not verified *any* by calling them, himself. Among some of the things students said the professor told them was that they could expect people who lived farther away to know less about the case, so they said that they fabricated the survey with this result in mind.

Some of the students said they *would* have come forward sooner, had they known their misrepresentations would be used to help sway a judge making such an important decision. Another law professor had said publicly after the announcement, "The point is to *teach* students, not obtain their labor."

University vice superintendent Diana Demetrulias announced her office would launch an investigation immediately that day, and said that it could take all week. She stated, "We will initiate this in the morning. We take very seriously any scientific misconduct or suggestion of that. We will be working on it." Another spokesman from the university said in regards to this finding that disciplinary measures for dishonest work can range from writing a paper or community service, to suspension or expulsion.

Chief Deputy DA John Goold exclaimed, "Oh, my God. It certainly sounds like this would affect the underpinnings of the judge's decision. If he is aware of impropriety, he can notify the parties to be in court tomorrow, to address the falsity before the court."

In court, Dave Harris cross-examined Professor Schoenthaler, by questioning his motives. He suggested Scoenthaler may have been seeking public recognition, and implied that the survey was poorly drafted, giving students motive and opportunity to falsify their data. The professor testified that nobody hired him or paid him to do that survey or a smaller one back in May. He said he had hoped to provide a public service and possibly to save some taxpayers' money.

Mark Geragos only said publicly on the matter, "Hypothetically speaking, one should never put any credence in anonymous sources."

Shortly thereafter, Dave Harris cited the fraudulent student surveys when he requested the judge to either keep the trial in Modesto, or at least to keep it as close as Sacramento. Girolami denied the request, indicating the survey and testimony from the professor who administered it "were not given much weight" in making his decision. This I could understand. As I mentioned at the start of this chapter, with the type of media circus we were seeing daily out front of that courthouse, the ruling was certainly no surprise, with or without the fraudulent student surveys.

Normally, murder trials aren't considered much of a source of revenue, when one district accepts taking on another county's case. However, the Peterson case was different. After Judge Girolami ruled that *local publicity* warranted the trial to be hosted in a more neutral environment, *four* counties jumped into the lottery pool to host the trial of the new millennium. Cheers of triumph rang out at the convention bureau, when the decision came down that San Mateo County won the sweepstakes to have the double-murder case. Attorneys from both sides of the case asserted that they were pleased with the final choice.

San Mateo won the contest by showing that their 150-seat, public courtroom was ready, open and available, and that the San Francisco Airport is only minutes away for jet commute of lawyers and experts. Conveniently, there happened to be a large vacancy on the San Mateo County Superior Court docket at the right time, rendering the Modesto judge's decision that much easier. The county appeared to be anxious to host the trial with apparent O.J.-type dimensions, which could last for six months or so, which could draw up to 500 journalists and 200 witnesses, and which might generate some $17 million in local spending. It's been described as being proportional to a temporary office park. The Laci Peterson case seemed to be a prize worth cherishing for San Mateo County.

The trial would be held in Redwood City, the San Mateo county seat, which is about 90 miles west of Modesto, on the San Francisco peninsula, and has a population of about 75,000 residents.

11

Potential Closing Arguments

Before I get started, I believe it's important for me to mention a few points. If I were prosecuting this case, final summation is a special area I'd be spending literally hundreds of hours preparing—particularly for a murder trial, which our society considers the ultimate crime. Closing arguments are uniquely important and should be treated somewhat differently in the overall trial strategy of the lead attorney than those of other felony cases. My summation, if I were prosecuting this defendant, would be, perhaps, several hundred transcript pages long. But for the purposes of this book I will make some key points and keep it relatively brief. I should mention also, that one of the main reasons for this minimizing is because my *projected* closing arguments are, naturally, limited under these circumstances, since at this time I don't have at my disposal the actual witnesses' testimony from the trial to come. Having this future information, of course, would have an enormous influence on the content of my final presentation.

[A final note about the prosecution's case, before I begin: If any prosecutor trying this case actually attempts to say Scott made *two* trips to the San Francisco Bay, instead of just one trip to dispose of the bodies, he must be secretly working for the defense, because a jury would surely come back with a "not guilty" verdict, just to spite such an absurd assumption. A tabloid, as well as a popular, nightly panelist, who normally seemed very sharp and competent in her interpretations of the state's evidence, actually tried to float this theory. Her reason? She thought the defendant would *not* have disposed of the body in broad daylight with people around, when he said he went fishing. What this panelist is failing to realize is the enormity of the San Francisco Bay. It stretches for many miles in all directions, and obviously, on Christmas Eve, there would be even *fewer* people there than usual. All Scott would simply need to do is wait for the nearest passing sailboat to drift beyond a close visual distance, then slip, there goes pregnant Laci's small body over the side. It wouldn't be hard at all for a guy like Scott to be careful in carrying out his plot during the day, with the freshly-murdered victims tightly wrapped (like figs in a blanket) in a blue tarp along with some bricks, secured with duct tape, and packaged on the floor of his boat. His only problem, which probably got him a little panicky, was his embarrassing performance of trying to back his boat trailer down the boat ramp without having much experience backing trailers up.]

Prosecution:

Ladies and gentlemen of the jury, good afternoon.

I wanted to start out by thanking each and every one of you for all your outstanding patience throughout the length of this enduring trial.

In a murder trial, if a prosecution team were presenting a circumstantial case based on statistical evidence alone, it would certainly be a good day for the defense. However, in this case, we, as prosecutors, will be using much statistical data *to support* both the circumstantial and physical evidence we do have, but certainly we'll not be considering this as evidence by itself, unless overwhelming circumstances prove otherwise.

For example, it's been determined within U.S. criminal history that, in 9 out of 10 cases in which *pregnant* women had been killed, the perpetrator was, in fact, the *impregnator*.

This statistic, alone, puts Scott Peterson in an extremely small percentile, if he, in fact, were innocent. In other words, there's a 90 percent (an A-grade) chance that he *did* do it, and only a 10 percent (a low F grade) chance that he *didn't* do it. Again, this is simply because Laci happened to be pregnant at the time.

So, starting out, it doesn't look good for Scott. This fact establishes from the get go that the odds are against him.

Let's now add to this statistical equation the fact that Scott provided the investigators with a peculiar alibi.

Let's assume that some people actually do go fishing on Christmas Eve. Let's face it—Scott's boat was certainly not the only boat out on the bay that day. In fact, I'm sure there were quite a few others, almost perhaps, as many as on any other day. But in how many of the other fishing, sailing, or motor boats was the occupant all by himself? I doubt very many.

So, not only is the alibi itself "fishy," but Scott also happens to have no one to *corroborate* his alibi.

This narrows that 10 percent (chance that he could be innocent) down even further, that Scott could be anything but guilty, perhaps now to only a 5-percent chance that he could be innocent.

Now, let's continue to add to that statistical equation the fact that, 3 months later, sure enough, the remains of his wife and unborn son do wash up near the spot of Scott's *supposed* alibi at the Berkeley Marina. This, then, would drop that percentage down to, perhaps, a 2- or 3- percent chance that Scott could possibly be innocent.

As the prosecutor I would like, at this time, to read a statement by **Mark Geragos**, the defendant's lead lawyer, who had responded publicly regarding Laci and Conner's bodies washing on the shore near where the defendant went fishing, prior to Mr. Geragos being hired by the defendant. Here is that exact quote: "It would be hard pressed to find a prosecutor who couldn't put together an indictment, let alone a conviction. It would have to be the greatest of circumstances and coincidences to be otherwise. When you put all that together, there are people sitting in state prison convicted on less evidence than this."

Now let's assume for a minute that Mr. Geragos is going to change his story and claim that anyone could have put those bodies in the bay. Especially since this location was obviously no secret: the entire world knew the Modesto Police were looking for Laci's body in San Francisco Bay, because everybody knew that *that* is where Scott claimed he went fishing on Christmas Eve, the day his wife disappeared.

Now, the only flaw in this "other killer" theory is that all it requires is for anybody to take one look at the autopsy report, to see that the bodies of Connor and especially Laci had been decomposing in the seawater for months. This would mean that, if the "other killer" theory is correct, this person would have needed a pond of seawater in his backyard, in which to let the bodies decompose, so that when he brought them back to the bay, they'd be in the same condition in which they were *actually* found. In other words, it would be doubtful that, if the bodies had been in a backyard or a trunk of a car for the duration of that time (several months) when the police were looking in the bay, that the remains would still be in that kind of condition.

More realistically, Laci was a small person in a vast ecosystem of water, along with with tens of thousands of different types and sizes of creatures, as well as a whole multitude of other decomposing debris and plant life. No matter how advanced the police technology was, or no matter how long they searched, the likelihood of finding her under those types of conditions would, realistically, be very slim.

So, more than likely, her body did, in fact, eventually rise to the surface, after a certain amount of underwater erosion loosened the head and hands, shackled to cement weights, from the rest of her body. As enough tides came in, she and her son *did* eventually wash up.

Also, more likely, Scott felt compelled to use the fishing alibi against his better judgment, since he knew he was seen by several other people at the Marina, who could fairly easily identify him, his truck, and his boat. Scott knew that at least someone had to have seen him towing his boat that day, if not at the marina, then just as likely in the parking lot by his warehouse, or just about anywhere he went that day, for that matter.

Well, since Mr. Geragos has already made his opinion in the case public, changing his opinion now at least proves *one* thing: the defense lawyer in this case is admitting he was wrong. (Pause) Well, how do we know that he's not wrong now? (Pause) In other words, as soon as he's hired by the defense in a case of this magnitude, suddenly he says he was wrong and for some reason adamantly believes another theory directly favorable to the defendant who hired him.

Of course, that is the defense lawyer's job, and I'm certainly not denying that, and there have been times in history, when it *was* the prosecution who was wrong, and not the defense. However, as prosecutors, we need only to seek the truth. We believe the truth stands strongly in this case, because the evidence concretely supports it.

Now, let's further add to that equation: the most shocking news of all that was delivered to Laci's family—the Amber Frey affair.

[Several of Laci's family members, back when Amber came forward, announced publicly that they were dropping their support for Scott—Brent and Amy, for example, Laci's brother and half sister. Sharon Rocha and Ron Grantski remained neutral, at least at this stage in the ever-developing case against Scott.]

Before I discuss Amber, I want to mention a few more things about the victim and the killer.

As we know, Laci and Conner's bodies washed ashore. Shortly thereafter, DNA verified their identities. No weapon ballistics or blood evidence from Laci was found, leading investigators to believe that she had been strangled. As the evidence will continue to show, we believe, without any doubt, the person responsible for this shocking atrocity, is none other than Scott Peterson, the defendant, Laci's husband.

To illustrate what this unfortunately, but truly, means, the defendant would have had to put his own "loving" hands around his unsuspecting wife's neck. One can only imagine the rush of thoughts that must have permeated the young, pregnant woman's mind, in her last few minutes of consciousness, knowing the imminence of her untimely death. As Laci looked into the cold murderous eyes of the man whom she had considered her loving husband, he slowly squeezed his masculine fingers harder and harder around her throat, until her last dying gasp. The man who was supposed to love her had decided, for some insane reason that was unknown to Laci, that she must die and must endure not only the terrible suffering of her last moments before death, but must die with something that only could have lingered on her struggling, dying lips, the unanswered question of **"why?"**

But now we do know **why**. There are probably *several* reasons; however, here is the reason that we believe actually triggered Scott Peterson's fatal decision.

Amber Frey announced publicly that she had met Scott on November 20, 2002. She admitted to having had a romantic affair with him, which implies that they were very recently sexually active. Or in other words, the affair was "hot on the pan." This now adds purpose and reason to why Scott felt compelled to commit the unthinkable.

Apparently, Scott had found that the sex he was having with Amber was good. This is not surprising, since Amber keeps herself in shape by going to the gym regularly. Scott, apparently, with this new relationship with Amber, began to experience a *longing* to be single again. To be single…with no strings attached.

He already had lied to Amber, by saying he had "lost" his wife, which we confirmed from the wiretapped phone call admitted into evidence. Naturally, everyone's question is, "How did he 'lose' his wife several weeks **before** she was 'lost'?"

When Amber Frey asked him this exact question, the defendant responded that he couldn't explain it to her right then, and that he needed to protect them both.

Ladies and gentlemen, this was indeed a case of **self-fulfilling prophecy** on the part of Scott Peterson. Evidently, the defendant, for some uncanny reason, already knew he was going to "lose" his wife, several weeks before she *was* lost. How convenient to know in advance about something, which would reassure a new lover that she had nothing to worry about. Either that, or Scott Peterson just happened to be the world's luckiest man, and actually had his lie mysteriously come true.

Scott knew that, if he divorced Laci "legally," it would probably take as long as a year to be completed, mainly because of the complications of both Conner and the real estate being in both spouses' names. By that time, Amber would be long gone. Not to mention that she'd be "shattered" by the discovery of the colossal lie he had told her. Scott knew he had to prevent this from happening.

Amber owned her own home. Scott told Amber truthfully that he owned *his* own home. But what he didn't tell her was that he still had a wife, who legally *owned* half of his house, too.

Again, I'm sure killing Laci was the last thing in the world Scott really *wanted* to do. In fact, I would say he was almost as repulsed by the idea as much as anyone else would be. But there comes a time in every man's life, when he finds himself stuck between a rock and a hard place, where there simply *is* no other way out, other than an extreme course of action. He simply had to weigh and balance the alternatives. Since Scott, for reasons of his own, probably had determined that the rest of his life would be better suited with *Amber* rather than with Laci, this was one of the most extreme decisions Scott would ever have to justify.

It was either pay child support for the next 18 years and alimony until the day that Laci remarries, with *no* insurance payoff, or simply eliminate the child support and alimony payments before they even begin, and on top of that, be rewarded for his bold crime with a fairly sizable life-insurance settlement.

Scott relied heavily on two factors. One, he knew that everyone would find it extremely hard to believe that a person of his character would actually commit such an atrocity. Two, he knew, unlike a lot of men who just work in offices every day, that he was a somewhat skilled outdoorsman, trained and experienced in various methods of disposal relating to his work in the fertilizer industry, and he had a college education from a somewhat prominent university, as well. So, he felt more intelligent and more privileged than the average person, which only served to escalate his confidence in carrying out the perfect crime, not to mention building his ego to the point that he felt more deserving of the option of murder.

So, let's now take a closer look at these compelling factors that Scott seemingly relied upon so heavily. The two cases that come to mind in which the prime suspect in a murder investigation gambled heavily on the "disbelief" factor are those of O.J. Simpson and Lizzy Borden. For example, in the Simpson case, O.J., because of his fame and fortune alone, knew that people would be saying, "No, there's just simply no way the 'Juice' would do this. Why would a man who has everything just throw it away over one woman, like that?" But, again, Simpson already knew that an overwhelming number of people would be saying that. It wouldn't take any special genius to figure this out, if one were in his shoes. Lizzy Borden knew the "disbelief" factor would be even more overwhelming in her case. Certainly there were no axe-wielding murderers roaming her neighborhood with any apparent motive for the crime, but to believe that such a harmless girl from such an upstanding family could possibly stoop to this level of evil, by murdering her parents for their money, again was apparently even more unthinkable. Having this basic knowledge, and being unlike most young women of her status, she actually had the balls to carry it out. But ultimately, both these defendants were acquitted for largely no other reason than what *they* already knew before committing these murders, the power of the disbelief factor. (It is true, however, that in the O.J. case, other factors, including race, influenced his acquittal.)

The other factor Scott relied upon, along with his outdoor skills, was that he felt assured that Laci's disappearance would only muster about as much media attention as did the Evelyn Hernandez case. Maybe there would be one local newspaper article, and after enough time elapsed, he thought, it would be pretty much forgotten altogether, as a lot of these disappearance cases are. He knew that, since they were a married couple, this fact would justify finding any DNA from either of them at the home, which he probably *did* expect police to search. Any high-tech, forensic examinations of his boat and truck, or continued monitoring of his whereabouts, lifestyle, and behavior, he did *not* expect, because he knew, like everyone else, that these types of investigations are more consistent with *actual* homicide cases and generally not used for the average "missing persons" case. To him, that's all this was going to be, simply another missing persons report, among thousands already out there on milk cartons, postcards, etc. He figured it would be years, if ever at all, before her remains would turn up.

Unfortunately, in this case, Scott didn't listen to his better angels. It was the dark side, to him, that appeared to be the better option, as if the crime would be almost *foolproof* that he could pull it off. He knew an average person probably *would* get caught, but Scott certainly didn't consider himself average. He believed in his own mind that only an exceptional guy like himself *could* successfully pull this one off. He had made the final decision regarding his future—that it would be in his best interest to get a late-term abortion. Except, in Scott's case, the abortion was not just to terminate Conner, but included Laci, as well. How would she **not** get in the way in Scott's new life with Amber? Oh no, Laci wouldn't be mad about Scott leading her on, all the way right up until the birth of Conner, and then saying, "I want out," as if there's no such thing as alimony or child support. Scott gave in to the temptations of selfishness and greed. He felt he had the disposal skills and charisma to get away with it. As we can see, Scott most certainly was **not** expecting or prepared for the national media attention the case almost immediately received. He may have even *picked* Christmas Eve on purpose to commit this crime, knowing this one holiday, above all others, surely would be the one for which the fewest reporters and police would likely leave their families and come out to investigate. Especially since the majority of missing person cases filed are not even necessary, since, more times than not, the missing persons simply show up the next day.

He wasn't expecting national media attention, so he figured Amber would have no way of finding out who he *really* was. He was confident enough in his ability to dispose of these bodies quickly and permanently, and he obviously didn't expect the remains to ever surface, at least not so soon. But there *was* massive media attention, and Amber *did* find out, and she came forward. The bodies *did* eventually surface, showing both Scott's hastiness and his lack of experience at body disposal. Scott, during the police-recorded conversation with Amber, even tried, as a last attempt to persuade her not to go to authorities, to use charm and romance to prey on her previous love for him, all to no avail.

We heard from Bruce Peterson (no relation to Scott), the previous owner of the boat that Scott needed for his notorious Christmas Eve fishing trip. When police took this gentleman out to inspect the boat as evidence, Bruce said he noticed cement residue in the bottom of the craft, that hadn't been there before. Eyebrows were already being raised about Scott's new boat. *One*, most people considered the day he chose for christening the vessel with its maiden voyage to be significantly strange, Christmas Eve, which, of course, was also the day his wife disappeared. *Two*, he told investigators he was fishing for sturgeon that day. Well, the boat is only 14 feet long, which, by common sense, is way too small to be pulling in *this* kind of fish, which averages six feet in length. A small, aluminum boat like that is made for lake fishing, and to take it out on the vast and severely choppy San Francisco Bay is a bit extreme—unless, of course, he needed a much larger and deeper body of water in which to sink a body, where it would be less likely to be recovered, than from a lake. *Three*, he had just gotten the boat very recently before his wife's disappearance, and he had hidden it over at his warehouse, so that nobody in the family knew of the boat, until after Laci had vanished. And *four*, he purchased the boat within a day of telling his mistress that he "lost" his wife. Now, are all these factors just coincidences, as well? I'm sure Mr. Peterson would like you to think so.

We know that Scott made a fatal error when he inspected his boat for evidence he may have left behind, before returning it to his warehouse that deadly day. When attempting to carry out the perfect murder, he overlooked the pliers he had left under one of the boat's seat cushions, which had a strand of Laci's hair in them.

December 10, 2002, when Scott purchased the boat, was just three weeks after he had met Amber Frey at the Elephant Bar in Fresno. Interestingly, this was the same day that Amber had asked him if he'd ever been married, to which Scott responded with a sob story about having "lost" his wife. This was no coincidence. It makes sense that the young man was well obsessed with his new lover by this point and had to come up with a serious plan of action, to cover his monumental lie.

One last thing before I conclude. Scott, when asked publicly whether police might find blood in his truck, said that yes, it wouldn't surprise him because he remembered cutting his knuckle on his toolbox the day Laci disappeared. Now, members of the jury, if you could all hold your hands out in front of yourselves for a second and see if any of you happened to cut yourself last night, you know, enough so that you would've bled in your vehicle, too.

I know there have been times in the last couple of years when I've cut myself, when I was, in fact, bleeding, but I also know that I've been able to wrap it with some type of bandage before it ever got in my truck. But, gosh, the last time I cut myself badly enough to bleed on anything at all, where there would be enough traces of blood evidence to be discovered, would probably be only once in a span of years. But Scott not only cut himself like this within a year of Laci disappearing, not only within a month, not only within a week, but actually on the *day* she was reported missing. But like all these other coincidences, I guess this was just another coincidence, too. Right, Scott? (The prosecutor could then look over at Scott for dramatic purposes.) From Scott's standpoint, though, it's understandable that he needed an excuse to explain to police the reason for fresh blood being found in his truck around the time Laci disappeared.

As do any prosecutors evaluating the evidence in a murder case, we seriously have to consider three factors before formally charging a suspect. These three points are as follows, motive, opportunity, and physical evidence.

Some cases are successfully prosecuted when only two of these three pieces of the investigative pie are solved. But in this case, we went farther than that. Not only do we have all three, but we even considered the *strength* of each of these three principles.

Did this defendant have a significant motive?

Yes. We were all shocked, when Amber Frey came forward to reveal the affair Scott had been hiding from investigators and Laci's family, especially when this was confirmed on the wiretapped call, in which Scott, in his own words, admits to Amber that he claimed he had "lost" his wife only weeks before Laci's disappearance.

Did the defendant have the opportunity to commit the murder?

Absolutely. He claimed he went fishing by himself on Christmas Eve, the day Laci disappeared. The defendant had no other person as an alibi to confirm his whereabouts.

Is there physical evidence tying the suspect to the homicide?

Indeed, there is. Laci's hair was found in Scott's boat, which he claims he launched that day for the very first time, so we know Laci could *not* have been in the boat before. Plus, it was determined during execution of the search warrants, that Scott had washed only the clothes he wore that day, and had mopped the floor, even though it had just been mopped the day before. The most condemning element of *physical* evidence was the location of Laci and Conner's bodies. They washed up in the same bay where the defendant told investigators he had been fishing when the victims disappeared.

Did the defendant have the physical means to carry out such a crime?

Sure enough, he was driving a truck with a loaded gun in the glove compartment, and with a boat in tow, the day his wife disappeared.

And the list goes on and on…

Ladies and gentlemen of the jury,…does the fact that 90 percent of all pregnant, murdered women were killed by their lovers, *and* that Scott went fishing by himself Christmas Eve day, when his wife vanished, mean that he killed her?

(Pause)

No…it does not.

Does the fact that Scott Peterson told Amber Frey that he had "lost" his wife, three weeks before Laci disappeared, mean that Scott murdered Laci?

No…it does not.

Does the fact that Scott secretly bought a boat shortly before Laci vanished, then only used it on the day she disappeared, and that one of Laci's hairs was found in the pliers on that boat, mean that Scott murdered Laci?

No...it does not.

Does the fact that Laci's murdered body and that of her child, washed up on the shores of San Francisco Bay, within the actual location of where Scott said he was fishing when Laci went missing, mean that Scott killed her?

No...it does not.

Do *any* of these pieces of evidence and statistical information, *by themselves*, mean that Scott Peterson murdered his wife, Laci?

(Pause)

No...they do not.

But when you put all these factors together, as they *did* fall naturally into place while the case developed, and step back for a minute to look at the big picture, all these pieces of evidence point to *one* person, and one person *only*. (Prosecutor then pivots to point his finger directly at the accused.) And that person is none other than Scott Peterson. The probable likelihood of Scott actually being innocent is so remote that this possibility drops to the range of perhaps one one-hundredth of a percent.

In fact, you could remove a large portion of the evidence against Scott Peterson and *still* have more evidence than what was needed to convict most people sitting on death row today.

Ladies and gentleman...any verdict other than guilty not only would thwart justice, but might send out the *wrong* message to hundreds of thousands of other young men who may, sometime in their lives, be faced with a similar dilemma.

Also, a commonsense glance at the overall facts would indicate that a person would have to be pretty naïve not to be certain of guilt beyond a reasonable doubt.

I now ask each of you, ladies and gentleman of the jury,...for the sake of justice...for the sake of the missing woman's mother, Sharon Rocha...her father, Dennis Rocha...her stepfather, Ron Grantski...her brother, Brent Rocha...and her sister, Amy Rocha...who all know exactly who murdered their beautiful loved one, and who I'm sure you all know as well. That person, of course, is none other than the defendant, Scott Peterson!...Now I ask that you return the *right* verdict...a verdict of **GUILTY** and convict this man responsible for the heinous murders of Laci and her son, Conner...*who now cry out from their graves*...for justice.

Thank you.

(Prosecutor nods reassuringly to the jury and then takes his seat.)

(Potential) Defense Closing Arguments

If I were to take on a client for defense, first I would want to be assured of his innocence. For example, I would request that this defendant take a full polygraph exam and pass. If the case were not high profile, I would contact the prosecutor, to see what significant evidence is being held against this individual. In fact, I would be up front with my reasons for inquiring, telling the prosecutor that I was considering taking on this defendant's case. That way, the prosecutor would be more willing to show his hand of cards, because he would know that if I were to see that he has a strong case against this defendant, I might be inclined to decline representing him. Thus, the prosecutor could expect a less talented lawyer to take the case.

In the Peterson case, I'm more inclined to believe I'd be defending a guilty person, and therefore, under normal conditions, would decline to offer representation. But with the kind of defense I've seen so far, I thought it would be in everyone's interest to present a few arguments I would certainly include to a jury.

A classic example of where the prosecutors dropped the ball in a high-profile case is, of course, none other than Marcia Clark and Chris Darden, in the O.J. Simpson case. One of the ways they succeeded in failing was similar to the way a child practices piano for the first time all week, a half hour before his or her teacher comes over. Those of you who remember 5th grade, when a lot of us used to practice this way, know from experience that it doesn't work. We now know, as mature adults, especially if we have kids who are going to start piano lessons soon, how <u>we</u> would do it, if we were taking lessons again. Imagine if you were to sit down at the piano a half hour after your music teacher leaves, while the new information he or she just taught you is fresh in your mind, and you started practicing right then for a half hour, and then a half hour daily, until he or she arrived again the following week. *You* may not think you're any good, but your teacher would say, "Wow, you *are* serious. That sounds really good." Imagine if you were to continue this practice, as mentioned, for an entire year, which technically is what we were supposed to do in the first place. We all say this is how we are going to do it, but when it comes down to it, many of us don't. Procrastination, distractions, family holidays, and general excuses get in the way.

Marcia Clark and Chris Darden decided to capitalize on their newfound fame while still in the middle of the trial. They were described, by several, reliable sources, as being seen at many of the local nightclubs on a nightly basis, throughout the duration of the trial. They, obviously, celebrated too soon. I'll say this much, evidently they were not working on their closing arguments during this time, when they should have been. I personally have a different philosophy regarding this type of fame, and how it can be far more effectively employed—**Bust your rear by burning the midnight oil every night on the case during the time it is pertinent so, that you don't go down in history as one of the world's biggest losers.** I'm no protester of celebrating, especially in the high social circles this newfound status would bring a person. However, if the media are coining the case another trial of the century, you'll find your fame is every bit as strong for at least another year after the trial, if not longer. So, if you feel compelled to party every night because of your fame, why not wait until it's over…and be a winner! This way you can bask in far more glory *and* not have to feel guilty about being there, because you've already *won* the "Super Bowl."

Right now, the Peterson case is considered to be the closest thing to the trial of the new millennium. If I were the lead attorney for either side in this case, believe me, if ever there were a time in my life to put my greatest piece of work out there for the world to view, I would, without hesitation, make my performance, especially the final summation, my magnum opus.

When a professor grades your paper, he's not stupid. He knows which papers were written the night before, versus the ones that had been worked on daily since the assignment was given. The grades given will always reflect this. Something that has been worked on over time can be honed, modified, improved, and fortified with much more proper meaning, thought, and insight, than something which might still be good, but was only worked on more briefly.

I should mention here, as well, that even with closing arguments as strong as these, I've seen cases lost simply because there wasn't enough adequate case-in-chief presented. For example, not enough effective witnesses, not enough thorough cross-examination, etc. A good, final summation is no substitute for a good case-in-chief, but in a murder trial, which America considers to be the ultimate crime, a decent trial lawyer should do more than a good job of both.

I am not ashamed to admit it. If I were bestowed the honor of being hired as the lead defense lawyer in a high-profile case such as this—yes, indeed, I would be trying to win an Academy Award.

But, again, I am not the one. So, instead, I will give a relatively small sample of my possible closing arguments for a trial of this nature, which should at least give some demonstration of the passion I would include. This is my free trial consultation. May those in practice use my insight to more effectively seek justice.

(In addition, I will also include what, perhaps, the real defense might include in *their* closing arguments, as opposed to just my own. For example, I don't think I'd be able to bring myself to say such awful things about Amber Frey. Again, be forewarned that there will be some very offensive remarks being directed at different participants in the trial, so I remind readers once more, that these are only *hypothetical* or *imaginary* arguments but *are* based, of course, on true circumstances, true people, and true places relating to the case.)

Defense:

Ladies and gentlemen of the jury, let me start out today by thanking each of you for your patience during this very trying ordeal. Your tolerance and cooperation have been greatly appreciated. The good news is that we are at least approaching the beginning of the end.

I would like to start out by talking about a witness whom the prosecution brought forward, the convicted felon who was burglarizing the house across the street from the Petersons on the morning Laci disappeared.

There was some speculation in the beginning that Laci, upon leaving to walk her dog, may have been a partial eyewitness to this burglary and thus succumbed to her ultimate fate because of it. But police were a little set back by Scott Peterson who arrogantly refused to take a polygraph **because that was his constitutional right.**

(Raising my voice here) **But the prosecution actually had the audacity to put this burglar on the stand…as a key witness!** (Pause) **A dirt-ball, low-life criminal!**

This person had absolutely nothing to lose at this point, and everything to gain, by simply telling the prosecution what they wanted to hear, to help them to build a stronger case against Peterson.

Here is what this individual had to gain. He may have been looking at a third felony strike for this burglary. Do you think that, if he had testimony valuable to the trial of the millennium, then the DA's office wouldn't cut him some slack? (Pause) **I bet they would drop all charges against him, but only <u>after</u> he testifies and only <u>if</u> it is favorable to the prosecution!**

A skilled career criminal, with a rap sheet like this man's, is also a skilled liar by trade. When a person like this needs to come up with a quick hustle, to score some dope, what does he do? He lies. He lies about his car stalling down the street, so that he can more effectively panhandle some gas money off you. Except, guess what?...**There's no car down the street.** But this individual knows from street experience that most people would be more inclined to give him money, if they thought it was for a one-time, legitimate purpose, rather than the truth, which is to get his next heroin fix.

But, also, sometimes this individual has learned that a lie can come across as genuine, if he does one thing...(Pause) temporarily believe the lie in his own mind. This is what actors actually do, when being filmed, to outwardly appear more sincere and genuine to their audience.

If someone were to report this suspicious individual to police, when he's about to commit a burglary, he would be professional enough in his trade to have already thought up a lie for being in the neighborhood. Again, a lie.

Career criminals live a life of lies. They thrive on it.

Ladies and gentlemen of the jury, **Scott Peterson is the complete opposite of this character.**

The man has never been in trouble with the law in his life.

No arrests, no convictions, nothing!

Why? Because the man is <u>not</u> a criminal!

He is nothing but a hard-working, upstanding citizen.

And he has proven that with an impeccably clean record.

(Sarcastically) Sure, this burglar just happened to see Scott Peterson loading a heavy tarp sack onto his truck the morning he was about to burglarize that house.

It would be a great deal more plausible that Laci may have happened to catch this suspicious man breaking into her neighbor's house, but because she was pregnant, she was no match for him, so he just took care of this witness…permanently.

The difference between cheating on one's wife and burglarizing homes professionally…**is a quantum leap!**

Hell, we've even seen presidents and congressmen cheat on their wives. I'm not saying it's right, but burglarizing homes? **My God!**

When the burglar was asked on the stand why he came forward with this information, he said that he felt for Laci's family, that he had a soft heart. **Soft heart?! What, are you kidding? Where was this guy's soft heart, when he was burglarizing this family's home?**

I just thought it might be interesting to consider the credibility of these individuals when determining which opposing testimony to believe, Scott's or the burglar's.

One way to compare would be to remember what the people who knew Scott best said about his possible involvement when Laci first disappeared. They said: No way! Not Scott. Absolutely not! Not in a million years would Scott be capable of this atrocious crime. Now, let's compare these people's testimony about Scott to the testimony of the burglary victim's regarding the burglar. After having $50,000 worth of family heirlooms, jewelry, and other life savings stolen from their home, while they were away visiting relatives for the holidays, if these victims had been asked if they thought the perpetrators might be involved in the disappearance of Laci on the morning of the burglary, I'm sure they would give a resounding, "**Yes!**"

    I want to mention the totally incompetent way in which police handled this investigation. After the lead detective dreamt up a theory within the first 8 hours of the investigation, the police worked the case backwards from there. In other words, if a lead came in, and it didn't fit their theory, they refused to investigate it. These *detectives* (saying the word with a sarcastic overtone) would investigate a lead, **only** if it fit in with their already "prefabricated" theory! In fact, the only evidence whatsoever that they say shows Laci left in a vehicle from her home that day rather than on foot, is because of what a dog handler interpreted.

    …**a dog handler!** Incredible. And they want to prosecute this man for a double homicide?

    Then, to add insult to injury, a very credible eyewitness had seen Laci walking her dog the morning she disappeared, and she tried for weeks to phone the tip in. The police, making one excuse after another, almost completely ignored her. Here was an actual eyewitness account of the missing woman herself, *the whole reason for the investigation*, just brushed off, as though it were meaningless. If a lead doesn't fit their theory, by golly, they won't investigate it! They *deliberately and maliciously* were ignoring key evidence. They didn't care if their only suspect might be innocent. They knew that there have been some cases in which the husband *was* guilty, so they ended their investigation right there. They weren't going to listen to anyone else. Period.

Unfortunately, this eyewitness has since passed away, but we did see her husband, a three-term city council member, take the stand to confirm the sighting.

(Here the prosecution most likely will object, due to hearsay. If it is overruled, then Geragos could continue.)

These so-called investigators actually expect you to believe the interpretations of a dog's behavior is more reliable than an **actual eyewitness** who is human, who knew Laci, who is very credible, and who was sure of the day, since it was an obvious holiday.

Ladies and gentlemen of the jury (he makes eye contact with all of them)…can you believe the audacity of these cops?

(Most likely, Geragos has pulled whatever strings he can, to examine the employment and disciplinary record of Detective Al Brochini. This is likely to occur, since Johnnie Cochran penetrated the LAPD personnel files, in an attempt to expose any delinquencies on Mark Fuhrman and found it surprising that no one else on the great "Scheme Team" was prepared to do this. What information Geragos may find, is unknown.)

The prosecution claims Detective Al Brochini found one of Laci's hairs in a pair of pliers on Scott's boat. But lo and behold,…we don't have just one hair, as the so-called detective originally contended, **but now we suddenly have two!**

Ladies and gentlemen, this overly ambitious detective, so hot to solve a big homicide case and get a notch on his belt, has *deliberately and maliciously* planted a second hair from Laci's brush, that he found in her bathroom, onto the innocent defendant's boat!

(If Geragos chooses to say this, the prosecution will most likely object, due to conjecture. If I were the lead defense lawyer on this case, I would not make this "evidence planting" accusation at all. I believe any intelligent juror would scoff at this notion as being absurd. The prosecution will undoubtedly contend that the hair just naturally split into two over time while in the envelope. I thought I'd print it like this anyway, because I heard that this is Geragos's biggest gun.)

Now let's talk for a minute about Scott's infidelity as a motive for murder.

Laci caught Scott cheating in 1998, but she forgave him, and they went on with their lives. If it weren't for Laci's disappearance, none of us would even know about Amber Frey.

Can you imagine how many times Scott continued this practice throughout his marriage? Can you imagine how many times Laci simply didn't catch Scott or was too embarrassed to talk about other incidents of him cheating. Laci showed good common sense as a person, and it is common sense not to talk about the negativities of your own husband, which ultimately reflects badly on you, as his wife. Laci, especially, would adhere to this principle, since she was high up in social circles. As a general rule of thumb, most people won't tell you about something as embarrassing to them as a spouse cheating.

So, now that we know Scott apparently had no qualms about cheating on Laci, let's take a look at Amber Frey.

(Let's go ahead and assume the defense had subpoenaed Josh Hart, the male stripper, to testify about the bizarre relationship *he* had with Amber, which would exemplify the "total disregard for a pregnant female's husband" concept, that we'll elaborate on in a minute.)

Amber Frey already had a kid!

Why in the world would a guy like Scott, with <u>his</u> family background, be interested in an unwed mother?

Does the prosecution actually expect you to believe that Scott would want to raise someone else's kid for the next eighteen years, **when he was about to have his <u>own</u> son, his own flesh and blood?!**...Finally, his own child, something Scott had been waiting years for, someone he had built a whole nursery for, with his bare hands. (Not to mention that, usually all males, deep down inside, want their first born to *be* a son.)

Does the prosecution expect you to believe that he would throw away the opportunity to have this child with Laci, a former cheerleader? Isn't this the ultimate American dream? Your wife, the mother of your children—was a cheerleader. How much prouder could you be?

All for what?...A masseuse? A woman who gives men massages for a living? Many people would parallel this to prostitution. Just look up "massage" in the phone book, and what do you see? It's about the same as looking up "escort." You'll see Amber's phone number, that's what you'll see.

For those who think Amber Frey was only in the legitimate end of the massage business, think again. Look at all these damning, nude photos of her, in all kinds of provocative positions, which had been sold publicly, prior to her involvement. **That**, ladies and gentlemen, is the real Amber Frey. **Taking money for sex!**

(Perhaps Mark Geragos, who is already famous, could pass on some of the dirty work to his colleague, Kirk McAllister. Perhaps he could sub-out the "Amber" part of the closing arguments to his associate, as is done in most high-profile murder trials. Perhaps Geragos, as lead attorney for the defense team, may also direct McAllister to conduct Amber's cross-examination as well. In that way, Kirk would be the attorney most prepped for this type of a closing argument. Hey, Kirk, you only live once, you know. You might as well go down in history as a great one, by taking a victory for your client. Why not be a winner? Why not let this conquest show on your resume for the public to see. In that way, you can be hired in the future by some of the really "big" names. Go on, Kirk! Show the world what you can do for your clients, when they pay you the big bucks! You've got nothing to lose. Why don't you just go ahead…and do it!)

We heard from the body builder/babysitter whom Amber's father hired to guard his daughter, while she was a teenager. (This is assuming, of course, that this person will be subpoenaed and will testify. Let's further assume that, during cross-examination, the defense lawyer will get this witness to admit that part of her hiring criteria had to with a "sexual" problem of Amber's, which, of course, would explain Amber's unusual age to be needing a babysitter. Here is, perhaps, what a clever lawyer could do, to exploit such an opportunity.)

We now know the real reason why this "babysitter" was really hired. Amber was no baby! She was a full teenager! A teenager who couldn't control her own body!

(His gray hair and wizened, aged features show decades of established and mature, legal expertise. He appears, at this moment, the master, in heroic proportions, of the courtroom. McAllister pivots toward the jury, as would Abraham Lincoln. With his palm up and fingers fanned out in a curved upward position, he looks directly into the eyes of the jurors with a penetrating glare from within his deep-set eyes, wizened from age. In a deep, yet golden voice, he speaks…)

They needed a big, body-builder woman to hold back this tough little one. Otherwise, Amber had to go out there and "do" everything with two legs and a penis, just to satisfy her own selfish and insatiable appetite for biological pleasure...at the expense and total disregard for the females of any other men.

(At this point the prosecution immediately rises. "Objection, your honor! He's trying to make something out of nothing!"...**Judge**: "Overruled."...The closing arguments then continue.)

Amber had a sister, Ava, who was only three years older than she. We know Amber's sister is *one,* too. Where does she work?...In a massage parlor! (Again, the factual information is based on public interviews from reputable publications. **No** tabloids were used in writing these arguments, or this book, for that matter.)

You can only imagine what this young teenager must have learned from having a sister like *this* coming home every night, especially if she spoke freely. Glorious stories of romance, passion, and adventure, coupled with wads of green cash in Ava's hand, which Amber could see with her very own, naïve eyes. Of course, the sister was already over eighteen at this time, so there was nothing the father could do to stop her. But Amber was still a juvenile, her father, a successful contractor, had to work for a living and couldn't watch Amber all the time, so he hired the female body-builder instead.

(For those who think this is a bit too extreme to ever become a reality, I'll remind them of what Johnnie Cochran said about Mark Fuhrman in his closing arguments. Mark Fuhrman, just like Amber Frey, was the key pivotal witness in *that* trial of the century. Johnnie called Mark a genocidal racist, the root of all evil, and he even compared him to Adolph Hitler! He was bringing up issues such as Martin Luther King and slavery, which *are* important concerns in other contexts, but which really had nothing to do with the deaths of Ron Goldman or Nicole Brown. This was all done with not much more evidence than what they already have on Amber Frey. Johnnie inflamed the inner passions of the jurors. And guess what?...He won.)

We know Amber is fairly tall for a female, about 5' 10". You just know a teenager like this, who I'm sure, was tall for her age, probably thought she knew everything. She felt she had the world at her fingertips.

To illustrate this "rebellious" type of behavior that we know Amber harbors, let us take a look at a small, more recent example. The police investigators gave her very specific instructions on the subject matter she would be allowed to touch on during the recorded telephone conversations she was to have with Scott Peterson. However, Amber *blatantly* ignored the officials and deliberately and maliciously steered right into those topics she was forbidden to discuss, which was a flagrant act of disrespect to these officers. She, without warning to the detectives, jumped right into an investigation of her own. I am somewhat sympathetic toward Amber for giving perhaps more priority to having her heart broken, but this is no excuse, when the rest of the entire world is sitting on edge for the results of these double-murder inquiries. These were obviously very seasoned veterans of homicide investigation, and I don't believe **any one of us** would have demonstrated that level of rebelliousness under these same high-profile circumstances.

Now back to Amber as a teenager, and why this fits in.

Both Fresno and Modesto have their "skid row" parts of town. (This could be explained further since this is a San Mateo County jury.)

She knew where these boulevards were. Having a sister like that, how could she *not* know?

Since she was fairly tall for a young teenager, and with her bleached-blond hair, whom would the men in these cars prefer to pick up?...Her? Or, the forty-year-old woman down the street with missing teeth?...She had no problem out there.

(Geragos should see if Amber's juvenile record is sealed or not, because if it isn't, he might be able to have a field day.)

We were hoping to find, on her juvenile record, an incident where she may have gotten into the car of a decoy. But with the kind of Amber we've seen so far, she was too smart to get caught.

(With fascination, some of the female jurors stare back at him, their mouths slightly parted in awe. In the courtroom, seated one row behind the defense table, are Jackie and Lee Peterson. A smug and pleased look appears on Jackie's face, behind the tubes coming out from her nostrils, while she slowly nods her head in approval. It's a look that reads, "I can't wait to write him another fat check for this one.")

Scott Peterson is not stupid. He knew what this woman was all about. Just like the rest of the floozies with whom he cheated on Laci. As far as Scott was concerned, they were all for one purpose and one purpose only—**straight sex!**

Would a young man of Scott's caliber and success just throw away the ultimate American-dream wife that he had, all for someone else's leftover piece-of-ass?

Or would someone of Scott's character be willing to commit capital murder and possibly face the death penalty, all over...just another public toilet, such as Amber?

Ladies and gentlemen of the jury, you saw that woman on the stand. Between the time of Scott's arrest and the trial, **Amber Frey managed to become pregnant yet again, and has already had the second baby! She doesn't even know who the father of *this* one is!** (He can hold up the child's birth certificate bearing no name for the father.)

For those of you who don't think it's true, just look at this birth certificate—father listed as—**"unknown!"**

Laci, on the other hand, not only was a cheerleader, but also was a schoolteacher, and was considered to be a good cook, housekeeper, and host. Now, who would you want to be the mother of your children? Laci or...the other woman?

(As a disclaimer, I should mention: I don't personally have this type of opinion about Amber. In fact, earlier in the book, I praise her. I am simply illustrating the necessary type of power a high-profile defense attorney should possess, when he is being paid top dollar, so that he can demonstrate to his worldwide audience that he really can pack a punch worth every dollar of his fiduciary responsibility to his client and his client's financiers. Again, high-profile defense lawyer Johnnie Cochran demonized Detective Mark Furhman, the pivotal prosecution witness in the other trial of the century, by calling him a genocidal racist, among other things, resulting in success for Cochran and his client.)

The statistic is that somewhere around 40% of all married men have, at some point in their marriages, cheated on their wives. Even though we know that cheating on Laci was nothing new for Scott, to go from adultery to murder is an entirely different ballgame. It's like going from peanut league to the majors in one reckless shot. Dr. Henry Lee said that to imply the pliers and hair found in the boat meant that Scott was guilty of murder would be too much of a quantum leap. Likewise, the idea that Scott's cheating on his wife means that he murdered her, is also a quantum leap. Regardless of these circumstances, it is still <u>not</u> very probable that Scott made this enormous jump. Going from something "petty and common" to something "brutally hardcore and rare" is the farthest thing from reality in terms of the character of this defendant.

> Defense counsel continues:
> Amber Frey meant nothing more to Scott than a common prostitute. But Scott actually "did" her twice, unlike most of her customers, who only do her once.
> So, Amber now thought that this meant it was on!

(I could just picture how most of these jurors might stare back with gaunt looks on their faces, some women showing only poker faces with puckered lips, others with jaws dropped in astonishment.)

> To illustrate Amber's feelings at the time, she made absolutely sure she got Christmas pictures taken of her with Scott, so she could include them in her Christmas cards.
> And all along, Scott was just sarcastically thinking—"Sure it's on, Amber. Sure it is. You are the one, ha, ha, ha," while knowing, full well, that he had a real wife at home, someone he had built the American dream with, someone who was giving him a son, someone whom he knew many other men wished they could have. (Here, he can hold up the photo that shows Scott trying to hold back this total smirk on his face, as he stands behind Amber, next to the Christmas tree.) Again, ladies

and gentlemen, Amber not only meant *nothing* to Scott, but based on her character and comparing it to his, it would have been almost *ludicrous* to assume a person like Amber could've actually meant anything to a guy like Scott.

Now, everyone, I would like to shift gears into another point here. Let us just imagine for a minute what might have happened in the Chandra Levy case, if the circumstances had been slightly different. For example, let us assume for a second that Chandra was **not** the one who disappeared, but that Mrs. Condit, the congressman's wife, was the one who vanished, with everything else still being the same.

Under circumstances of a nationwide search for a congressman's wife, Chandra Levy would have, no doubt, come forward, the same way Amber Frey did, to publicly disclose her affair with the married congressman. Law enforcement and the general public would be simply *stunned* that a U.S. congressman would murder his wife of 25 years for a young, sexy intern, even though *this*, as we know, is *not* what happened!

Now let's further assume, that Condit just happened to be *fishing*, by himself, when his wife disappeared. Even Ron Grantski, Laci's stepfather, testified that *he* also went fishing on that same Christmas Eve morning, so what if Condit actually *was* just fishing?!

Instead of trying to sue the tabloids, today Congressman Gary Condit would most likely be in state prison, totally f#!*%d.

(The judge at this time reminds Geragos to watch his language in lieu of being charged with contempt. He reminds Geragos of the public apology the defense lawyer was forced to make to the district attorney after calling him a "piece of crap" during jury selection.)

I'm sorry, Your Honor. Ladies and gentleman, Congressman Gary Condit, under **these** circumstances, would, in fact, today...be sitting on death row, wrongfully convicted!...And everybody knows it!

Ladies and gentlemen, by this one example alone, we can all see with startling clarity, that with a few simple coincidences, it could have been any one of us who became a victim of circumstance. (Pause) And it just so happens, that the entire reason we are even in this courtroom at all, and having this trial, is for no other reason...than the fact that my client...with a crystal clear record...Scott Peterson...with no criminal background whatsoever, and a sterling reputation with friends and family, as well as with the whole community...**is** such a victim of basic circumstance.

Now let's talk about the bodies that washed ashore near the location of Scott's fishing alibi.

(Geragos may be forced to let Kirk McAllister perform this portion of the closing arguments, as well, because of the foolish public statement Geragos already locked himself into regarding the bodies washing up in the bay.)

The minute it was announced that the remains were positively identified as that of Laci and Connor, **I never, not even for one minute, ever thought Scott had anything to do with this.** Here's why:

The police, as we know, were scouring the bottom of the bay for months during the search for Laci.

The police, with help from the FBI, were using millions of dollars worth of the latest technology in underwater sonar scanning equipment, for this purpose.

This magnificently assembled search team had the national media scrutinizing their every move, for all the world to see.

(Voice escalates here with a slight Shakespearean flare) But even with this overwhelming public pressure and the additional surge of energy and determination spawned from their experience with the Chandra Levy search, they still turned up...absolutely no bodies.

Not even <u>another</u> body from any other missing persons case.

All they found was a tarp and an old boat anchor.

But as the search only ended in futility, the public soon shifted its focus onto the latest national crisis, the war with Iraq.

Then lo and behold, while the public was distracted by the war, the bodies of Laci and Conner just mysteriously wash up on shore, right where the vortex of the search had taken place. And it wasn't the police who found them! It was a person walking her dog!

How could these high-tech explorers have missed this?

Not even the slightest hint or clue of a body, but Laci and Conner's remains were there the whole time, right under the detectives' noses...**or were they?**

The reason, ladies and gentlemen...is because there were no bodies in this location at the time of the search.

What does the prosecution think the real killer was watching on TV during the search for Laci...*I Love Lucy?*

The killer knew where the prime suspect's alibi was, as did the rest of the world.

It doesn't take a rocket scientist, let alone a skilled killer, to figure out where to put the bodies, if he wants to frame another man for it—to end the investigation and make sure that he, the killer, will never be arrested for it.

Everyone knew the reason why police were searching this particular body of water for Laci—**it was the location of Scott's alibi.**

Any experienced killer could see that this provided an absolutely golden opportunity to pin the murder on someone else—the innocent, committed husband of the victim.

The innocent husband, who, unfortunately, happened to have a peculiar alibi.

The innocent husband, about whom the real killer couldn't care less.

The innocent husband, who just, unfortunately, happened to have a media circus following him around, wherever he went.

If it weren't for the high-publicity nature of this case, the real killer would never have learned the location of Peterson's alibi, and thus would never have dropped the bodies there.

To me, this is far too much of a coincidence for these bodies just to mysteriously turn up later, exactly where the police originally were searching intensively for them.

I thought it was curious that the remains were discovered, **not by police, but by ordinary citizens, just walking by.**

This killer knew that all he had to do was to get those bodies into the bay some way, somehow, and when they washed up, this would nail the prime suspect, an innocent man, Laci's grieving husband.

In this way, another man goes down for the murder, not the killer.

The Iraq War provided the most perfect, inconspicuous cover for this purpose.

(Pause)

If Scott did, in fact, kill his wife and unborn child, then why on God's Earth would a reasonably intelligent man, such as he, deliberately place himself where only he knew this body might turn up?

I mean, couldn't he at least have thought that a "fishing" alibi on the day of Christmas Eve might seem a little *fishy* to the average person, let alone, a homicide detective? So rather than use the Berkeley Marina parking receipt, wouldn't it make more sense for an intelligent guy like Scott to provide a department store receipt, showing that perhaps he did some last-minute Christmas shopping? And if the receipts were from later in the day (i.e., he had to rush back from the bay, to make up for lost time dumping her body, so as to still establish the "shopping" alibi), he could always say that he was looking for just the right gift, and that, naturally, there were long lines at all the stores.

(Pause)

In a court of law, a person must be found guilty beyond a reasonable doubt and to a moral certainty to be convicted of a crime.

Ladies and gentlemen of the jury, if this is not a seriously reasonable doubt, I don't know what is.

(Pause)

Ladies and gentlemen, sometimes it's easy to overlook the fact that our American criminal justice system is only human, that our law enforcement officials sometimes do make mistakes, and that, sometimes, innocent people are charged with crimes.

I've always been an advocate for the individual rights our U.S. Constitution guarantees us. This is the beauty that sets our system apart from other nations—our individual liberties, rights, and freedoms. We have fought wars over the centuries to protect this great cause, and here's why: Certainly we could prevent ourselves from committing a crime, but you cannot necessarily prevent yourself from being charged with one. So, if you or a brother, sister, son, or daughter of yours is wrongfully accused of a crime, wouldn't you want every guarantee our constitution provides for them? And if, God forbid, a wrongfully accused person is convicted, who, then is the victim then?

Ladies and gentlemen of the jury, even though this case has become a high-profile spectacle, this doesn't mean that Scott Peterson should not be entitled to these same rights and guarantees that we all have. These laws and guarantees were drafted to protect **all** of us, not just those who *haven't* been tried by the media. Scott Peterson is just as entitled to these legal guarantees that our great country provides, every bit as much as you and I are.

Ladies and gentlemen of the jury, as you can see, we have raised what we believe to be several, *solid,* reasonable doubts. However, by the laws that govern our American criminal justice system, we need only to raise **one.**

Ladies and gentlemen of the jury...

I say you acquit him. (The reason I say a defense lawyer should use the term "acquit," instead of "not guilty," when addressing the jury, is because it shows the panelists you are giving them a boost of respect, by letting them see you assume them to be intelligent, and are not just spoon feeding them. Remember, by this time, many of the jurors might have developed a little ego, by having survived this long as a "trial of the century" juror, and might think they've become fledgling experts *themselves* at legal terms and courtroom politics. Plus, as any experienced trial lawyer will tell you, it is the most intelligent of the jurors who have the greatest influence on the remaining jurors. I believe that, especially in a murder trial, it's imperative to show your jurors a generous level of respect regarding their legal knowledge.)

Thank you.

(Lead defense counsel now takes his seat.)

12

End for Now

♦

(To be continued in Volume 2—The Trial)

This book was already written by the time the made-for-TV movie about Laci, *The Perfect Husband*, aired. However, before it went out to print, I wanted to include a few comments about this movie, my opinion and thoughts on it.

I've chosen to start by mentioning what I like about the film, then I'll talk about the various characters and roles they were trying to portray, and then I'll mention a few things about the flick that I felt could stand some improvement.

I liked the intensity of the opening search scenes, because I felt they were a good representation of the mass effort that the search became.

I thought the actor portraying Scott deserves an "A." Of course, nobody could be exactly like Scott except Scott, but under the circumstances, I felt that the actor did extraordinarily well. For example, one way this character differed from the real Scott was due to the fact that, since this was a professional actor, he was able to appear more convincing of his innocence than the actual Scott was able to do in his limited public appearances. Also, I thought this actor looked to be closer to 35 years old, instead of 30 that Scott was at the time of Laci's disappearance.

I'm just going to tell it as I saw it. When I saw a big guy with a gray beard stumble into the room and say, "Hey, what's goin' on?" I knew this was supposed to be Ron Grantski. Thinking it was kind of funny, I chuckled a bit. I can see why the Rochas were visibly upset by the way this film was presented. I would be, too, if I were they, and here's why. First, let's look at the Sharon Rocha character. From what I understand, the real Sharon Rocha was the most upset family member regarding this presentation. The actress playing Sharon's part, I felt, did a good job of acting like a mother who's missing a daughter. But the problem *is* that Sharon Rocha is *not* Dorothy Moxley. Sharon Rocha is Sharon Rocha. In other words, I don't believe this actress really studied the behavioral mannerisms of the real Sharon Rocha from the public interviews and what not. I really got the impression that this actress simply did her own thing, you know, portraying what *she* would be like if she had lost a daughter. It was a convincing performance in that regard. However, it was nowhere near the image or personality of the real lady we all saw in the news conferences. The real Sharon Rocha, I believe, has a more stately appearance, almost like a slightly older Hillary Clinton stereotype. I'm not really saying she looks like Hillary; it's just that Mrs. Rocha has a more prominent and aristocratic look, plus a more aware and authoritative appearance. I also believe that one of the reasons Laci's case received the explosive attention it did was due not only to Laci's beauty, but, to her mother's beauty, as well. For being middle aged, Sharon is still a stunningly attractive, prominent, and stately-looking lady. This, I believe, lent itself well to the connection between the media and politics, and its subsequent growth in this case. The actress, however, played the role with a slightly more gullible and naïve appearance, not excessively so, but almost a little dumpier and lamer in her appearance. She's not an actress I would've picked to bring more central focus to the character. It's just that it seemed her whole demeanor and personality were in different generation and personality categories. I believe this actress had a good idea for something close, but clearly *not* what I'd be looking for, as a director, to portray Laci's mother. I can only give her performance a "C-."

The Dennis Rocha character was completely in left field compared to Laci's actual father. The real Dennis Rocha is fairly short, stocky and dark, his mustache is gray from age, and he does wear a cowboy hat. He has a thick accent that is fairly common among many Central and South American immigrants. The actor playing this character looked absolutely nothing at all like Dennis Rocha—he was tall, light-skinned, and only had a slight accent. They made him look like a big, tall all-American cowboy/rancher type, which he definitely was not. Because of the casting error here, I can only give this actor a "D."

The actor and actress playing Scott's parents were usually shown together. They did a fairly realistic job with the mother and the emphysema tubes for her face, and the few lines she had were usually in defense of her son, so that was good. The actor playing Scott's father, Lee Peterson, had too much of a beaker face. I simply think they should have used a better-looking actor, more filled out, and around his same age, to play that part.

The brother of Laci was an interesting attempt at the real Brent Rocha. I believe this actor *did* more carefully study the real Laci's brother, but you can, of course, only come so close to a real likeness. But one slight problem I saw with this character was that, when he stood next to the Scott character, communicating with him, for lack of a better term, the actor came across as slightly more nerdy than the real Brent Rocha. This, again, became more noticeable when he was seen next to the Scott character, who was almost a little "studlier" than the real Scott. Overall, I'd have to give the actor who played Brent Rocha a "B."

One problem I caught with most of the younger characters is that the actors playing those roles were actually about 5 or 6 years older than the real participants were. For example, I thought the actor playing Scott appeared to be about 35 years old instead of just 30, and I thought the Brent Rocha actor looked about 35 years old instead of 31. I realize they can't be perfect, but there were some differences in hair color and skin complexion, as well, including the eyebrows, etc.

There was another scene in the movie that was totally mischaracterized, and added to the dismay of the Rochas. This is the scene where the Dodge dealer showed up at Sharon Rocha's house to return Laci's Land Rover to the family. It never happened that way. In reality, the Rochas noticed Scott's new truck in the driveway and that Laci's vehicle was missing. When they found out he had traded her vehicle in, the first thing the Rochas did was go down to the dealership where, of course, they were immediately recognized. The SUV was immediately given back without question. Again, *they* went to the dealership, and not the other way around. I don't see the significance of why the director reversed the scene like that; maybe it was just easier and less cluttered to present it that way.

The biggest disappointment of the whole movie was, by far, the Amber Frey character. I'm not sure why the producers chose to downplay this character's significance, but I do have some ideas as to why, and I'd like to discuss them. Everybody knows Amber was a bleached blond, slender, and tall all-American girl who was into *some* bodybuilding and limited nude modeling. The real Amber Frey stood out in a spotlight well—more so than Laci's friends, for example. But in this dramatization, Laci's friends stood out as the clear *90210* cast, and Amber only appeared like a meek, sheltered, librarian type on the side, even appearing a little frail. Instead of being the young, vivacious 28-year-old that Amber was, the actress they chose looked about 35 or 36 and was shown more as a motherly type, who was raising her daughter. The real Amber not only has long bleached-blond hair, but also has full lips and big eyes, photogenic qualities that really stood out in the media coverage. But the actress playing the part had thin lips and small eyes, as well as what appeared to be red, or just mousy, dishwater-brown hair. As we can see from her photos with Scott, the real Amber was quite tall, but the actress was much shorter. Again, all these observations were very disappointing; she neither looked nor acted anything at all like the Amber the public was so interested in. I have a theory as to why the producers made such an obvious blunder.

One reason, I believe, the Rochas were so visibly upset about the way the movie was made is because it definitely appeared to be skewed in Scott's favor. It almost leaves the viewer thinking, "Hey, this guy really might be innocent." The Amber Frey character is instrumental to Scott's guilt or innocence in his trial, and it was this knowledge that gave the producers the signal that, if they want to air the movie this early in the game, they had better be careful that they don't assassinate the young man's ability to get a fair trial. This, in turn, put Scott's character in a much more favorable light, as far as the Rochas were concerned, and could, of course, affect the state's ability also to get a fair trial for the prosecution. In other words, I believe, the producers feared the Petersons might sue, before the Rochas would consider that an option.

So, stepping back for a second and separating myself from the prosecution and defense and just neutrally looking at the *real* Amber Frey, yes I see someone for whom this man might feel compelled enough to commit murder. But when I step back and look at the actress playing Amber in the movie, *no*, I don't get that same feeling. In fact, I get more the feeling that this affair could have been no more harmful than the basic cheating, but no, not something that would lead to murder. Now the producers, I believe, were fearful that, if they overdid, say, the blondness and attractiveness of the Amber character, then they would catch heavier flack from the other side. For example, the *National Enquirer* came under some earlier criticism for referring to Amber as a blond bombshell, which she obviously was not, but she clearly was no meek librarian, either, as the film portrayed her. (By the way, in my opinion, here are some blond bombshells—Pamela Anderson, Marilyn Monroe, and Loni Anderson. These women are all from different generations, but all delivered a proven formula in looks. Amber Frey does stand out a bit, but again, she's obviously *not* a bombshell.)

The actress in the movie also sounded really sappy towards Scott on the phone, nothing at all like the real Amber in the recorded phone transcripts, who was, in contrast, grilling Scott and very suspicious of his involvement with Laci's disappearance. The actress, however, would tell Scott she loved him, and that she didn't think he had anything to do with his missing wife, which was not anything at all like the actual transcripted calls.

The biggest difference between the real Amber Frey and the actress was this: The real Amber definitely has a strong look that is hard to forget—the whole world knows what Amber looks like. The actress, on the other hand, could easily be forgotten, just the plainest Jane they could've found, with no redeeming features, whatsoever. With any television or movie studio, the Amber-type look is very popular and obviously not hard to find. In fact, the "Amber" look is considered in Hollywood to be the most dime-a-dozen look available. But despite this propensity, the directors must have had a deliberate intention behind their "downplay" of this character. For example, Amber herself is fairly tall, about 5' 9" or 5' 10", at least, with big hair and big features on her face. The actress they chose to play her was tiny, maybe 5' 1" or 5' 2", skinny, meek, and very soft spoken.

What were they doing here?

The actual Amber was about number 3 in importance in the story. First Laci, then Scott, then, naturally, Amber.

But, no!

The producers made her only about the tenth most important character in the film, giving not only family members and other characters more emphasis, but also giving many of Laci's friends more central roles.

One more thing about the Amber character is that they seemed to emphasize the fact that she had her own child already. This may be true in real life, but for the purposes of a made-for-TV movie, I don't think the directors were giving proper levels of priority to different elements of the case. For example, it really appeared that the producers had definite opinions as to what certain people were supposed to be doing, but quite frankly, they were completely lost and were simply taking guesses in other areas. For example, because this was a made-for-TV movie, it's sole purpose really was nothing more than entertainment, so if I were directing this film, I would have completely left out the fact that Amber already had a kid. I just don't believe the general viewing public would really need to see *that* for the purposes of this film alone. My overall assessment of the actress playing Amber: I'd only be able to give her a "D-." I just didn't feel she even came close to making the part believable. In fact, as I said before, I believe the producers had a little bit of a political motive behind their choices here. Who knows, maybe the director has an unfaithful marriage and doesn't think it's fair that Scott is being prosecuted for an infidelity-inspired murder.

I want to remind you that I only viewed this drama in its entirety one time, so I'm strictly going on what I remember without having studied it in depth. One of the main characters in the film was a very preppy-looking guy, with a receding hairline and usually dressed in a sweater, who was supposed to be one of, I guess, Scott's friends, or perhaps, Laci's. Please forgive me because maybe I was just supposed to know who this guy was, but to be honest with you, I couldn't really figure out at the time who he was actually supposed to be. I thought maybe he was supposed to be Renee Tomlinson's husband (and if so, the actress playing his wife didn't look a thing like the Renee Tomlinson I met). Anyway, there was a scene in which this guy approaches a group of national reporters having lunch at a café, because he overheard them talking "smack" about his buddy, Scott. There was some finger pointing and raised voices here.

That was great for the dramatic purposes of Hollywood, but in reality, I can attest (since I basically transcended from neighbor at the searches to reporter in the field) that these types of attitudes never existed between the media and the friends and families involved. All appeared to have very respectful and mutually beneficial relationships. The only animosity I saw generated from this activity occurred when certain family members reacted adversely to a few, too pointed questions, such as when Lee Peterson snapped back at a reporter sarcastically with, "How would you goddamn feel?"

The director might've failed to see the big picture in terms of giving the Amber Frey character enough significance that Scott might kill Laci for her. There was a female actress playing one of Laci's friends (the wife of the preppy guy in the sweater) who, I thought, would have made a good Amber. She was a young, attractive, blond girl with full features. Likewise, the actress they used to play Amber, I thought, would have made a good friend of Laci instead and especially would've made a good wife for the preppy guy (by the way, I believe this couple possibly were supposed to be playing the characters of Heather and Mike Richardson, Scott and Laci's best man and matron of honor). The way the producers cast them was the complete opposite of how I would have chosen to use these actresses, and if you look at the film realistically for what it is, the way they chose to do it opposes all common sense. Under these conditions, I would have switched actresses between the Amber and Laci's friend's character. I figured the producers must have left it this way for an ulterior reason. I believe that, whatever the producer's reasons may have been for playing down the Amber character, it was a mistake.

One particularly funny scene in the movie was, I'm sure, most people's favorite part, the segment where they're about to arrest Scott, and he turns around sporting this bright, new, orange face. His hair, eyebrows, and a thick, new goatee were all died a bright Easter-egg orange. At first when viewing this scene, before Scott turned around, I was wondering why they changed the story to include him already parked and removing golf clubs from his trunk, when everybody knows he was waving to the police, like a smart alec, and was pulled over just before reaching the golf course. But then, of course, I understood right away why they did that, because they wanted his newly disguised face to be a surprise, which it was. It struck me as quite funny. I also wondered for a second why they didn't do a more realistic version of the goatee. For example, Scott's goatee had more of a blended highlight than a straight dye, but then I again realized, that this movie was filmed in one month, which didn't allow the actor enough time to grow a real one, and they simply used what they had to work with under those conditions.

Again, back to the preppy guy with the sweater. My favorite scene with this actor was the part when Scott was being driven into the jail, and *this* friend of his was standing there with the crowd, looking into the vehicle at Scott's new, orange face, and showing look of total disbelief, and with his jaw dropped in a state of utter dumbfoundedness. This, combined with the young man's preppy image, looked like some typical yuppie with a graduate degree at about age thirty, standing there with this look of total bewilderment on his face, as he stared at Scott's new, orange face through the window, while standing in the crowd of about 200 persons holding signs that read "murderer." I was, as a matter of fact, laughing quite hard when I saw this actor maintaining this facial expression.

With a case this fresh and vivid in people's minds, from seeing the family members on TV almost every night, I simply wouldn't film something this important without actually doing it right. For instance, if I directed or cast this film, the difference between my version and this one, would be that I don't believe anyone would be nearly as upset after seeing mine. I know most people would consider that very hard to do under these circumstances. I think everybody, including both families, would be laughing and would enjoy the movie, mainly because they would see how extremely well chosen the actors and actresses were. I'm sorry, but even though this director picked a good "Scott," the fact that he deliberately chose the wrong "Amber" makes, in my opinion, and in the opinion of many others, including the Rochas, this film, I wouldn't say an *utter* failure, but it did fail to some degree. When it has this level of importance assigned to it, the satisfaction of both families involved would be of utmost priority to me throughout the beginning, middle, and end of filming this motion picture. Again, that's how I'd do it for this type of picture, a made-for-TV movie, which caters mostly to family viewing.

However, for a major motion picture for the silver screen, I'd do it a little differently. It would not make everyone happy, but to do it for this particular venue, the popularity and glamour of the film would need to be emphasized. The actors and actresses I would cast in these roles would be as popular as the case itself. For example, Scott, Laci, and Amber could be played by Ben Affleck, Jennifer Lopez, and Britney Spears. Besides their obvious popularity, here's why I would cast these stars. Everybody I know has said that Scott looks like Ben Affleck.

Not only do J. Lo. and Laci look similar, but both have that award-winning smile. J. Lo. has played in similar roles, and both of them are about the same age. The fact that Ben and J. Lo. were in a relationship was just a coincidence and had nothing to do, actually, with my choice. To most, the Britney Spears pick would seem the oddest choice of the three, but here's why I selected her. Both Amber and Britney have the slender, blond, all-American image that many associate with Barbie Dolls. Both currently hold the status of most popular young, slim, blond, attractive American female on Planet Earth—Britney because of her rock-stardom and Amber because of her role in the case of the new millennium. Both girls are in their twenties. Though, I do realize that they don't look that much alike. For example, Britney has more of a symmetrically perfect face, whereas Amber has some of Britney's same features but has a much longer face from top to bottom. But I hope I make myself clear on *why* I chose her, which is because someone like her would attract the proper amount of attention necessary to highlight the Amber character correctly, in contrast to how she was *actually* perceived by the general public (which, of course, the producers of the made-for-TV movie utterly neglected).

This case is seeing a huge amount of attention, even though, there are several other high-profile trials going on simultaneously, such as those of Martha Stewart and Robert Blake, not to mention Kobe Bryant and Michael Jackson. And, even more astonishing, the Peterson case participants were not even famous prior to the investigation, as the other defendants already were. Perhaps the status the trial of the new millennium might provide enough incentive for one of these superstars to accept such a role. Whether or not any of these actors and actresses actually would accept these roles is another story, but remember Arnold Schwarzenegger's philosophy—don't go for the small contests, go for the absolutely biggest challenge available. I believe, with a cast like that one, producers would be looking at a similar success to "Batman," "Pirates of the Caribbean," "Lord of the Rings," etc. I mean, with a cast like *this*, who wouldn't go to see it?

This popularity reminds me of a huge promotional event that was supposed to take place a number of years ago, the Mike Tyson/Tony Mandarich fight. Tony Mandarich was labeled by *Sports Illustrated,* at the time, as the "Incredible Bulk." He was a young, fresh out of college, NFL football player, weighing in at about 325 pounds, about 6' 6", white, and pure muscle, with absolutely zero body fat. He was so fast that he could apparently run a 100-yard dash in near-record time. This man was determined to fight Tyson, who was then at the pinnacle of his career, because Mandarich believed it to be impossible for Tyson to defeat him. He believed that, if he were allowed to train for a few months, so as to stay within the rules of boxing, and he went the necessary number of rounds with Tyson, by using his world-record strength and stamina, that there was simply no way he could be defeated by a man half his size. Mike Tyson, on the other hand, knew that, regardless of how great an athlete Tony Mandarich was, Tyson had defeated every major contender in the entire world until then, so how could someone as inexperienced as Mandarich possibly defeat a champion like him. Now, you tell me. Who wouldn't want to see a match up like *that*?

Pay-per-view was supposed to air the event; however, it was later cancelled. The reason, from what I understand, was because Tyson's promoters, as well as other officials in the boxing world, didn't think it would be fair for this man, Tony

Mandarich, who was not a boxer, to get a shot at Tyson before other, more seasoned contenders, working their way up the ranks, could get a chance. To say the least, like millions of other Americans, I was rather disappointed. It was the uniqueness of this particular event that, I believe, gave it its popularity. If nothing else, it sure would have been interesting to see what may have happened in that match. There didn't appear to be any legal or moral issues holding back the airing of such an event. For example, the pay-per-view interview of O.J. Simpson, in which he stood to make about $30 million, was cancelled for reasons such as those. But in this case, I believe they should have let both athletes train a few months for the bout and then just let it happen. As I said, if nothing else, it would've been stunning to see a match-up between two of the world's best and most determined athletes going at it hard, generating ratings similar to those of a presidential debate.

We will now find out what happens to Scott Peterson in his trial.

Regarding jury consultation, there is a sure-fire way that the prosecution could guarantee a conviction. It is a little underhanded, though, but with all the strong evidence against Peterson, I don't think the DA's office would actually feel the need to use it, and I would tend to agree with them. What I mean is this: They could pull the race card from the bottom of the deck. Those factors we discussed in Chapter 6 are *not* as circumstantial as the rest of the case we've been hearing so much about, meaning that there is an actual eyewitness to a possible murder-for-hire plot, an eyewitness who turned out to be a lot more credible than what most of us originally thought.

Just as Johnnie Cochran did in O.J.'s case, the prosecution in this case could arouse the inner passions of some jurors to the point of no return, by using race. I'll keep this brief, but through surveys and focus groups to corroborate the findings, the prosecution ideally would want at least one, if not several people, of Hispanic descent on that jury. If the DA achieves this, he's set. (Also, San Mateo County has a large Asian population. This should work well, too, because Asian females would more likely side with a girl like Laci.) All the prosecutor needs to do is provoke some thought about a possible racial motive that ultimately led to this total disregard of human life, the possibility of Scott Peterson having made the choice to abort his unborn child and wife for possible racial reasons. Say, for example, that he decided that he wanted to have whiter children, by seeking to replace Laci with Amber Frey, and then corroborating this possible motive with the Nazi Low Rider evidence, including the Cory Carroll testimony. If the prosecution ultimately chose to use this argument, the jury would not even deliberate, they would all just rise to their feet and announce, "We have arrived at a verdict, your honor...we find the defendant...*guilty* as charged!"

A few final comments about Scott Peterson before his trial.

Scott's not going to win an acquittal just by appearing to be conservative, as if he wasn't the *type* to murder. The only way he is going to have any chance of succeeding is by doing what he already does best, by being a good lady's man and charming a few of the those female jurors. This way, he'll at least possibly end up with a hung jury. Let me explain.

I'm sure Jo Ellan Dimitrius, the defense's jury consultant, is already coaching Peterson daily on this absolutely necessary endeavor, in order to produce the maximum result at trial for the benefit of the defendant and his family. (As I mentioned previously, Jo Ellen Dimitrius was the defense's jury consultant in the O.J. trial, who, through various means, such as focus groups, determined that the ideal juror favorable to O.J. as a defendant would be females between 20 and 40 years old, preferably black. Johnnie Cochran stuck loyally to his jury consultant's findings. Marcia Clark, on the other hand, turned her back on *their* jury consultant, who told her prosecution team the same thing. Marcia said that that it was all nonsense, and that she would overcome any inhibitions any of these jurors might have. Here, I should point out, is a classic example of a strategic blunder. Clark failed to realize that, in making her decision, she was not stockpiling every possible factor to continue building the odds in her favor. Cochran, as a true fighter, understood this principle. Which in essence meant that every little bit adds up and *does* count.)

Every day before going into that courtroom, Scott needs to do himself up just right, like he's about to go out on a hot date. He needs to give those women on the jury a treat, a treat they normally don't get. Scott needs to *give* those female jurors what they want every day they are in that courtroom looking at him. Without over-doing it, of course, he needs to focus specifically on every little aspect of his appearance and demeanor that a female juror might actually find to be sexually appealing. He needs to conduct this endeavor with class and perfection, so that not only will the female jurors possibly be a little intrigued by him, but also that male jurors may become interested in what Scott may really be doing to achieve this *way* with women.

Jail officials allow Peterson, as an inmate, to get a certain amount of exercise each week, so this is an activity he needs to utilize. Since a defendant is innocent until proven guilty, and because of the high-profile nature of both the defendant and his celebrity attorney, it should be no problem for Jo Ellen to be allowed in to the facility Scott is being held at to make sure he is getting just the ample amount of sun for his face daily, so that he'll be showing a fresher and healthier glow. Scott knows, through years of experience as a player, how to make himself look his best. Most people can come to some determination as to how this is best achieved. For example, through proper diet and exercise, as well as appropriate fashion sense, a person can usually maximize whatever looks they've got. Scott, who has naturally good features, should have no problem with this. He could use, for example, a little moustache comb to perfectly groom his eyebrows. He needs not only to make a natural amount of eye contact with some jurors, but he also should show a natural level of concern for his predicament, as well as show just enough love to some of these female jurors, so that they will believe he appreciates them.

All he really needs to get is for one female juror to say, "Hey, I really kind of like him."

I wanted to bring up a few things regarding the intense local coverage of the Laci Peterson case. I'm sure the vast majority of local reporters sincerely appreciated the unique opportunity to cover such a widespread reaching story. There were, however, one or two creampuff, local journalists, who, I believe, in an effort to get a little extra attention, tried to boo-hoo all the national coverage. As I said, this, I believe, was done only in a weak attempt at trying to look as if they had something to stand up for, a half-hearted attempt to look like some kind of fledgling hero, for what only appears to be a very nebulous cause. You know, saying things like, "Hey, stop. This is not right," (while perhaps standing there with their hands on their hips not knowing what else to say, or not actually knowing what they're *really* trying to say). Making such comments could only provide someone like this with a false sense of security that they can't get in a normal way.

In fact, I've always felt quite the opposite regarding all the high-profile, national attention here in Modesto. I say, bring it on, the more the better. Likewise, if another high-profile case were to break here in our community, I would say—**Come on down!** In fact, I'd even invite some national reporters to use my backyard, if they needed to.

Now that the case is on the verge of going to trial, I'll make a final assessment in terms of Scott's guilt or innocence. Without going into any elaborate detail, if I were to weigh and balance all the factors we've discussed throughout this entire book, I would have to say, sure, there are some good points that the defense can argue, but with the magnitude of coincidences pointing at the young man's guilt, for example, Scott's self-foreseen prophecy to Amber of his wife's death a few weeks before it happened, his admission of bleeding in his truck on the day of the disappearance, Scott's secret boat and the handgun he was in possession of on that same day, Scott's highly suspicious behavior from the time Laci disappeared (mainly referring here to his refusal to speak to both law enforcement and the media, unlike *all* the other family members, who cooperated), the polygraph exam of Cory Carroll showing that Scott had murder on his mind and was shopping for options, Scott's bizarre Christmas Eve fishing trip he went on all by himself, and last but not least, the location of where Laci and Conner's bodies finally showed up—the San Francisco Bay, precisely where Scott said he had gone fishing. Just as Geragos said before being hired by the Petersons—"When you put all of it together, there are more people sitting in state prison today that have been convicted on less evidence than this." I have to agree with Geragos here, with the motive, the opportunity, the means to do it, and the physical evidence tying it all together, yes, I believe Scott Peterson is guilty.

As we know, very high-profile cases oftentimes lead to the enactment of new legislation. For example, in the Adam Walsh case, his father John Walsh, host of *America's Most Wanted*, was able to push the Missing Children's Act all the way through Congress and eventually to see it signed into law. This initiative simply brings the resources of the FBI into use in helping track missing children. In other words, it brings federal powers in to help assist at the local and state level towards finding missing children and investigating their cases.

In the Polly Klaas case, her father Marc was instrumental in having a new state law passed here in California. This was known as the "three strikes" law. This resolution simply stipulates that, if a perpetrator is convicted of a third, "violent" felony, he automatically must be sentenced to 25 years to life. An exception to this law would be, for example, if a defendant is convicted for the third time of a *non-violent* felony, such as "drug sales;" then, of course, this legislation would not apply.

Likewise, in the Laci Peterson case, a new, federal law was signed into action by President George W. Bush. This new federal initiative is called the Unborn Victims of Violence Act and is also known as the Laci & Conner Law. It basically recognizes the baby of a pregnant woman as another person when it comes to violent crime. Thus, it becomes a second homicide, if the two people are the victims of a malicious offense resulting in death. Although the bill was stalled on Capital Hill for several years prior to the Laci Peterson case, thanks to the new visible support of Sharon Rocha and Ron Grantski, the Laci & Conner Law was passed by the House and Senate with relatively easy margins.

Well, I've enjoyed this little conversation with you, and I do look forward to our next one, which should be coming out in just a few short months.

Brad Knight
Modesto, California
2004

APPENDIX

ARTICLE A
ARREST WARRANT

PEOPLE OF THE STATE OF CALIFORNIA)
           Plaintiff,)
vs.)
Scott Lee PETERSON   Defendant)

FILED 03 APR 21 AM 6:50

PROBABLE CAUSE WARRANT OF ARREST*
(P.C. §814 and §1427;
Peo. V. Ramey, 16 Cal.3d 263;
Peo. V. Sesslin, 68 Cal.2d 418.)

COUNTY OF STANISLAUS:
THE PEOPLE OF THE STATE OF CALIFORNIA:

To any Peace Officer of said State:

Complaint upon oath having been this day made before me by Detective Craig Grogan, I find that there is probable cause to believe that two counts of the crime of: 187 PC, homicide committed on or about Monday December 23, 2002 or Tuesday December 24, 2002, in the County of Stanislaus by **Scott Lee Peterson**, date of birth, 10/24/72.

YOU ARE THEREFORE COMMANDED forthwith to arrest the above-named Defendant and bring him/her before any magistrate in Stanislaus County pursuant to Penal Code Sections 187.

The within named defendant may be admitted to bail in the sum of:

NO BAIL   Dollars.

WITNESS, my hand this 17th day of April 2003.

Judge of the Superior Court
County of Stanislaus, State of California

IDENTIFICATION INFORMATION

AKA* _____ Address _____ Phone ▇▇▇▇

N/A _____ Business: Trade Corp

Name: **Scott Lee Peterson**

Address 523 Covena Ave

Phone ▇▇▇▇

DOB 10/24/72   HT 6'-0"   WT 200   Hair: brown   Eyes: brown

DDL# ▇▇▇▇   CII# _____

FBI# _____ SS# _____

Local Agency # 02-142591

Other Information None

*An arrest under this warrant does not initiate a criminal proceeding. After arrest, submit all reports and copies of this warrant and affidavit to the District Attorney who will review for a complaint. Retain original of this warrant and affidavit as evidence.

Article B
Probable Cause Declaration

Article C
Booking Register

ARTICLE D
CRIMINAL COMPLAINT

STANISLAUS COUNTY SUPERIOR COURT
STATE OF CALIFORNIA

THE PEOPLE OF THE STATE OF CALIFORNIA,

vs.

SCOTT LEE PETERSON
(DOB: 10/24/1972)
(IN CUSTODY)

DEFENDANT(S)

No. 1056770

State of California)
County of Stanislaus) ss.

FILED
03 APR 21 AM 10:05
SUPERIOR COURT
COUNTY OF STANISLAUS
BY _____
              DEPUTY

COMPLAINT - CRIMINAL

MFD 02-142591
Booking #558289

On April 21, 2003, K. VELLA, STANISLAUS COUNTY DISTRICT ATTORNEY'S OFFICE, complains and alleges, upon information and belief, that said defendant(s) did commit the following crime(s) in the County of Stanislaus, State of California.

COUNT I: On or about and between December 23, 2002 and December 24, 2002, defendant did commit a felony, MURDER, violation of Section 187 of the California Penal Code, in that the defendant did willfully, unlawfully, and feloniously and with malice aforethought murder Laci Denise Peterson, a human being.

SPECIAL ALLEGATION: It is further alleged as to Count I, MURDER, that the defendant acted intentionally, deliberately and with premeditation.

ENHANCEMENT: TERMINATION OF PREGNANCY. During the commission of the murder of Laci Denise Peterson, the defendant, with the knowledge that Laci Denise Peterson was pregnant, did inflict injury on Laci Denise Peterson resulting in the termination of her pregnancy, a violation of Section 12022.9(a) of the California Penal Code.

COUNT II: On or about and between December 23, 2002 and December 24, 2002, defendant did commit a felony, MURDER, violation of Section 187 of the California Penal Code, in that the defendant did willfully, unlawfully, and feloniously and with malice aforethought murder Baby Conner Peterson, a fetus.

SPECIAL ALLEGATION: It is further alleged as to Count II, MURDER, that the defendant acted intentionally, deliberately and with premeditation.

THE FOLLOWING SPECIAL ALLEGATION APPLIES TO BOTH COUNTS:

SPECIAL ALLEGATION: It is further alleged as to Counts I & II, MURDER, the defendant committed more than one murder in the 1st or 2nd degree in this proceeding, and is a special circumstance within the meaning of Penal Code section 190.2(a)(3).

KD:kv
(Disk #3)

All of which is contrary to law in such cases made and provided, and against the peace and dignity of the People of the State of California.

Said Complaint therefore prays that a warrant be issued for the arrest of said defendant(s) and that said defendant(s) be dealt with according to law.

I certify under penalty of perjury, at Modesto, California, that the foregoing is true and correct.

Dated: 21 April 03   K. Vena
                             Complainant

Index

A
Adams, John 61
Aguillera, Herman 205
Alameda County Sheriff 68, 70
Angel of Justice 73, 110

B
Baden, Dr. Michael 146, 147, 263
Baehr, Jeff 69
Barbieri, Paula 75
Beard Brook Park 48
Berkeley Harbor Patrol 68
Berkeley Marina 31, 32, 35, 58, 62, 67, 68, 133, 159, 192, 280, 284, 292, 302, 342, 376
Bible Retreat 108
Boyers, Stacey 61, 183
Brochini, Detective Al 73, 188, 269, 292, 363
Brown, Nicole 269, 368
Buehler, Detective Jon 150, 152
Bush, George W. 228, 324, 397

C
Cal Poly 14, 15, 24, 196, 198, 258
Candlelight Vigil 62, 293
Carroll, Cory 216, 221, 330, 331, 393, 396
Cheerleader 13, 72, 365, 370

Chief of Police 62, 94, 143, 144
Clark, Marcia 356, 394
Cliff/Rescue Dive Team 69
Cloward, Sgt. Ron 61, 66, 68, 133, 135, 157
Cochran, Johnnie 269, 313, 314, 363, 367, 370, 393, 394
Condit, Gary x, 3, 12, 71, 309, 320, 372, 373
   congressman 309, 372, 373
   scandal 3, 12, 71, 309
Coroner's Office 142, 229, 240, 241, 248
Covena Avenue 26, 28, 38, 59, 61, 86, 87, 118, 120, 126, 186, 218, 219, 229, 231, 232, 327
Cowlings, Al 270
Crogan, Detective Craig 123
Cuesta College 18

D
Darden, Chris 313, 314, 356
Davis, Governor 88
Del Monte 50
Del Rio Country Club 84, 165, 287
Distaso, Rick 288, 309, 310, 329
Dodge Dakota 25, 112, 119, 153
Don Pedro Dam 50

Downey High School 13
Dry Creek 44, 45, 48, 60, 288

E

East Bay Suburbs 106
East La Loma Park 32, 38, 44, 57, 59, 61, 62, 65, 115, 127, 187, 215, 289, 305
El Vista Bridge 48
Ellesworth, Lori 183

F

Fertilizer 27, 98, 108, 124, 148, 347
Fertilizer Conference 98
Fieger, Jeffrey 306, 309, 310
Fixer-upper 30
Fleeman, Connie 135, 136, 137
Flores, Paul 197, 198, 199, 200
Fort Bragg 99
Frey, Amber 31, 63, 72, 73, 92, 93, 94, 99, 109, 125, 180, 181, 189, 210, 212, 222, 280, 287, 293, 295, 304, 326, 331, 344, 345, 346, 351, 352, 353, 358, 364, 365, 367, 368, 370, 371, 372, 383, 384, 385, 387, 393
Frey, Ron 100
Fuhrman, Mark 215, 269, 363, 367

G

Garza, Renee 13, 183
Geragos, Mark 122, 157, 166, 220, 229, 231, 239, 241, 259, 262, 269, 279, 280, 281, 283, 286, 299, 304, 310, 313, 315, 319, 324, 329, 330, 336, 342, 365
Girolami, Judge Al 240

Golden Gate Bridge 201, 205, 206
Golden Retriever 32, 126, 239, 305, 331
Goldman, Ron 368
Gomez, Gloria 111
Good Morning America 95, 98
Goold, Chief Deputy DA John 188, 232, 336
Grantski, Ron xiii, 13, 33, 84, 112, 151, 163, 166, 167, 190, 195, 211, 213, 228, 251, 290, 344, 355, 372, 380, 398

H

Harris, David 132, 240
Hart, Josh 109, 364
Hedges, Sheriff Patrick 200
Helicopter 44, 45, 60, 61, 142
Hernandez, Evelyn 1, 95, 201, 202, 203, 205, 206, 300, 348
Hetch Hetchy 62
Highland Drive 38, 59
Highway 50, 52, 60, 62, 150, 263, 303, 316
Hoffinger, Dean 104, 106
Hull, Sabrina 59
Huston, Kelly 67, 116, 151, 155, 156

I

intern 372
Iraq War 99, 157, 376

J

Jackson, Michael 390

K

King, Larry xiv, 76, 233, 234, 260, 262, 266, 291, 313

King, Melvin 214, 217, 221
Klaas, Marc xiii, xiv, 3, 34, 76, 307
Klaas, Polly 6, 96, 213, 397
Knight, Brad ix, 398
Krigbaum, Amy 59

L

La Loma Park 26, 32, 38, 44, 57, 59, 61, 62, 65, 115, 127, 187, 215, 289, 293, 305, 331
Lee, Dr. Henry xiii, 237, 241, 260, 262, 263, 264, 266, 267, 269, 371
Lengel, Matt 67
Levy, Chandra x, 3, 12, 71, 207, 208, 309, 320, 372, 374
Levy, Susan 66
Lie Detector 36, 84
Lockyer, Attorney General Bill 149, 151, 152, 154, 315

M

Madera County 103
Maderas Ranchos 103
Manson, Charles 74, 239
Marks, Jack 61
McCluskey, Dena 207, 208
Mistress of Death 73, 110
Mitchell, Vivian 125, 128, 137
Modesto Bee xiv, 65, 163, 239
Modesto Police xiv, 35, 40, 54, 57, 58, 68, 69, 73, 76, 92, 93, 100, 121, 123, 133, 134, 135, 137, 142, 143, 144, 148, 152, 154, 157, 167, 170, 173, 207, 231, 281, 313, 342
Modesto Rotary Club 27

Modesto, City of 71
Modesto~Empire Railroad 50
Morro Bay 14, 18, 19
Motive 92, 104, 107, 177, 199, 205, 210, 213, 216, 301, 326, 332, 333, 336, 348, 352, 364, 386, 393, 397
Muna, Frank 217, 219

N

national media 3, 12, 71, 135, 156, 161, 164, 165, 196, 206, 268, 349, 374
Nava, Margarita 288
Nazi Low Riders 214, 221, 222
New Year's Day Brunch 64
New Year's Eve 62, 63, 293

P

Pacific Café 18, 19
Pera, Detective Holly 203
Petersen, Kim xiii, 55, 56, 85, 144, 167, 170, 172, 195, 228, 249
Peterson, Connor 151
Peterson, Jackie 60, 87, 88, 123, 124, 143, 155, 162, 173, 174, 175, 176, 178, 179, 180, 181, 194, 195, 230, 233, 251, 252, 279, 317, 327
Peterson, Janey 89
Peterson, Lee 17, 65, 82, 127, 173, 174, 175, 176, 177, 178, 179, 180, 221, 233, 234, 253, 287, 299, 326, 369, 381, 387
Pioneer Religion 102, 103
Player Haters 107
Players 106
Polygamy 102

Polygraph 34, 36, 37, 111, 215, 216, 217, 218, 219, 221, 306, 355, 359, 396
Pornography 109

R

Ralston, Gene 133, 134
Ralston, William 49
Red Lion Hotel 57, 59, 64, 92, 169
Redwood City 338
Reward 38, 55, 56, 67, 129, 170, 230, 321
Ridenour, Doug 35, 66, 71, 86, 87, 93, 113, 118, 142, 144
Robert's Auto Sales 111, 112
Rocha, Amy xiii, 84, 90, 91, 119, 288, 355
Rocha, Brent 49, 60, 84, 90, 117, 181, 231, 355, 381, 382
Rocha, Dennis 16, 38, 63, 84, 113, 153, 166, 167, 213, 306, 355, 381
Rocha, Sharon 25, 33, 56, 63, 84, 88, 91, 143, 151, 162, 166, 169, 172, 195, 211, 228, 229, 230, 234, 248, 282, 286, 292, 303, 315, 318, 322, 323, 324, 327, 344, 355, 380, 382, 398
Rowlands, Ted xiii, 285
Ryder, Winona 158, 160, 308

S

Saltzman, Brad 64, 169, 233, 234, 235
San Francisco Bay 1, 11, 32, 49, 67, 113, 125, 132, 141, 147, 151, 159, 196, 201, 202, 236, 248, 289, 294, 302, 340, 342, 350, 354, 397

San Joaquin River 60, 62
Sawyer, Diane 95
Scheuch, Art 104
Schoenthaler, Professor Stephen 334
Sex Addict 102
Shack 24
Shapiro, Robert 269
Sheriff's Dept. 70
Shodin, Dru 97
Sibley, Shawn 98
Simi Valley 285
Simpson, O.J. x, 3, 74, 156, 210, 241, 267, 269, 270, 278, 347, 356, 392
Smart, Kristin 197, 198, 200, 258
Southern Pacific Railroad 50, 51
Stanislaus County xiv, 39, 44, 50, 56, 57, 62, 82, 116, 121, 137, 142, 145, 150, 151, 152, 155, 163, 165, 188, 189, 213, 232, 248, 253, 277, 280, 291, 312, 313, 315, 316, 334
Stanislaus Superior Court 240
Staynor, Gary 55
Steele, Sgt. Ed 66
Stewart, Martha 28, 390
Stough, George 40
Sturgeon fishing 31, 114
Sund/Carrington Foundation xiii, 56, 85, 129, 166, 167, 170, 228

T

Todd, Steven 40
Torrey Pines Golf Course 150
Tradecorp 27, 28, 117
Tuolumne County 69, 133
Tuolumne River 44, 60

U
Urquidez, Albert 59

V
Van Susteren, Greta xiv, 236, 263
Vintage Faire Mall 53

W
Walsh, John 34, 307, 397
Wasden, Roy xiv, 62, 94, 143, 144, 148, 154
Wecht, Dr. Cyril 241, 260, 262
Weidman, Les 56, 248

Y
Yosemite Blvd 26, 48
Yosemite Slayings 55, 56, 207

978-0-595-34750-6
0-595-34750-9

Printed in the United States
33516LVS00002B/123